European Communism

D0222858

European History in Perspective
General Editor: Jeremy Black

Benjamin Arnold   *Medieval Germany*
Ronald Asch   *The Thirty Years' War*
Nigel Aston   *The French Revolution, 1789–1804*
Nicholas Atkin   *The Fifth French Republic*
Christopher Bartlett   *Peace, War and the European Powers, 1814–1914*
Robert Bireley   *The Refashioning of Catholicism, 1450–1700*
Donna Bohanan   *Crown and Nobility in Early Modern France*
Arden Bucholz   *Moltke and the German Wars, 1864–1871*
Patricia Clavin   *The Great Depression, 1929–1939*
Paula Sutter Fichtner   *The Habsburg Monarchy, 1490–1848*
Mark Galeotti   *Gorbachev and his Revolution*
David Gates   *Warfare in the Nineteenth Century*
Alexander Grab   *Napoleon and the Tranformation of Europe*
Martin P. Johnson   *The Dreyfus Affair*
Ronald Kowalski   *European Communism*
Paul Douglas Lockhart   *Sweden in the Seventeenth Century*
Kevin McDermott   *Stalin*
Graeme Murdock   *Beyond Calvin*
Peter Musgrave   *The Early Modern European Economy*
J. L. Price   *The Dutch Republic in the Seventeenth Century*
A. W. Purdue   *The Second World War*
Christopher Read   *The Making and Breaking of the Soviet System*
Francisco J. Romero-Salvado   *Twentieth-Century Spain*
Matthew S. Seligmann and Roderick R. McLean
Germany from Reich to Republic, 1871–1918
David A. Shafer   *The Paris Commune*
Brendan Simms   *The Struggle for Mastery in Germany, 1779–1850*
David Sturdy   *Louis XIV*
David J. Sturdy   *Richelieu and Mazarin*
Hunt Tooley   *The Western Front*
Peter Waldron   *The End of Imperial Russia, 1855–1917*
Peter G. Wallace   *The Long European Reformation*
James D. White   *Lenin*
Patrick Williams   *Philip II*
Peter H. Wilson   *From Reich to Revolution*

European History in Perspective
Series Standing Order
ISBN 0–333–71694–9 hardcover
ISBN 0–333–69336–1 paperback
(*outside North America only*)

You can receive future titles in this series as they are published by placing
a standing order. Please contact your bookseller or, in the case of difficulty,
write to us at the address below with your name and address, the title of the
series and the ISBN quoted above.

Customer Services Department, Palgrave Ltd
Houndmills, Basingstoke, Hampshire RG21 6XS, England

European
Communism
1848–1991

RONALD KOWALSKI

palgrave
macmillan

First published in 2006 by
PALGRAVE MACMILLAN
Houndmills, Basingstoke, Hampshire RG21 6XS and
175 Fifth Avenue, New York, N.Y. 10010
Companies and representatives throughout the world.

PALGRAVE MACMILLAN is the global academic imprint of the Palgrave
Macmillan division of St. Martin's Press, LLC and of Palgrave Macmillan Ltd.
Macmillan® is a registered trademark in the United States, United Kingdom
and other countries. Palgrave is a registered trademark in the European
Union and other countries.

ISBN-13: 978–0–3336–8458–0 (hardback)
ISBN-10: 0–3336–8458–3   (hardback)
ISBN-13: 978–0–3336–8459–7 (paperback)
ISBN-10: 0–3336–8459–1   (paperback)

This book is printed on paper suitable for recycling and made from fully
managed and sustained forest sources.

A catalogue record for this book is available from the British Library.

A catalog record for this book is available from the Library of Congress.

10 9 8 7 6 5 4 3 2 1
15 14 13 12 11 10 09 08 07 06

Printed in China

Contents

Preface   vii

Chapter 1:   Introduction   1

Part I   Theoretical Foundations

Chapter 2:   The 'Founding Fathers'   11

Part II   The Parting of the Ways

Chapter 3:   German Social Democracy   37
Chapter 4:   Russian Marxism   59
Chapter 5:   War and Revolution   81

Part III   Communism in the Soviet Union

Chapter 6:   The Rise of Stalinism   103
Chapter 7:   Late Stalinism to Gorbachev   127

Part IV   Communism in Europe

Chapter 8:   Communism in West Europe since the
             First World War   151
Chapter 9:   Communism in East Europe   171

Part V Disintegration

Chapter 10:   The Collapse of Communism in
the Soviet Union and East Europe   203

Conclusion   224

Appendix A: The Disintegration of the Soviet Union   229

Appendix B: The Collapse of Communism in East Europe   231

Notes   234

Select Bibliography   251

Index   258

Preface

A comprehensive history of European Communism would extend to countless volumes and require the collaborative work of many historians. This work focuses on what the author judged to be the most critical issues in its evolution, both in theory and in practice. This judgement as well as the more detailed interpretations offered in the final text remain my own responsibility. No one else is culpable for my foibles.

Yet a few dues must be acknowledged. My colleagues at Worcester offered their usual comradely encouragement. Others gave much of their time discussing issues I was unsure of but I shall spare naming them lest they become 'guilty by association'. I am much indebted to them, as I am to anonymous readers of the manuscript who suggested a number of helpful revisions. I must also thank the series editor, Professor Jeremy Black, for his great patience in awaiting the completion of this book. My editors at Palgrave (Terka Acton and Sonya Barker) were long suffering too yet always highly supportive. Many mitigating circumstances contributed to my failure to produce the manuscript more swiftly, including the sudden withdrawal of funding to finance the research leave that I had anticipated to complete the writing of and revisions to the text. The Scottish poet Rabbie Burns was certainly correct in his conclusion: 'the best laid schemes of mice and men gang aft agley'. Last but far from least my daughters, Anna and Helen, warrant special mention. They propped me up in our collective time of troubles. Jenny would agree, I'm sure, that this book be dedicated to them.

The reader will find the endnotes are quite extensive. Yet to avoid too many cumbersome distractions I have sought, where I deemed sensible, to include references to the sources in the body of the text.

Chapter 1: Introduction

In the summer of 1989 Francis Fukuyama published his controversial essay 'The End of History?' As he clarified in a subsequent book, the end of history meant that 'a remarkable consensus concerning the legitimacy of liberal democracy as a system of government had emerged throughout the world over the past few years as it conquered rival ideologies like hereditary monarchy, fascism, and most recently communism.'[1] Within months of his initial pronouncement Fukuyama appeared to have been proved correct. The Communist states set up in East Europe after 1945 fell like ninepins in the autumn of 1989 (Appendix B). By the end of 1991 the motherland of Communist revolution, the Soviet Union, had collapsed, with remarkably little bloodshed and, at the time, little regret amongst its citizenry (Appendix A). The successor regimes hastened to embrace the principles of the free market and of liberal democracy, with varying degrees of commitment and success. Since the 1980s China too, under the auspices of a Communist government, had adopted a form of capitalist economics, if not democracy, to stimulate growth. Communism was dead, certainly the model of it inspired by the Soviet Union. Its core features, a centralised command economy and the denial of individual freedom, as the Marxist historian Eric Hobsbawm concluded, are 'neither possible, desirable, nor ... necessary'. The epoch begun with the publication of *The Communist Manifesto* in 1848 had ended, it seemed, in abject failure.[2]

Whether the ideals that inspired Communism have been consigned to the rubbish heap of history is a different question. It is important to grasp their longevity. Deriving from the Latin *communis* (common), Communism, according to the definition contained in the *Oxford English*

1

Dictionary, envisaged a society in which ownership of property would reside in the hands of the collective, or community, not the individual. In this society all would work for the common good. Its roots have been seen in the visions of a self-governing society of citizens elaborated by ancient Greek philosophers such as Plato and Aristotle; in the Christianity of the New Testament, which posited that the meek and the poor would inherit the earth (since the Reformation, in particular, various Christian sects have sought to create communities in which property was held collectively and goods were allocated according to need); to the communal landholding espoused by Gerrard Winstanley and the Diggers during the English Civil War; and to François Babeuf and the Conspiracy of Equals during the French Revolution. Important as these visions are they are not central to this book. Modern-day Communism, a term coined by the French revolutionary socialist Etienne Cabet in 1840, was the product of developments in Europe, the western part of it at least, from the late seventeenth to the early nineteenth centuries. First, the scientific revolution, a major influence upon the eighteenth-century Enlightenment, led many political thinkers to conclude that just as the natural world could be understood, and mastered, by the application of reason, so too could reason be applied to the social world to ensure progress, freedom and justice. Secondly, the French Revolution revealed that men and women had the power radically to recast politics and society, although it soon became clear that political liberty *per se* produced neither economic equality nor social fraternity. Thirdly, the Industrial Revolution, which began in Britain in the last decades of the eighteenth century and gradually spread across Europe, had a twofold impact. On the one hand, it heralded an unprecedented increase in production, which potentially offered a life of material well-being to all that hitherto had been unthinkable. On the other, it created a working class, a 'proletariat' to employ Marxist terminology. It was bereft of property and economic security and consigned to the 'dark satanic mills' of industrial capitalism, and a life of grinding labour, impoverishment and squalor.

In the 1820s and 1830s the parlous condition of the working class precipitated the emergence of modern socialism, at first in Britain and France. Socialism defies any easy definition. In practice it evolved into a complex and heterogeneous phenomenon. At the risk of simplification, one could say that nineteenth-century socialists feared that liberalism, which championed a more representative political system, if one still confined to the educated and propertied middle classes, and even radicalism, which espoused the further devolution of political power (the vote) to 'the masses', would lead neither to democracy nor social justice as long as property and wealth remained in the hands of the minority of pluto-crats. If political democracy was to be properly secured it had to be underpinned by the social ownership of property, or at the very least some measure of social control over it. Socialism, however, is not the con-cern of this book. The reason is that the intellectual mainsprings behind European Communism were Karl Marx and his lifelong friend and fellow thinker, Friedrich Engels. The 'founding fathers' of Communism dis-missed all their socialist precursors as 'Utopian', and constructed their own theory of 'scientific socialism'. Admittedly, between the 1850s and 1917 the distinction between socialism and Communism was of much less significance than it later acquired. The parties inspired by Marx and Engels usually called themselves Social Democratic, a title grudgingly accepted by them. Marx himself often used the terms interchangeably. One notable exception was in *The Critique of the Gotha Programme* (1875), which had been adopted by the German Social Democratic Party (SPD). In it he elaborated upon Cabet's earlier thinking. Socialism, he argued, was the system that would immediately succeed capitalism after the proletariat had risen to overthrow it. Socialist revolution, he continued, would create a state administered by the workers. This new state would expropriate the capitalists and introduce collective ownership. Yet some of the characteristics of the capitalist order would survive, especially the distribution of rewards according to work done. It only gradually would evolve into the higher stage of full Communism, an egalitarian and state-less society in which each person would work willingly according to his or her abilities. The unlimited growth of production that Marx envisaged would permit the distribution of goods according to the needs of all. Yet it was only in 1918, when the Bolsheviks assumed the name after coming to power in Russia in October 1917, that a self-professed Communist Party came into existence.

Accordingly, it is with Marx's and Engels' theoretical legacy that we must begin. However, this legacy is far from unproblematic. As James White emphasised in his elegant and meticulous reconstruction of the development of Marx's thought, there is no consensus on what Marx's ideas in fact were: 'how Marx's ideas should be interpreted remains largely a matter of opinion'.[3] This problem is not simply an academic one. It plagued Marx's followers from the late nineteenth century. For example, the leaders of the SPD, the largest Marxist party in Europe on the eve of the Great War, drew radically different conclusions from the works of 'the master' from those drawn by their Bolshevik counterparts.

In part, these differences can be explained by the failure of Marx and Engels to bequeath a complete and unambiguous exposition of their thinking to their successors. Furthermore, after Marx's death in 1883 Engels' own rather simplified account of what Marxism was muddied the waters even more. In addition, Marx's early writings, in which he sought to outline the philosophical and methodological premises that underlay his thought, remained unpublished until the 1920s and 1930s.

Yet it remains inadequate to account for divergent interpretations of Marxism simply by reference to the contradictions and *lacunae* within the body of Marx's and Engels' writings. It is also necessary to understand the particular contexts in which Marxism was received. In an interview in January 1879 with the *Chicago Tribune*, which centred on his critique of the Gotha programme, Marx insisted that '[m]any of its points have no significance outside of Germany. Spain, Russia, England [*sic*], and America have platforms suited to their peculiar difficulties. The only similarity in them is the end to be attained.' At the end of the nineteenth century Eduard Bernstein, the architect of Revisionism within the SPD, elaborated upon this point in his famous book *The Preconditions of Socialism*:

> it is well known that there are great differences between different countries. Even in countries at an approximate equal level of industrial development we find very significant political differences and great differences in the intellectual tendency of the mass of the people. Peculiarities of geographical situation, rooted in customs of national life, inherited institutions, and traditions of all kinds create ideological differences.... Even where socialist parties began by accepting the same presuppositions as the starting point of their operation, so they have, in the course of time, been compelled to adapt their activity to the special conditions of their various countries.

Over twenty years later, in 1921, he explained the resurgence of authoritarianism in Russia after the October Revolution by reference to its own 'peculiarities'. Bolshevism, he concluded, was 'a specifically Russian phenomenon that derive[d] from long centuries of absolutism and habituation to the worst kinds of oppression'.[4] Marxist movements and Communist regimes elsewhere in Europe also were shaped by the particular circumstances in which they found themselves.

The structure of this book requires a little explanation. Part I offers a brief account of the development of Marx's and Engels' own thought (the interested reader can find a definitive treatment in White's work). Important in itself to an understanding of the history of Communism, it will also provide the reader with some insight into its contested nature. Marx himself denied that he had produced a holistic system, and towards the end of his life distanced himself from those who claimed to have grasped the grail of Marxism. It also highlights the sketchy and at times conflicting nature of their thinking on how a Communist society should be constructed. This meant that it was possible for their successors to embrace quite different strategies, while claiming to be following consistently in their footsteps. Their inability, too, to comprehend adequately the growing power of nationalism in the modern world also left their followers with little practical guidance on how to deal with this problem.

Part II examines the development of Marxism in West and East Europe in the late nineteenth and early twentieth centuries. Its focus will be primarily on Germany and Russia. This is not an arbitrary choice. As the Polish intellectual historian Andrzej Walicki rightly observed, 'before World War I, Marxist ideology was most influential in [these] two countries'.[5] German Marxism, as embodied in the doctrine of the SPD, was the dominant influence in the Second International. Founded in 1889, it was a heterogeneous and loosely structured organisation, whose member parties did not all subscribe to Marxism. Its history was bedevilled by the attempts of the SPD to impose its own *credo* on it. Russian Marxism, at least in its Leninist form, proved to be the most influential in the twentieth century. Moreover, although still a predominantly backward peasant society, Russia underwent the first Communist revolution. Part II ends with an explanation of why this was the case, and why Germany, and the West more generally, were able to resist the challenge posed by Communism at the end of the Great War.

Part III deals with the rise and consolidation of Stalinism in the former Soviet Union, the most important, if tragic, episode in the history of European Communism. It begins by exploring the interaction between circumstances and ideology that condemned the first Communist revolution to the terrible human suffering wrought by the forced collectivisation of agriculture, and then by the Great Terror of the later 1930s. It closes with an analysis of the halting attempts to reform the Stalinist system after the old dictator's death in 1953. Admittedly, little of theoretical import then emerged. Yet the period warrants some detailed consideration as it illustrated how Communism in practice could be sustained without resort to the murderous policies of the Stalin era. Mass terror was eliminated, and replaced by more sophisticated methods of

Communist control, but the fundamental characteristics of the system (one-party rule and a centralised command economy) survived intact. Their survival was eventually to lead the Soviet Union into a situation where economic stagnation and political corruption were the order of the day.

Part IV returns to a comparison of Communism in West and East Europe since the end of the First World War. In the West it was a political failure, as no Communist Party succeeded in coming to power there. It has long been fashionable to attribute this failure to the 'Bolshevisation' of the Communist Parties of West Europe, their subordination to tactics imposed by the Stalinist regime in the Soviet Union. Such an explanation is too simplistic, as we shall see. Whatever the shortcomings of West European Communism in practice, in theory Western Marxism (or neo-Marxism) proved to be remarkably fruitful as those inspired by Marxism grappled with the problems posed by the absence of revolution in the West, and the emergence of Stalinism in the Soviet Union. Western Marxists provided many fascinating additions to, perhaps revisions somewhat at odds with, Marx's intellectual legacy. Their sheer diversity precludes a systematic treatment here, but the contribution of the Italian Communist Antonio Gramsci has been singled out. Important and insightful as his work is, it has also been seen as one of the sources of Eurocommunism, the strategy adopted in the 1970s by the Italian, French and Spanish Communist Parties to secure at least a share in political power. Approaching Communism in West Europe in this way did mean that less was said on the history of the Communist International (Comintern) than some might deem to have been warranted. However, I would defend my approach on two grounds. First, I stand by my conclusions in Chapter 5 that the prospects of Communist revolution in the West were remote. There were moments (Italy in 1920 and Germany in 1921 and 1923) when there might have been some reason to anticipate the spread of revolution across Europe, but they proved to be false dawns. Spain in the late 1930s was another. In this instance there can be little doubt that Stalin sought to contain the onset of a radical social revolution lest it jeopardise his pursuit of an alliance with Britain and France against the threat posed by Nazi Germany. Secondly, and more pragmatically, I reckoned it would lack any justice to recent monographs and documentary collections on the Comintern to offer a potted account of their findings. They are included in the bibliography and I fear that it is the task of the inquisitive reader to explore them in order to confirm if my judgements are correct. In the East, Communist Parties did come to power after 1945, largely but not exclusively as a result of the expansion of Soviet influence throughout the region in the closing years of the Second World War. The imposition of the Stalinist system was to be the source of subsequent challenges to the Communist order. Major opposition to Stalinism arose first in Yugoslavia in the late 1940s, somewhat ironically as initially the Yugoslavian Communists had been more Stalinist than Stalin, and later in Hungary, Poland and Czechoslovakia. To varying degrees the Communists there introduced reforms to ameliorate the most odious characteristics of Stalinism, and establish their own national paths to socialism, in order to gain popular consent to their rule. Their attempts to create a socialism with a (more) human face ultimately came to nought.

The final section, Part Five, examines the dramatic, and unforeseen, collapse of Communism in East Europe in 1989 and the Soviet Union in 1991 unwittingly set in train by Mikhail Gorbachev. His initial intention was limited: to revitalise a regime that had sunk into economic stagnation. As his attempts to do so foundered in the face of bureaucratic obstruction to reform he resorted to increasingly radical measures. The consequences of his actions, and of his refusal to sanction the use of naked force to prop up regimes that were bankrupt and corrupt, led to a series of remarkably non-violent revolutions that swept Communism away. The book concludes with some reflections on Communism, in theory and in practice, and what relevance, if any, it has for the twenty-first century when global capitalism appears to be in the ascendant.

A few final observations are warranted. Marxism and European Communism are vast and complex subjects. For better or worse, they have been amongst the greatest influences on the history of Europe, and the world, since the middle of the nineteenth century. The literature on them is encyclopaedic, encompassing economic, philosophical and political analyses, as well as more traditional historical accounts. Much of it too has been partisan, seeking either to demolish or defend (rarely after 1991) the Communist project. This is unsurprising. One does not have to concur wholly with the early Soviet historian M. N. Pokrovskii that history is the most political of all sciences to accept that the political standpoints of historians consciously or unconsciously influence their interpretations, not least with respect to such a contentious phenomenon as Communism. To deny such influences in this book would be foolhardy. Whilst I may be critical of the theories and practices of Marx and his self-professed followers, my own reservations about the much-heralded virtues of global capitalism no doubt still lead me to be sympathetic to those in the past and present who question them. I have sought to be historical and objective but it is only fair to alert the reader to the possible biases in this account.

PART I
Theoretical Foundations

Chapter 2: The 'Founding Fathers'

Any history of European Communism ought to begin with the ideas of Karl Marx and Friedrich Engels. Their own political activities are of less importance. In part, this was the consequence of their sporadic involvement in the emerging workers' movement, which had little lasting practical impact; and in part, on the fact that their ideas only became widely influential in the late nineteenth century, in the era of the Second International when mass socialist parties appeared. As Hobsbawm pointed out, 'with the partial exception of Germany, no Marxist movement of significance . . . existed before Marx's death in 1883'.[1] Admittedly, in the later 1840s Marx and Engels had become associated with the embryonic organisations of émigré German socialists, chiefly in Paris, Brussels and London. The League of the Just, little more than a propaganda group of several hundred artisans established in Paris in 1836, gradually fell under their ideological influence. Renamed the Communist League in June 1847, they wrote *The Communist Manifesto* for it in 1848. Despite its subsequent fame the initial response to it (as later to *Capital*) was muted. The Revolutions of 1848 also embroiled them in politics as they vainly sought to direct the disjointed workers' revolution in Germany in a radical direction. The ultimate failure of these Revolutions led to the disintegration of organised workers' movements, in Germany and in Europe generally. The League itself was dissolved on Marx's urging in 1852. For the next decade they remained largely detached from everyday politics. Marx himself devoted most of his energies to journalism (his major, if inadequate, source of income) and to theoretical work. Thereafter, they did play a leading, at times reluctant, role in the International Working Men's Association (the First

11

International), set up by leaders of the London Trades Council and their counterparts in France in September 1864. Marx was prevailed upon to give its Inaugural Address and draw up its Provisional Rules. He continued to provide it with intellectual and political leadership until its demise in 1876, although he only attended one Congress in person, in the Hague in 1872. It was not a large organisation, with a membership never exceeding several thousands, nor a very influential one, nor wholly Marxist. As Engels conceded, its role in the famous Paris Commune of 1871 was overshadowed by that of the Blanquists. Its other major weakness was its lack of a following in Germany. The moving force behind the development of a growing workers' movement there in the 1860s was Ferdinand Lassalle, whose ideas and tactics were scorned by Marx and Engels (see Chapter 3).

Their ideological legacy, however, was to prove massively influential. Precisely what it was, for reasons suggested in the Introduction, was the subject of much confusion and debate. This confusion permitted self-professed Marxists to pursue quite different political strategies, while claiming to be following in the footsteps of the 'founding fathers'. Bernstein wearily remarked in his *Preconditions* that it had become possible to 'prove *everything* out of Marx and Engels'.[2] Why this had come to be the case first requires an analysis of their theory of history: historical materialism.

Theory of history

The problem with historical materialism is that Marx and Engels failed to produce a definitive statement of what it was. As Karl Kautsky declared in the Preface to his *magnum opus, The Materialist Conception of History* (first published in German in 1927), the charge that Marxists hitherto had 'neglected to give a systematic and comprehensive account and justification of this conception' had prompted him to undertake this task in his two-volume, 1800-page tract. The nearest that the 'founding fathers' had come to doing so was in one of their early collaborative works, *The German Ideology*. It was written in 1845 and 1846, but published only in 1932. Isaiah Berlin concluded that despite being a 'verbose, ill-organised and ponderous work' it contained 'in its lengthy introduction the most sustained, imaginative and impressive exposition of Marx's theory of history'. David McLellan concurred, but proclaimed it to be a 'masterpiece' of immense clarity and cogency.[3] Subsequent developments in their thinking on history were never again presented in such a systematic fashion, which helps explain the continuing debates about what the materialist conception of history was. As more of their writings, especially Marx's early philosophical ones, were published in the twentieth century, commentators emphasised the apparent differences within his work: the early (humanist) Marx; the mature (determinist) Marx; and even the late ('senile') Marx.

An all too common approach to the materialist theory of history has equated it with an economic, even a technological, determinism, an interpretation forcefully advanced by Gerald Cohen in *Karl Marx's Theory of History: A Defence* (1978). Marx himself shares some responsibility for such an interpretation. In *The Poverty of Philosophy* (1847) he incautiously remarked that '[I]n acquiring new productive forces men change their mode of production; and in changing their mode of production... they change all their social relations. The handmill gives you society with the feudal lord; the steam mill society with the industrial capitalist.' Elsewhere, Marx and Engels repeatedly contended that the economy was the factor which determined all other phenomena, ideological, political and social. In the oft-quoted preface to *A Contribution to the Critique of Political Economy* (1859) Marx outlined what is often taken to be the quintessential statement of his position:

> In the social production of their life, men enter into definite relations that are indispensable and independent of their will, relations of production which correspond to a definite stage of development of their material productive forces. The sum total of these relations of production constitutes the economic structure of society, the real foundation, on which arises a legal and political superstructure and to which correspond definite forms of social consciousness. The mode of production of material life conditions the social, political and intellectual life process in general. It is not the consciousness of men that determines their being, but, on the contrary, their social being that determines their consciousness.

In his 1888 Preface to *The Communist Manifesto* Engels reiterated 'the fundamental proposition' of historical materialism: 'in every historical epoch, the prevailing mode of economic production and exchange, and the social organisation necessarily following from it, form the basis upon which is built up, and from which alone can be explained, the political and intellectual history of that epoch....'

Marx and Engels applied this 'proposition' to explain how, as they stated at the beginning of the *Manifesto*, 'the history of all hitherto existing society' had unfolded. In recognisably economic-determinist terms, they argued that the productive forces of society had a tendency to grow. Their development eventually would lead to a fundamental contradiction, when the existing relations of production, or property relations, became an obstacle to the further growth of these productive forces. At this point a revolution was necessary, to free these forces from the fetters constraining them. They employed this rather abstract schema to account for the emergence of capitalism from feudal society. However, as Rodney Hilton remarked, they failed to articulate fully and unequivocally their understanding of this transition.[4] For example, in the *Manifesto* they suggested that the massive expansion of trade that followed the opening up of the Americas and the East doomed the old feudal guild system of production in West Europe. No longer could it produce sufficient goods to satisfy the demands imposed upon it. It was replaced, first, by the manufacturing system, which in turn was superseded by mechanised industrial production as markets continued to expand. Consequent upon this economic transformation the political power of the rising commercial and industrial bourgeoisie increased. The bourgeoisie then carried out a political revolution, to destroy all remaining feudal barriers to the unfettered development of capitalism. Later, in *Capital*, Marx offered a different explanation of the rise of capitalism, the 'really revolutionising' one. While not denying the importance of an expanded world market as a stimulus to the development of capitalist manufacturing, none the less he emphasised above all else the process of the 'primitive accumulation' of capital within feudal society itself. This gave rise to the growth of a minority of capitalist producers, who amassed ever more property in their own hands. In the process, those who earlier had possessed their own means of production (peasant proprietors and guild craftsmen) were converted into a mass of property-less wage workers.

What constitutes a genuinely Marxist theory of the transition from feudalism to capitalism is a question for others to pursue. What is certain is that for Marx and Engels capitalism was not the end of history. Its growth would lead to a future contradiction when capitalist relations of production themselves would impede economic development. At this stage the preconditions for socialist revolution would be mature. Their reasoning demands some further exploration. As capitalism grew, production was becoming ever more centralised and concentrated in large industrial enterprises. In part, this centralisation and concentration was the result of technological progress, necessary if growing markets were to be satisfied. But new, and costly, technology could be introduced profitably only in large-scale industry. Furthermore, technological progress and the consequent increased output of goods led to periodic crises of over-production. In these crises, small-scale enterprises were either destroyed, or absorbed by their larger, more efficient competitors, so advancing the process of centralisation and concentration. In the process, however, the capacity of increasingly large-scale industry to produce goods in quantity was rising dramatically, so establishing the material preconditions for socialism. As they declared in *The German Ideology*, 'slavery cannot be abolished without the steam engine and the mule and spinning jenny...in general, people cannot be liberated as long as they are unable to obtain food and drink, housing and clothing in adequate quality and quantity'.

Moreover, the concentration of the means of production in the hands of an ever diminishing number of capitalist magnates had critical political and social consequences. On many occasions Marx and Engels argued that the economic logic of capitalism eventually would destroy the middle class, 'the small manufacturer, the shopkeeper, the artisan, the peasant...'. Their extinction was inevitable, so swelling the ranks of the proletariat, the gravedigger of capitalism. Forced under capitalism to live in dire poverty it would be driven to overthrow it. Towards the end of the first volume of *Capital* Marx spiritedly concluded:

> Along with the constantly diminishing number of the magnates of capital, who usurp and monopolise all advantages of this process of transformation, grows the mass of misery, oppression, slavery, degradation, exploitation; but with this grows the revolt of the working class, a class always increasing in numbers, and disciplined, united, organised by the very mechanism of the process of capitalist production itself. The monopoly of capital becomes a fetter upon the mode of production, which has sprung up and flourished along with, and under it. Centralisation of the means of production and socialisation of labour at last reach a point where they become incompatible with their capitalist integument. The knell of capitalist private property sounds. The expropriators are expropriated.

Stirring as Marx's conclusion was, it provided little guidance to just how far capitalism must develop before it was ripe for revolution. Marx and Engels frequently posited that socialism could be constructed only on the foundations laid by the most extensive growth of capitalism. This alone, they explained again in *The German Ideology*, would create the requisite material wealth, 'because without it, want is merely made general, and the struggle for necessities and all the old filthy business would necessarily be reproduced'. Moreover, Marx's 'Preface' of 1859 also implied that socialist revolution could only follow the fullest development of capitalism:

> No social order ever perishes before *all* the productive forces for which there is room in it have developed, and new, higher relations of production never appear before the material conditions of their existence have matured in the womb of the old society itself.   (emphasis added)

Premature attempts at socialist revolution, he later cautioned in a letter entitled *Against Carl Herzen*, were bound to fail as long as 'the material conditions, which necessitate the abolition of the bourgeois mode of production, and thus, the final overthrow of bourgeois political authority, are not as yet created'. However, these pronouncements were of little practical use to their followers. Kautsky conceded that Marx and Engels had left no absolute formula for determining when the preconditions for socialism were present. The Russian Communist Nikolai Osinskii elaborated on this issue shortly after the October Revolution. Marx spoke, he contended,

> only about the forces which lead towards socialist revolution.... He does not specify the degree of development which they must reach for the tendencies... that are preparing the revolution to become the immediate prerequisites, the moving forces of the revolution.... In other words, he does not indicate the signs by which it is possible to say that a country has become ripe for socialist revolution.[5]

There is little to be gained by pursuing this question in the abstract, bar concluding that Marx and Engels provided no measurable economic criteria by which to gauge when socialism was possible; but it was to be of later significance, especially in understanding the final division in the ranks of the Russian Marxists, as Part II will reveal.

However, Marx's and Engels' theory of history is not reducible just to an economic or technological determinism, to the impersonal workings of economic forces. Conscious and willed human action remained integral to it. In *The Holy Family* (1845) they trenchantly denied that history was a supra-human process, with its own innate purposes:

> History does nothing; it 'does not possess immense riches', it 'does not fight battles'. It is men, real, living men, who do all this, who possess things and fight battles. It is not 'history' which uses men as the means of achieving its own ends. History is nothing but the activity of men in the pursuit of their ends.

Nevertheless, 'real, living men' (and women) did not make history in a vacuum, simply according to their desires. The circumstances in which they found themselves placed constraints on their actions. As Marx explained in *The Eighteenth Brumaire of Louis Bonaparte* (1852), '[m]en make their own history, but they do not make it just as they please ... but under circumstances directly encountered, given and transmitted from the past. The tradition of all dead generations weighs like a nightmare on the brain of the living.' As well as this ideological 'muck of the ages', the material conditions encountered circumscribed the objectives that men could pursue.

To return to the transition from feudalism to capitalism, Marx and Engels did not see it as an impersonal process. In the final chapters of the first volume of *Capital* Marx argued (simplistically, many historians now would claim) that commensurately with its growing economic power the rising bourgeoisie had fought consciously to win political supremacy. Ultimately it had

> employ[ed] the power of the State, the concentrated and organised force of society, to hasten, hothouse fashion, the process of transformation of the feudal mode of production into the capitalist mode, and to shorten the transition. Force is the midwife of every old society pregnant with a new one. It is itself an economic power.

Similarly, the future transition to socialism required that men and women again, in this case the proletariat, must act to destroy the old bourgeois system and then proceed, wittingly, to construct the new socialist order. The *Manifesto* was unequivocal on this point:

> the first step in the revolution by the working class is to raise the proletariat to the position of ruling class, to win the battle of democracy.
> The proletariat will use its political supremacy to wrest, by degrees, all capital from the bourgeoisie, to centralise all institutions of

production in the hands of the State, i.e. of the proletariat organised as a ruling class.

For Marx and Engels, the development of capitalism itself would engender within the proletariat the political will necessary for it to carry out socialist revolution: 'The very living conditions of the proletariat under capitalism', the misery, oppression and degradation referred to above, 'would bring it a consciousness of its own inhumane situation and hence make it aware of its need to liberate itself.'

This consciousness would emerge in stages. At first, capitalism would transform 'the mass of the people...into workers', would place them in 'a common situation...a class as against capital...'. At this stage the workers would constitute what, in *The Poverty of Philosophy*, Marx termed a 'class in itself', still unaware of its common interest in overthrowing capitalism. They would be driven to struggle, initially by strikes in separate factories, for measures to better their daily lives, such as wage increases. Gradually they would coalesce, to seek other common objectives, especially the eight-hour working day. 'And in this way,' Marx reaffirmed in a letter of November 1871 to F. Bolte, 'out of the separate economic movements of the workers there grows up everywhere a *political* movement... a movement of the *class*, with the object of enforcing its interests in a general form, in a form possessing general, socially coercive force.' It would become transformed into a 'class for itself', conscious of its common bonds and its revolutionary purpose. This belief was enshrined in the Provisional Rules of the First International, where Marx began by proclaiming that 'the emancipation of the working classes must be conquered by the working classes themselves...'. Later, in 1879, in their *Circular Letter to Bebel, Liebknecht, Bracke et al.*, the leaders of the recently formed SPD, Marx and Engels again denied that 'the workers [were] too uneducated to free themselves' and thus would have to rely on leadership external to them for their liberation. The task of the Communists, 'the most advanced and resolute section of the working class', was not to substitute themselves for the workers and act on their behalf, as Joseph Femia has suggested. Rather it was to counsel the workers of their ultimate goals, help them to organise and urge them to act in a united and determined manner. As Marx stated in his interview with the *Chicago Tribune* in January 1879, '[t]he working classes move spontaneously, without knowing what the ends of the movement will be. The socialists invent no movement, but merely tell the workmen what its character and its ends will be.' Despite fleeting Jacobin flirtations in the late 1840s, they had no truck with Blanquism, the notion that a self-appointed revolutionary elite could overthrow capitalism and maintain itself in power until such time as the majority of the working class could be mobilised or re-educated to support it. Their assessment of the capacities of the proletariat spontaneously to acquire a revolutionary consciousness has proved to be wildly optimistic. Yet the claim, recently reiterated by Neil Harding among others, that Leninism was 'wholly a child of Marxism in respect to the basic foundations of its theory of the party' is wide of the mark.[6] Lenin's proposition that a vanguard of intellectuals alone could bring a revolutionary consciousness to the workers (see Chapter 4) was at odds with Marx's and Engels' fundamental ideas.

Were this to be the final word on their theory of history then the conclusion drawn many years ago by Maurice Meisner, that it was a combination of deterministic and activistic elements, might seem to be apt.[7] While, in the final analysis, economic development was seen to have underpinned historical progress, human action remained essential if the evolution of society from a lower to a potentially higher stage was to be realised. Discussing how socialist revolution would come about, in *Reason and Revolution* Herbert Marcuse, a leading Western Marxist theorist, deftly captured this feature of what he termed 'the Marxian dialectic':

> The revolution depends upon a totality of objective conditions: it requires a certain attained level of material and intellectual culture, a self-conscious and organized working class on an international scale, acute class struggle. These become revolutionary conditions, however, only if seized upon and directed by a conscious activity that has in mind the socialist goal. Not the slightest natural necessity or automatic inevitability guarantees the transition from capitalism to socialism.[8]

On occasion, however, Marx and Engels subscribed to a decidedly more voluntarist position, one which emphasised the potential of human action to accelerate the process of change, even to leap the stages of history that Marx had outlined in the Preface of 1859. There he had delineated what many, incorrectly, have taken to be his definitive schema of history: 'In broad outlines Asiatic, ancient, feudal and modern bourgeois modes of production can be designated as progressive epochs in the economic formation of society.' The implication of his argument is clear: all societies develop through economically determined stages, in a uni-linear manner. This process of development would culminate in the creation of

Communism. How Marx reconciled this schema with his journalistic writings of the mid-1850s on China and India when he lamented the innate resistance of Asiatic society to 'disintegration and economic evolution', as Hobsbawm observed, remains somewhat mysterious![9]

Marx's and Engels' thinking on Germany in the late 1840s illustrates their voluntarist propensities. Still adhering to the view that 'all collisions in history' were rooted in the 'contradiction' between the forces and relations of production, they denied that capitalism would have to be developed 'fully' before socialist revolution was possible in Germany. They defended this proposition in *The German Ideology*:

> Incidentally, to lead to collisions in a country, this contradiction need not necessarily have reached its extreme limit in this particular country. The competition with industrially more advanced countries, brought about by the expansion of international intercourse, is quite sufficient to produce a similar contradiction in countries with backward industry (e.g. the latent proletariat in Germany brought into view by the competition of English industry).

They clung to this view until 1850. On the final page of the *Manifesto* they declared that Germany, while much less advanced economically than either Britain or France, could become the first battleground of socialist revolution: 'the bourgeois revolution in Germany will be but a prelude to an immediately following proletarian revolution'. As late as March 1850, in an *Address of the Central Committee to the Communist League*, they insisted that the task of the German workers was to make the bourgeois democratic revolution 'permanent', to drive it forward towards socialism, a fleeting idea later taken up and elaborated by Trotsky, as we shall see in Chapter 4. However, they soon abandoned this whole notion. Recovery from the economic crisis of 1847, they later concluded, precluded revolution in the near future. Socialist revolution in Germany now demanded the extensive development of industry, the work of some decades at least. To think otherwise, Marx thundered at the September 1850 meeting of the Central Committee, would be to be deluded by 'the revolutionary phrase'.

Marx and the Russians

While their exaggeration of the prospects for socialist revolution in Germany can be discounted as a passing aberration, the dramatic *volte-face* on the part of Marx in the 1870s cannot be dismissed quite as simply. As White observed, after Marx had completed the first volume of *Capital* in 1867, his investigations into backward societies caused him to doubt whether the system of capitalist production that he had spent decades analysing must necessarily expand on a global scale. Russia became a major focus of his attention. He planned, apparently, to use his studies of it as the framework for the third volume of *Capital.* Detailed analysis of Russian society led him to conclusions contrary to the histori-cal schema outlined in the 'Preface' of 1859. Haruki Wada also has pointed out that by 1875, when he was correcting *Capital* for publication in French, Marx had begun to consider the possibility that Russia might evolve in a manner quite different from West Europe.[10] Three years later he was convinced that this was the case.

His conclusions were laid out, unambiguously, in his famous letter to the journal of the Russian Populists, *Otechestvennye Zapiski* (Notes of the Fatherland). Drafted in November 1878, it was only released by Engels after Marx's death. In it he denied that the 'historical sketch of the genesis of capitalism in Western Europe' contained in *Capital* was 'a historico-philosophical theory of the general course fatally imposed on all peoples, whatever the historical circumstances in which they find themselves placed'. Russia itself still had the chance to avoid 'all the fate-ful vicissitudes of the capitalist regime'. He clarified his views on Russia's possible future two and half years later, in response to a request from the Populist revolutionary Vera Zasulich. In a letter dated 8 March 1881 (itself the summary of four earlier drafts) he repeated that Russia's devel-opment along Western capitalist lines was not inevitable. This would be the case only if private property became dominant in it. In Russia this was not yet so, since communal peasant property persisted on a wide scale. As for its prospects of survival, he concluded:

> The analysis in *Capital* therefore provides no reasons either for or against the vitality of the Russian commune. But the special study I have made of it...has convinced me that the commune is the fulcrum for social regeneration in Russia. But in order that it might function as such, harmful influences assailing it on all sides must first be eliminated, and it must then be assured the normal conditions for spontaneous development.

These 'harmful influences' were not the product of inexorable laws of economic development. Rather, they were the consequence of 'state oppression, and exploitation by capitalist intruders whom the state has made powerful at the peasants' expense'. All was not lost. The pretensions of the state could be resisted. Provided a revolution, a peasant revolution, moreover, came soon enough, the commune could be saved. Then, it could act 'as a regenerating element of Russian society and an element of superiority over the countries enslaved by the capitalist system'.

For the commune to become the basis of socialism in Russia two additional obstacles would have to be overcome. First, it must 'shake off its primitive characteristics and develop directly as an element of collective production on a national scale'. These steps, ironically, could be achieved by looking to Western capitalism, and 'appropriat[ing] its positive achievements', 'build[ing] into the commune all the positive achievements of the capitalist system, without having to pass under its harsh tribute'. Secondly, the isolation of the communes from each other, which had produced 'a central despotism above the communes', also had to be surmounted. For Marx, this problem could be resolved with 'the utmost ease. All that is necessary is to replace the "*volost*" ... with a peasant assembly chosen by the communes themselves – an economic and administrative body serving their own interests.'

The Preface to the second Russian edition of *The Communist Manifesto*, of January 1882, reiterated this optimistic message, but with a notable *caveat*:

> If the Russian revolution becomes the signal for proletarian revolution in the West, so that the two complement each other, then Russia's peasant communal land-ownership may serve as the point of departure for a communist development.

This linkage of the socialist potential of the commune to revolution in the West in all probability was the work of Engels, not of Marx himself. By the 1890s, under the cajoling of the so-called 'father of Russian Marxism', G. V. Plekhanov, Engels' reservations about the commune had grown. In his *Russia and the Social Revolution Reconsidered* (1894) he concluded that it had already been destroyed by the development of capitalism. Even if revolution in Russia sparked off a victorious socialist revolution in the West it was now too late to save the commune as the basis for the construction of socialism in Russia. The Russian peasants, he added, had 'already forgotten how to cultivate their lands for the common good'.

There is little reason to doubt that Marx's letters on Russia lacked 'good faith', as Walicki suggested. His last studies, so White persuasively argued, had led him to abandon his attempts to construct a universal theory of history.[11] However, his letters had little impact at the time, and have been neglected in much that subsequently has been written on Marxism. Moreover, Marx's own conclusion, which endorsed the Populists' belief that socialism could be established in Russia without it first having to experience capitalism, was suppressed by the country's first self-professed Marxists, led by Plekhanov. Their own Marxism was based on the determinist premises of Marx's 'Preface' of 1859, with Plekhanov insisting that the level of any country's economic development dictated its political structure. Marxists elsewhere in Europe shared similar views. Yet their determinist reading of Marx was unsurprising, since, as Lucio Colletti commented, the bulk of what they had to guide them was Marx's economic writings of the 1850s and 1860s.[12] Engels belatedly recognised that this was the case. In a letter to Joseph Bloch, written in September 1890, he admitted that

> Marx and I ourselves are partly to blame for the fact that younger people sometimes lay more stress on the economic side than is due to it. We had to emphasise the main principles vis-à-vis our adversaries, who denied it, and we had not always the time, the place or the opportunity to allow the other elements [politics, law, ideas] involved in the interaction to come into their rights.

Engels' admission is not without its own irony. Even before Marx's death his own exposition of Marxism had come to emphasise that the economy was 'the *ultimately* determining element in history'. In his *Anti-Duhring* (1878) he argued that

> the economic structure of society *always* furnishes the real base, starting from which we can alone work out the ultimate explanation of the whole superstructure of juridical and political institutions as well as of the religious, philosophical, and other ideas of a given historical period.

Moreover, greatly influenced as many of his contemporaries were by the work of Charles Darwin, Engels increasingly equated historical processes with those of the natural world, so imparting to Marxism an almost evolutionary determinism absent in Marx's own thinking.

Many commentators, it is true, have argued that Engels was not as sophisticated a thinker as Marx. For instance, in *Capitalism, Socialism and Democracy* (1943) the émigré Austrian economist Joseph Schumpeter astutely remarked that Engels' account of Marxism might have obscured Marx's own meaning. McLellan concurred, pointing out that the late Engels removed much of 'the subtlety out of Marx's ideas'. Yet it was Engels who mattered most in the late nineteenth and early twentieth centuries. As Christopher Arthur aptly claimed, *Anti-Duhring* was 'the most influential textbook on Marxism ever written'. Kautsky professed that it 'first made the materialist conception of history entirely accessible to me'. Bernstein concurred, agreeing that it was the later writings of Engels which provided 'the mature and refined version' of historical materialism. Engels' interpretation, combined with an understandable ignorance of the richness of Marx's own thought on the part of leading Marxists of the time, led to what Berlin scathingly described as 'the half-positivist, half Darwinian interpretation' of Marxism that dogged European Communism until the inter-war period.[13]

Engels' efforts, well-intentioned as they were, to present a coherent and systematic account of Marxist thought have masked the fundamental problems with which the late Marx was grappling. His own theory of history was left unfinished at the time of his death. In fact, he doubted if he could construct any general theory. Besides, much of what else they had to say on other, more particular issues was also open to conflicting interpretation, or very fragmentary. It is to these issues: their views on the peasantry, their vision of the politics and economics of socialism, and their attempt to understand the growing power of nationalism, that we now must turn. Let us begin with the peasantry.

The peasantry

It is commonly held that Marx and Engels were contemptuous of the peasantry, and discounted its revolutionary potential. In truth, in much of their work they predicted that the peasants would meet the same fate as other small producers. In *The Peasant Question in France and Germany* (1894) Engels concluded that capitalism would extinguish 'the lifestrings of small production in agriculture'. The position of the peasants, he continued, was 'absolutely hopeless'. Preservation of their farms would prove to be 'absolutely impossible' since 'capitalist large-scale production [was] absolutely sure to run over their impotent antiquated system of small production as a train runs over a pushcart'. Their survival would be undermined further as industrial capitalism also deprived them of vital earnings from handicrafts. Until the 1870s this prognosis appeared to have been confirmed by the rapid growth of large estates in Britain, the United States and even Germany.

Not only was the demise of the peasantry, its transformation into a rural proletariat, inevitable, it was also welcome. In Marx's and Engels' eyes, the peasantry, certainly the property-owning peasantry of the West, was a backward, ignorant and reactionary class. Its sole purpose was to protect its property against the encroachment of large-scale agrarian capitalism. As such, the peasants were, in the words of the *Manifesto*, 'not revolutionary, but conservative. Nay more, they are reactionary, for they try to roll back the wheel of history.' They were also a potential bulwark of counter-revolution. 'Immured in the idiocy of rural life' they would be prey to manipulation by the landlords and bourgeoisie, become 'a bribed tool of reactionary intrigue', and resist the threat to private property posed by socialism.

The only solution to the ills of the countryside lay in socialist revolution. The duty of the socialist state was to nationalise the existing large capitalist estates and hand them over to the rural proletariat for communal cultivation. Demands for their division into smallholdings were to be resisted. Land division would destroy the economic progress already made towards more efficient and productive forms of agriculture. It also had dangerous political consequences, simply strengthening the class of small peasant proprietors innately hostile to socialism. They hastened to add, nevertheless, that the creation of collective agriculture should not be forced upon an unwilling peasantry. Coercion would only convert it against socialism. Persuasion and force of example would lead it to see the material advantages of collective agriculture. In the meantime it was to be left in possession of its smallholdings.

However, their dismissal of the peasantry was not total. In his 1870 'Preface' to *The Peasant War in Germany*, Engels had insisted that the proletariat could mobilise the 'small peasants' as well as agricultural workers to support the revolutionary cause, provided it was able to convince them that socialist revolution alone offered them 'salvation' from their oppression and poverty. In his *Critique of the Gotha Programme* Marx concurred, deriding Lassalle for his dismissal of the peasantry as 'one reactionary mass'. Moreover, he had lauded the revolutionary potential of the communal peasantry in Russia, as we have just seen. The few of their followers (Vollmar in Germany, Lenin in Russia) who looked to the

peasantry for support no doubt were swayed to do so by the circumstances in which they found themselves, rather than by the prescriptions
of the 'founding fathers'. Yet to cast them as wholly heterodox in relation
to the spirit of Marxism is one-sided, as again its ideological legacy
is open to interpretation.

The politics of socialism

Marx and Engels failed to provide, as Tony Polan pointed out, 'any
rigorous exposition . . . of the institutions of an emancipated society'. Why
this was the case is not completely clear. They professedly were more
concerned with analysing capitalism than with elaborating utopian
blueprints for a future society. Marx frankly conceded in an 'Afterword'
to the second German edition of *Capital* that he was more interested in
the 'critical analysis of actual facts, instead of writing recipes . . . for the
cook-shops of the future'. Arguably, they also believed that after the
victory of the revolution any problems in constructing a socialist society
would be solved, as Carl Boggs suggested, 'organically and also quite
rapidly'.[14] Marx's own reflections on the experience of the Paris
Commune of 1871 appear to bear out this contention. In *The Civil War in
France* he averred: 'The working class did not expect miracles from the
Commune. They have no ready-made utopias to introduce *par decret du
peuple*. . . . They have no ideals to realise, but to set free the elements of
the new society with which old collapsing bourgeois society itself is pregnant.' Yet one motif runs consistently through their writings. They
equated socialism with democracy. For them, the dictatorship of the
proletariat, the political system that would replace the old bourgeois
state, was synonymous with democracy. They anticipated that it would be
a government of the majority, one established by the workers themselves,
whom they expected to become numerically preponderant in a bourgeois
capitalist society. The problem was that they proffered two distinct, if
sketchy and contradictory, models of this (democratic) dictatorship.

One model, that adopted by the majority of socialists of the Second
International and by Social Democrats after the First World War, and
later by the Eurocommunists, proclaimed that it was possible to make use
of the institutions of the bourgeois–democratic state in the construction
of socialism. The *Manifesto* declared, as we saw, that the task of the proletariat was 'to win the battle of democracy', 'to raise [itself] to the position
of ruling class'. Having done so, it should employ the machinery of the

state to crush opposition from the bourgeoisie and lay the foundations of a socialist economy. Ultimately, when full communism was achieved and all 'class distinctions [had] disappeared', the need for a state of any sort would wither away and be replaced by a (nebulous) form of direct democracy in which the workers would govern themselves. Almost thirty years later, in his *Critique of the Gotha Programme*, Marx again implied that a democratic republic could serve as the revolutionary dictatorship of the proletariat. In some of their later writings they even held out the possibility of a 'parliamentary road' to socialism. In a speech in Amsterdam in September 1872, one primarily designed to repudiate anarchist denials of the need to seize state power at all, Marx concluded that in certain advanced 'democratic' societies 'such as America and England, and if I was familiar with your institutions, I might add Holland... the workers may attain their goal by peaceful means'. Later, he added that in France too, where parliamentary democracy had become consolidated under the Third Republic, the workers could exploit universal suffrage as 'an instrument of emancipation'. Elsewhere, revolution would remain necessary. Imperial Germany was a case in point, as Engels pointed out. There, 'where the government is practically all-powerful and the *Reichstag* and other representative bodies are without real power', the prospect of a parliamentary path to socialism was out of the question.[15]

On other occasions, they put forward a radically different vision of the revolutionary state. In *The Eighteenth Brumaire of Louis Bonaparte* (1852), Marx in passing implied that the task of the revolution was not to perfect, but to smash the existing state machine. Some twenty years later, in their Preface to the 1872 German edition of the *Manifesto*, Marx and Engels returned to this idea. Drawing upon 'the practical experience' of the Paris Commune, 'where the proletariat for the first time held power for two whole months', they now were convinced that 'the working class [could] not simply lay hold of the ready-made state machinery and wield it for its own purposes'. Instead, the existing state had to be destroyed root and branch, as Marx had outlined in his *The Civil War in France* (1871). The standing army and the police, whose essential purpose was to subjugate the exploited majority of the population, were to be abolished. They were to be replaced by a people's militia, which alone could quell counter-revolutionary opposition. Administration was to be conducted by democratically elected representatives of the working population, whose tasks would be legislative and executive, that is, to make and implement laws. Such a fusion of powers would eliminate the need for a professional bureaucracy. Bureaucratism was to be combated by ensuring that all elected officials were subject to instant recall. Also, they were to be paid only an average worker's wage, to eliminate the material bases of bureaucratic careerism. In addition, power was to be decentralised into the hands of local communes. A central government of sorts, composed of elected and revocable representatives of these communes, would remain necessary, to carry out 'the few but important functions which would still remain for [it]'. While these functions were never defined fully by Marx the most important was economic, 'to regulate national production upon a common plan'. So conceived, the commune state would be a form of direct democracy, in which the radical diffusion of power into the hands of the workers would lead to 'the authentic self-administration of the people'.

The 'true secret' of the Commune, Marx averred, was that it constituted 'the political form at last discovered under which to work out the economic emancipation of labour'. In his 1891 'Preface' to *The Civil War*, Engels repeated the injunction that all vestiges of state power were to be 'lop[ped] off at once as much as possible until such time as a generation reared in new, free social conditions is able to throw the entire lumber of the state on the scrap heap'. His impatience with the 'superstitious reverence' in which many German 'Social Democratic philistines' held the existing state was also palpable: 'Dictatorship of the Proletariat. Well and good, gentlemen, do you want to know what this dictatorship looks like? Look at the Paris Commune. That was the Dictatorship of the Proletariat.' Marx himself may have been less unequivocal than Engels but in an article in *The World* in October 1871 he did describe it as a 'proletarian *dictature*'. Many of their followers were far from convinced. Kautsky and the vast majority of the SPD rejected the Commune as the model for the dictatorship of the proletariat, as did the Russian Menshevik leader Julius Martov. A notable exception was to be Lenin. In *State and Revolution*, written in 1917, he denounced all those socialists, especially Kautsky, who defended the democratic republic as the political superstructure appropriate to socialism, and came out in favour of a commune state.

Both visions of the revolutionary state were committed to some form of workers' democracy. Both also assumed the abolition, sooner or later, of state power *per se*. In Engels' famous maxim, ultimately 'the administration of men [would] be replaced by the administration of things'. In other respects they were profoundly different. The first model implied a continuing role for strong, centralised state power in the construction of socialism, the second the immediate dismantling of the old state.

Moreover, the commune-state model of direct democracy articulated by Marx, as Richard Hunt pointed out, was seriously flawed. Specifically, it lacked any criteria 'to delineate exactly what functions should devolve upon which levels of the administration, or specify any overall degree of centralisation to be achieved, or suggest how the inevitable conflicts of and jurisdictional disputes among the various levels would be resolved'. The experience of the Soviet Union, as Daniel Doveton argued, high-lighted other flaws in this model, in particular Marx's neglect of the separation of executive, judicial and legislative powers to be found in democratic polities. Its absence leads to minorities – in the Soviet case, even the majority – becoming subject to an absolute and untrammelled state power, claimed for itself by the victorious Communist Party.[16] Finally, doubts arise as to whether any form of democracy was possible as long as Marx's and Engels' again sketchy vision of how a socialist economy should be constructed was adhered to.

The economics of socialism

For such prolific writers Marx and Engels had surprisingly little to say about the economics of socialism. The reason once more seems to have been their aversion to Utopian 'recipes'. In the process of their historical struggles the workers, as Marx remarked in *The Civil War*, gradually would discover how to build a socialist economy from those prerequisites already 'pregnant' within bourgeois society. What they left to their followers did not amount to a detailed blueprint for the construction of a socialist economy, but rather, a series of broad principles. In particular, as they emphasised in the *Manifesto* and elsewhere, after the workers had won political power they must begin to abolish private property. They advocated the nationalisation of the land, banks, large-scale industry, and transport – the so-called 'commanding heights' of the economy, which were to be administered centrally by the new proletarian state. Small-scale enterprises would come under state control only gradually, 'by degrees'. As Marx later wrote in *The Civil War*, if the 'economical foun-dations' of the old capitalist order were not destroyed, if control over pro-duction was left in the hands of the bourgeoisie, then the workers would be unable to retain political power. The most important single act of the Commune, Engels later added, was that which established the principle of workers' control over industry, though neither he nor Marx offered much practical guidance on how to implement it.

However, their belief that after the revolution the workers should take the means of production into public ownership and administer them, does not determine how a socialist economic system should function. Echoing the argument expounded by the Polish Marxist economist Oskar Lange, in his *On the Economic Theory of Socialism* (1936), Scott Arnold has pointed out that it leaves open the question of whether it should be a market or a centrally planned economy.[17] Notwithstanding Marx's and Engels' failure to discuss this question in detail it is possible to infer from their scattered remarks that they saw no place for the market in a socialist economy. In the *Economic and Philosophic Manuscripts of 1844* Marx had launched a blistering attack on private property, commodity production and money, the characteristic features of a capitalist market economy, as the sources of human alienation and servitude. Human liberation required the elimination of the market. In the *Manifesto* and, later, in the *Critique of the Gotha Programme*, he declared in broad terms that under socialism the production and distribution of goods was to be subject to planning. In *Anti-Duhring*, Engels unequivocally summarised their views:

> The seizure of the means of production by society puts an end to commodity production, and therewith to the domination of the product over the producer. Anarchy in social production is replaced by conscious organisation on a planned basis.

Marx and Engels, it appears, had given no consideration to the concept of market socialism elaborated by some of their followers in the twentieth century.

They also offered little idea of how a centrally planned economy would function in practice, nor of its authoritarian potential. Although the Russian anarchist Mikhail Bakunin, in his *Statism and Anarchy* (1873), had warned that centralised economic power was incompatible with the diffusion of political power into the hands of the workers (and peasants), it was only later experience that alerted Marxists to the tensions between central planning and democracy, both economic and political. As Karl Korsch, a keen advocate of the devolution of power to workers' councils during the German Revolution of 1918–19, shrewdly observed, 'even in a fully socialised community there must still exist a conflict between the particular interests of individual producers and the universal interests of the general consumers'.[18] In theory, planning would resolve this conflict.

Yet the plan, if it is to satisfy the general needs of society, and not simply particular local demands, must be drawn up by a central authority. This authority alone would have the vision and, no less important, the information to determine what these general needs might be. Its task would be to issue instructions to all enterprises under its purview, specifying the nature and quantity of goods to be produced; to distribute supplies of materials and labour amongst them to ensure that their targets could be met; and to distribute the goods finally produced. The very experience of the Soviet Union since the 1930s, so Alec Nove emphasised, illustrated that a centrally planned economy was incompatible with workers' democracy in any shape or form. Even if the workers did possess the (Utopian) level of consciousness that would lead them to sacrifice their own particular interests for those of society at large, they simply would not possess the information to take decisions which would achieve this objective. In the complex industrial economy demanded by socialism, production could be regulated through the market. If the market was abolished, then its replacement by a centralised bureaucracy would become 'a *functional necessity*'. In that case, Nove concluded, '[b]elow the centre there are bound to be severe limits placed on the power of *local* or regional authorities, in order to ensure the priority of the general over the particular'.[19] In a nutshell, central planning and democracy, especially the direct democracy of the commune-state model, are mutually contradictory.

How Marx and Engels might have revised their views in light of the history of Soviet planning, and the authoritarian control of the 'New [bureaucratic] Class' that it spawned (see Chapters 7 and 8), remains a matter of idle speculation. For long, their followers subscribed to the principle of central planning, despite Lange's speculations on the feasibility of market socialism. It was the non-Marxist economist Schumpeter who was among the first to confront squarely the contradiction between central planning and democracy. A market economy, he insisted, was vital if democratic socialism was to be realised; wryly adding that 'there exists no more democratic institution than a market'. However, he conceded that the scope of the market should be confined essentially to the production and distribution of the consumer goods desired by 'each individual comrade'. Fundamental questions concerning investment to provide for greater production in the future, and, one might add, concerning other public goods such as education, remained matters for political decision, best taken by an elected congress or parliament.[20]

Nationalism and socialism

Nationalism proved to be another of Marx's and Engels' blind spots, which is not surprising in light of their perceptions of themselves as citizens of the world. Their cosmopolitanism notwithstanding, the economic logic of their analysis also led them to regard nations, and nation states and nationalism, as historical phenomena, which had evolved as a product of capitalism. Capitalism had overcome the feudal barriers and particularist loyalties which hitherto had separated groups sharing the characteristics of nationhood, such as a common language and traditions. They described this process in the *Manifesto*:

> The bourgeoisie keeps more and more doing away with the scattered state of the population, of the means of production, and of property. It has agglomerated population, centralised means of production.... The necessary consequence of this was political centralisation. Independent, or but loosely connected, provinces with separate interests, laws, governments and systems of taxation became lumped together into one nation, with one government, one code of laws, one national class interest, one frontier and one customs tariff.

The bourgeois nation states so created were themselves destined to be transitory. The development of capitalism was leading to the creation of a united and increasingly uniform world economy and society (the late Marx's thinking on Russia was not integrated into his consideration of nationalism). In turn, it would beget a global proletariat, one with 'no country', which, as they rather recklessly postulated in *The German Ideology*, ' "all at once" and simultaneously' would rise in revolution. Once in power, this nationless proletariat would seek to eradicate as swiftly as possible all sources of division and exploitation, economic, social and national, and establish a harmonious new world order.

Their understanding of the economic trajectory of capitalism also explains their opposition to the aspirations of the small, so-called 'unhistoric', nations of Europe to set up their own independent states. The birth of such states, to satisfy what they derided as 'the principle of nationalities', would run counter to the whole logic of capitalism. It would destroy the economic integration already brought about by capitalism and thus hinder the advance towards the envisioned international socialist order of the future. Accordingly, the aspirations of most Slavs in central and southern Europe were dismissed out of hand. As Engels

wrote in February 1849, they 'lack[ed] the primary historical, geographical, political and industrial conditions for a viable independence'. Self-
determination for the large 'historic' nations of Europe alone was
legitimate, as independent states in Germany, Hungary, Italy and Poland
would promote the development of capitalism, the growth of their
respective proletariats, and thus foster the eventual victory of socialism.

Exceptionally, however, they did advocate the break-up of large
multinational states, based on criteria other than the logic of capitalist
economic development. Poland was a particular case in point. The
Partitions of the late eighteenth century had divided the former Polish
state into three parts, which had become integrated into the Habsburg,
Prussian and Russian Empires. However, the benefits of such integration
were outweighed by more immediate political concerns which
demanded the re-creation of an independent Poland. First, the Partitions
had bound Germany to the reactionary Holy Alliance, the contrivance of
the 'prison house of nations', the Russian Empire. To free themselves
from its clutches the Germans had to struggle as much for Polish independence as for their own unity. As Engels concluded in August 1848,
'the restoration of a democratic Poland [was] the first condition for the
restoration of a democratic Germany'. Moreover, an independent Poland
was also seen as a vital barrier against 'the barbarian hordes... of Russia',
which Marx and Engels prophesied would intervene to suppress revolutionary movements in Central Europe (the crushing of the 1848
Revolution in Hungary appeared to confirm their worst fears). In the
1870s, after Germany had been united, they put forward a final reason
for Polish independence. Developing an idea first mooted with respect to
Ireland, whose oppression by England [sic] had divided the workers of
both countries, they insisted that international proletarian solidarity
would also be stymied by continuing partition. As Marx pointed out in a
speech of January 1875, until independence was regained the emerging
Polish proletariat would be deceived into rallying behind nationalist
rather than socialist goals, which would turn them against their German
and emerging Russian comrades. Their concern was that the proletariat
of oppressed nations would be blinded by chauvinism until national freedom was won. In other words, national self-determination (but still not
for the 'unhistoric' nations) was a necessary precondition of proletarian
internationalism.

Marx and Engels grossly misjudged the power of nationalism, as did
many of their followers, although Lenin (Chapter 4) was more sensitive
to its appeal. The workers of the world did not surrender their allegiance

to their respective nations and become the international class that Marx had predicted and hoped for. When the First World War broke out, most workers in Europe willingly went to fight their comrades. Almost all of their leaders abandoned their internationalist principles too, and urged them to do so. They justified their actions on the grounds that they were defending democracy, and the prospects for socialism, from reactionary enemies, often by appeal to the literal prescriptions of the 'founding fathers'. A few critical voices demurred but we shall return to this question in Chapter 5.

Conclusion

The contradictions in the ideological legacy bequeathed by the 'founding fathers' soon became evident in the divergent practice of the professedly Marxist-inspired political movements in the late nineteenth and early twentieth centuries. Its ambiguities allowed them to embrace quite different political strategies, confident that they were following consistently in the footsteps of their mentors. Boggs identified four major variants of Marxism that had evolved before the First World War: the orthodox–centrist, represented by Kautsky; the evolutionary–revisionist, represented by Bernstein; the vanguardist–revolutionary, represented by Lenin; and the radical Left, represented by Rosa Luxemburg.[21] Just what these variants were, and how they arose, are the subject of Part Two. It will focus, as Boggs does, primarily on German Social Democracy and Russian Marxism, and the circumstances which had led, by the end of the First World War, to the 'parting of the ways' between them.

PART II
The Parting of the Ways

PART II
The Parting of the Ways

Chapter 3: German Social Democracy

In the second half of the nineteenth century the locus of European socialism shifted from Britain and France to Central and East Europe, where it adopted a distinctively Marxist hue. By 1914 the German Social Democratic Party (SPD) was the strongest socialist party in Europe. It had a mass membership of over a million, with another two and a half million largely skilled workers affiliated to it through their trade unions; it had won four and a quarter million votes in the elections of 1912; and, with 110 deputies, it was the largest single party in the Imperial German Parliament (*Reichstag*). Its sheer size meant that it was also the dominant force in the Second International, a loose and ideologically diverse organisation of primarily European socialist parties upon which the SPD aspired to impose its ideology and tactics. German too, according to Moira Donald, was 'the lingua franca of the socialist world'. The leaders of the SPD were among the most renowned Marxist thinkers of their age. Karl Kautsky, the so-called 'pope' of Marxism, was described by Leon Trotsky as the International's outstanding theoretician.[1] Its status led many other socialist parties, including its much weaker counterparts in Austria and Belgium, to see it as a model to emulate. Its intellectual and political pre-eminence, combined with the fact that the conflicts over reformism, revisionism and nationalism, and the threat of war, which plagued all the parties of the International, were waged most intensely within it, warrants focus on it.

Why the German Social Democrats embraced Marxism requires some explanation in the first place. The large and growing labour movement in industrial Britain proved to be remarkably immune to Marxism, and revolutionary ideas generally, after the 1840s. As Ross McKibbin has pointed out, a combination of: deference to the Crown, increasingly seen as standing above partisan politics and ensuring fair play for all, regardless of class; the gradual accommodation of the working class within a more representative parliamentary system; virtually complete freedom for trade union action after 1875; and the absence of a radical intelligentsia, certainly since the early decades of the nineteenth century, all blunted the appeal of revolutionary politics.[2] Consequently, in Britain, the evolutionary path to socialism advanced by the intellectuals of the Fabian society, who believed that a democratic government in control of an efficient civil service at the central and local level could regulate the economy and introduce legislation to improve the welfare of the workers, had a much greater appeal than the class war espoused by Marxism. The welfare reforms introduced by the Liberal government of 1906–11 reinforced the belief in gradualism, and in the potential, if piecemeal, benefits to be gained from an alliance between the Liberals and the nascent Labour Party. Liberal polities had emerged elsewhere in West Europe. France was a case in point. It too had a liberal parliamentary system after 1871, under the Third Republic, which legalised union organisation and strike activity in 1884. Moreover, in France, and Italy too, a slower pace of industrialisation, which retarded the development of a large and concentrated working class, and the continuing appeal of indigenous radical and other socialist traditions (Jacobinism, anarcho-syndicalism, Blanquism, Proudhonism), thwarted the formation of unified mass Marxist parties.[3] Different conditions and intellectual traditions in Germany led to a much greater receptivity to Marxism. It is to these that we must turn.

The origins of German socialism: from Lassalle to Marxism

Until the middle of the nineteenth century industrial backwardness and the climate of political repression within the German Federation stymied the emergence of a mass socialist movement. Embryonic émigré movements, of artisans rather than industrial workers, did spring up, such as the League of the Just, initially influenced by Wilhelm Weitling's brand of Christian, cooperative socialism. The revolution of 1848–9 witnessed the formation of numerous workers' organisations, many of which allied with the Liberals in pressing for greater political and civil liberties as well as measures of social reform. The pusillanimity of most

Liberals, alarmed at the prospect of violent social revolution from below, created widespread disillusion in the emerging working class. The prospects for a coalition between labour and liberalism, on the British 'model', were limited, particularly as after 1848 most Liberals proved as eager as the governments of the German states to suppress all socialist associations.

Suppression notwithstanding, the rapid development of industry during the 1850s led to the emergence of an independent workers' movement in the 1860s. In May 1863, Ferdinand Lassalle established the General Union of German Workers (GUGW), whose roots lay in the workers' educational societies initially set up under the tutelage of the still radical Progressive Party. While it was certainly not Marxist in inspiration or programme, Marx himself, and his German disciple Wilhelm Liebknecht, acknowledged that it was the first mass socialist organisation in Germany. Its objectives were twofold: universal (male) suffrage and the democratisation of the state; and the creation of workers' cooperatives, to be funded by the newly democratised state, which would serve as the basis for a future socialist economy. Rejecting collaboration with the perfidious Liberals, Lassalle naively hoped to realise these objectives in partnership with the highly authoritarian Prussian state, which he saw as the only force able to bring about the unification of the country – something that he had also long desired.

Six years later, the rival Union of German Workers' Societies, which had refused to merge with the GUGW, gathered at Eisenach. Under the leadership of August Bebel and Liebknecht, it transformed itself into the Social Democratic Workers' Party (SDAP). A self-professedly Marxist party, it adopted most of the prescriptions that Marx had drawn up for the First International. Its mission, as Liebknecht recalled in his 1899 pamphlet *No Compromise – No Political Trading*, was to take the place of the cowardly bourgeoisie and, in keeping with the First International's rejection of alliances with the middle classes, independently to carry out the democratic revolution in Germany without which socialism was unthinkable. Democracy itself, however, could not be won through the ballot box but only after the existing 'police and military state' had been overthrown. With its bases largely in the southern states, it vehemently rejected the process of unification from above engineered in the 1860s by Otto von Bismarck, prime minister of Prussia, and supported by most Liberals, as it threatened to spread Prussian authoritarianism throughout Germany. Dislike and fear of Prussia as much as Marxist internationalism explained its opposition to the Franco-Prussian war of 1870–1, which was likely to lead to the incorporation of the south into the Prussian-dominated North German Confederation set up in the wake of the Austro-Prussian war of 1866. It was also a much more decentralised and democratic body than the GUGW. Annual congresses representing local organisations, not the dictates of a despotic leader such as Lassalle or his successor, J. B. von Schweitzer, determined policy.[4]

In May 1875, under pressure from the party members, 127 delegates from both parties met at Gotha, where they united to form the German Socialist Workers' Party (SAPD), renamed the SPD in 1890. Its programme was a compromise, Liebknecht admitted, with significant concessions to Lassalleanism. While welcoming the formation of a united party, in his *Critique of the Gotha Programme* Marx dismissed its manifesto as error ridden and confused. He venomously rejected the Lassallean ideas embedded in it, including reference to the 'iron law of wages', which implied that the workers could make absolutely no material advance under capitalism; the dismissal of all but the workers as 'one reactionary mass', which denied any revolutionary potential to the lower middle class and peasantry; producers' cooperatives as the basis for the future socialist organisation of the economy, instead of the nationalisation of the means of production; and the emphasis on the struggle of the German workers within national bounds, at the expense of forging links with their counterparts elsewere. Notwithstanding continuing tensions between the Eisenachers and the Lassalleans, with Liebknecht scornful of the latter's lingering belief in a parliamentary path to socialism, the Party prospered. Despite the Anti-Socialist Law of 1878, which banned Social Democratic organisations and newspapers, and trade unions (curiously, individual Social Democrats could still be elected to, and speak openly in, the *Reichstag* and the individual state legislatures within the federal German Empire), it made substantial progress. In the 1881 *Reichstag* elections it gained only 6.1 per cent of the votes cast and 3 per cent of the seats, while in 1890, when the Law was lifted, it won 19.7 per cent of the vote and 8.8 per cent of the seats. Oppression, combined with the failure of Bismarck's social welfare legislation – including health and accident insurance and a rudimentary old age pension scheme – to benefit the workers as much as the remaining Lassalleans had hoped, and continuing poverty and harsh conditions of work, best account for the Social Democrats' advance.[5]

Ineffectual as it was, the Anti-Socialist Law had a profound impact on the ideological development of the Party, as well as on the cultural evolution of much of the working class. First, the prohibition of party and trade union activities discredited Lassallean notions about what could be achieved in cooperation with the Prussian-dominated state. Liebknecht's warning of 1869, that in Germany 'the ballot box [could] never become the cradle of the democratic state', rang true. Secondly, the support of most German Liberals for such repressive measures (the Progressive Party was an honourable exception) confirmed the Party in its rejection of any future collaboration with them. Finally, the persecution and the transformation of the working class into *Reichsfeinde*, enemies of the state, led to its exclusion from the mainstream of German society. This exclusion, described as a process of 'negative integration', fuelled the creation of a proletarian sub-culture, underpinned by a myriad of vibrant educational and recreational clubs and associations established by the SPD to mobilise working men and women in support of its aims. In these circumstances, quite different from those prevailing in France and especially in Britain, the appeal of Marxism grew markedly.[6]

At its Halle Congress in October 1890 the recently legalised SPD resolved to draw up a new programme. It was adopted the following October when it met again at Erfurt. Exorcising the vestiges of Lassalleanism, it re-armed the Party theoretically on Marxist lines, at least the positivist, evolutionary and Darwinian–naturalist Marxism of Engels' *Anti-Duhring* (see Chapter 2). Its first, theoretical section, drawn up by Kautsky with Engels' assistance, sketched out a recognisably determinist prognosis of the future that will be familiar from the preceding chapter. The growth of capitalism, marked by a recurring series of crises, inexorably was creating the economic and political preconditions for socialist revolution. Capitalism's 'iron logic', as Liebknecht stressed, was driving it towards an unavoidable catastrophe, when the proletarian masses would rise in revolution, overthrow capitalism and resolve the crisis by the introduction of a planned socialist economy. However, as this catastrophe remained some time in the future, the programme incorporated a second (minimum) section, drafted by Bebel and Bernstein. It outlined the immediate objectives that the Party must pursue, to offer succour to the working class and to prepare the way for socialism. They included universal suffrage; the root and branch democratisation of the state; civil liberties for all, including women; a progressive income tax, to replace the existing system of regressive indirect taxation; social welfare legislation, including free education and health care; and laws to protect labour, most notably the eight-hour day. Even Lenin was moved to praise this programme eight years later, and to seek to 'imitate' it, with necessary modifications to take account of Russian conditions.[7]

The new programme appeared to have equipped the Party for a radical assault on the old order. Yet, Liebknecht once more observed, it was not without its tensions. The theoretical section, with its emphasis on the inevitable replacement of capitalism by socialism as a result of economic catastrophe, was in danger of reducing Marxism to little more than a form of social evolutionism, and the Party to fatalism and political passivity. Socialism, he countered as Marx had before him, would not fall as manna from heaven. Revolution remained necessary, and could only be brought about by the conscious and organised action of the proletariat. However, before 1914 the majority of the Party, and the trade unions, together with their comrades across Europe (Russia proved to be an exception), increasingly based their actions on the gradualist strategy implicit in the second section of the programme. Economic, political and social reform of the structures of Imperial Germany and the material improvement of everyday working-class life became their *raison d'être*. It is the material and ideological reasons for this conversion to evolutionary rather than revolutionary politics that we now must address.

Reformism and revisionism

The ink was barely dry on the new programme when fissures again appeared. A group of radical 'Youngsters' (*Jungen*), active worker propagandists according to Bernstein, was highly critical of the reluctance of the Social Democrat deputies in the *Reichstag* to support the celebration of May Day with strike action. Their criticisms were echoed by recently recruited youthful intellectuals and journalists, who presciently warned that focusing on advances within parliamentary channels would breed careerism within the leadership and demoralisation at the grass roots of the Party.[8] Yet the most serious challenge to the Marxist orthodoxy of the Party came from its moderate wing, which embraced the 'heretical' practice known as 'reformism'. At first, it was confined largely to the southern states of Hesse, Baden, Württemberg and Bavaria. As the leader of the Bavarian Social Democrats, George von Vollmar, pointed out, unlike the north the south remained heavily agrarian, with a large peasant population. It was likely to remain so, he continued, as agriculture was not subject to the same processes of concentration as industry. Consequently, the small peasant was not doomed to extinction but would survive as a major political force, and potential ally of the proletariat. The business census of 1895, which revealed that the number of small and medium-sized peasant holdings had increased by 3.5 per cent and 9 per cent respectively since 1882, seemed to substantiate Vollmar's argument. If the SPD was to make progress in the south, then it had to win over the peasants. By the mid-1890s Vollmar and his allies demanded that the Erfurt programme be revised, to include a section devoted to their concerns. Their attempts to conciliate the peasants went far beyond what Marx and Engels had envisaged (see Chapter 2). They insisted that specific concessions were required to secure peasant support, including the abandonment of the Social Democrats' traditional opposition to collaboration with other parties, particularly the Liberals, in order to pass budgetary legislation that would provide material assistance for the countryside. The fact that regional governments in the south were considerably more liberal than the Prussian government convinced many southern Social Democrats of the feasibility of constructing effective cross-party coalitions, especially after the lifting of the Anti-Socialist Law. The French and Italian Socialist Parties too, much less worker-based than the SPD, were inclined to seek backing from the peasantry, and from the lower middle classes more generally.[9]

The southerners' strategy provoked heated debates in the SPD. Its Cologne (1893), Breslau (1895) and Hamburg (1897) Congresses categorically rejected agreements with other parties. With the ageing Engels' support, Kautsky entered the fray, intent on refuting Vollmar's theoretical justification of reformism. The Breslau Congress accepted his long-held views that technological progress would lead in the end to the extinction of peasant farming. In his major treatise, *The Agrarian Question* (1899), he conceded that the growth of large-scale capitalism in agriculture would proceed more slowly than in industry. Nevertheless, he reaffirmed that despite the peasants' surprising resilience so far, ultimately they were doomed, whatever sops were granted to them. The task of the Party was not to offer them false hope but rather to try to prevent their mobilisation into the camp of counter revolution, for example, by promising not to expropriate their property. Russia, he acknowledged several years later, was a different case. Foreshadowing Lenin's own conclusions (see Chapter 4), he admitted that it was possible for the Russian proletariat to enlist the peasants as allies in the democratic revolution against the autocracy. He hastened to add, in his *The Driving Forces of the Russian Revolution and Its Prospects* (1906), that after the revolution had given them the land confiscated from the nobility they would become quintessentially petty-bourgeois property owners. As such it would be Utopian to imagine that they could be won over to support socialist revolution, for which conditions in Russia in any case were not yet propitious.[10]

Despite the SPD's condemnation of the participation of its members in regional and municipal government, reformism grew throughout the 1890s. Social Democrats in the south, principally in Bavaria, went their own way, as Vollmar and his allies vainly pursued peasant support. They entered into electoral alliances, 'cow trades' as Liebknecht mocked them, with the Catholic Centre and other bourgeois parties. In the interests of preserving party unity the majority turned a blind eye to these practices. Reformism also gained momentum from the rapid growth of powerful trade unions, which also had been legalised in 1890. Increasingly, the unions, and the workers whom they represented, directed their energies to securing immediate material advances. They knew and cared little for Marxism. The vast majority of ordinary workers, Liebknecht conceded, even those who were Party members, took no interest in theoretical debates. Their lack of interest in theory helps us understand Kautsky's repeated insistence on the need for intellectuals, who alone understood the historical inevitability of socialism, to instil political consciousness into the working class. As he wrote in his 1901 article *Revision of the Programme of Austrian Social Democracy*, 'socialist consciousness is something brought from outside into the class struggle of the proletariat, and not something arising spontaneously out of it'.[11] Without intellectual leadership it would merely acquire a 'trade union consciousness', to employ the term later coined by Lenin, who gleefully seized upon Kautsky's conclusions to defend his own conception of the need for a vanguard party of self-appointed intellectuals to impose its authority over the workers and lead them in revolution (see Chapter 4). But Kautsky himself was far from consistent on this question and should not be regarded simply as a prototypical Leninist. He certainly did not weigh in behind Lenin and unequivocally endorse his ideas on party organisation. As his grandson John Kautsky argued, more often he envisioned the task of the Party intellectuals as Marx himself had: not to substitute themselves for the proletariat but merely to educate it as to what its final goal was, to turn its spontaneous strivings in a revolutionary direction. Moreover, as he came to discover that the Party intellectuals were not as uniformly revolutionary as he had supposed, on occasion he denied that such education could be handed down. In his *The Intellectuals and the Workers*, written for the Party paper *Die Neue Zeit* (New Times) in 1903, he insisted that 'the proletarian himself must develop his own theory... he must be completely self-taught'.[12]

His doubts about the intellectuals, arguably, were nurtured by their role in the reformist debate. It flared up again at the end of the 1890s, when a group of Party intellectuals produced a fundamental reinterpretation of Marxism that was embraced by many reformist Party and trade union leaders as a theoretical justification for their practices. Bernstein was the leading proponent of what became known as 'Revisionism'. A close friend of Engels and an 'orthodox' Marxist in the 1880s, he too had condemned anything smacking of reformism, or 'state socialism'. Then, he remained certain that the capitalist system was destined ultimately for economic breakdown, a 'revolutionary catastrophe' which would bring the proletariat to power. During the 1890s his thinking changed. Despite his own protestations, in all probability he had become influenced by Fabianism as he had lived in exile in Britain since 1880. He professed that he had come to see the need to update Marxism in light of recent economic and political developments, in order to provide a suitable theory for contemporary socialist practice. He dismissed appeals to the writings of the 'founding fathers' as mechanistic and counter to the spirit of Marxism. Any work deserving of the name 'scientific socialist' had to analyse current economic, political and social developments, to ascertain the degree to which the premises and predictions of Marx and Engels remained correct. He laid out the conclusions of his own analysis in *The Preconditions of Socialism,* first published in 1899, in which he summarised arguments developed in a series of articles in the *Die Neue Zeit* between 1896 and 1898.

He began by criticising Marx's and Engels' quasi-Blanquist faith in 'the creative power of revolutionary force for the socialist transformation of modern society', a faith which he attributed to the influence of 'the radical Hegelian dialectic'. In a very different world from that foreseen by the 'founding fathers', revolution had become redundant. In support he cited passages from Engels' 1895 'Preface' to Marx's *The Class Struggles in France,* where he had emphasised 'legal methods' and 'parliamentary activity' as the best means now to ensure Social Democratic progress. He failed to mention that Engels had played down the need for revolution at the request of the leadership of the SPD itself. He then critically re-examined a number of Marx's other predictions. He granted that large-scale enterprises, and cartels, had emerged in some sectors of industry, such as coal, chemicals, electrical engineering, and machine construction, but were far from dominant in any country. On the contrary, industry in general had not become ever more centralised and concentrated in the hands of a diminishing number of capitalist magnates. Small and medium-sized businesses had not only survived but increased in number, especially in the consumer and service sectors. Other countervailing forces were also at work. Property ownership itself was increasing, as the appearance of joint stock companies had encouraged the proliferation of small shareholders. Large-scale capitalism had not taken over the countryside, where the peasants had proved to be remarkably tenacious. The middle classes too, including a new stratum of white collar workers, had grown markedly. The workers themselves had not been subject to ever increasing immiseration, and in most advanced West European countries their wages and standard of living had been rising, particularly during the economic upsurge of the second half of the 1890s. In sum, modern industrial societies had not undergone the polarisation foreseen by Marx, into a small minority of capitalist plutocrats and a vast and impoverished proletarian majority. Furthermore, the increase in middle-class and even working-class income in the advanced capitalist states of the West meant that the market for goods had expanded. This development, in conjunction with the evolution of a sophisticated system of credit and the capacity of the new cartels to regulate production, had done much to eliminate the possibility of over-production and so minimise the explosive crises which Marx had predicted. Unlike his more orthodox comrades, for Bernstein the victory of socialism would not be determined by the breakdown of capitalism. Quite the reverse, such a catastrophe would be fatal for socialism, which demanded not the destruction but rather the expansion of economic wealth.

The question facing Bernstein was that if socialism was no longer an 'immanent economic necessity', then how was it to be achieved? While as averse as Marx to providing blueprints of the socialist future, he sketched out proposals for its 'piecemeal realisation', as he described the process in an article in *Die Neue Zeit* of January 1898. His more detailed exposition in the *Preconditions* bore a striking resemblance to Sidney Webb's 1889 Fabian essay *The Historic Basis of Socialism*. Since the economic preconditions for socialism, in particular the centralisation of industry, were far from complete, it was necessary to construct the bases for the socialisation of production and distribution. To achieve this end, he supported (with echoes of Lassalle) the promotion of cooperatives: agrarian, consumer and producer. In particular, the powers of municipal governments were to be augmented, to permit them to establish communal enterprises. Avowedly borrowing ideas from Sidney and Beatrice Webb, he also advocated the gradual extension of 'Industrial Democracy', that is, increased trade union participation in the management of industry. All this could be done by parliamentary means. He likened the politics of socialism to 'organised liberalism', capable of evolving from the institutions of modern society without recourse to revolution or a dictatorship of the proletariat. '[T]he victory of democracy, the creation of democratic social and political organisations,' he averred, 'is the indispensable precondition for the realisation of socialism.' In Germany itself democracy could be attained only if Social Democracy abandoned its isolationist tactics and allied with those elements of the bourgeoisie and petty-bourgeoisie also bent on eliminating the reactionary feudal power of Prussian Junkerdom. The peasants were particularly important, in his eyes 'belonging to the working classes'. Accordingly, he accepted Vollmar's argument that the SPD must champion their demands for economic assistance, which in turn would secure their support in future elections. The 'final goal', he repeated, the actual structures of a socialist society, could not be laid out in advance. Its shape would be determined by 'the movement', which he understood, first, as the organisations which would press for socialism, and secondly, as the series of transformations through which society would pass under their influence. Socialism, he reiterated, was not a pre-ordained product of the impersonal processes of 'History', but rather a morally desirable goal which had to be fought for. It is little wonder that his attempt to provide the SPD with a new theoretical underpinning for its emerging practice was welcomed by reformist socialists elsewhere in Europe, prominent among whom were Jean Jaurès in France and Ramsay MacDonald in Britain. Revisionism, Kautsky complained at the Amsterdam Congress of the Second International in 1904, had become a European phenomenon.[13]

Revisionism provoked the ire of the Party's intellectual 'heavyweights', with Kautsky and Rosa Luxemburg leading the assault against it. Kautsky's own rebuttal of his old comrade's views, in his *Bernstein and the Social Democratic Programme* (1899), was surprisingly muted, possibly to avoid splitting the Party irrevocably. He agreed with Bernstein that the later 1890s had ushered in a period of relative prosperity and, consequently, of capitalist stability. In this conjuncture the emphasis on partial reforms to improve material conditions for the workers was appropriate. Bernstein, however, had mistaken this temporary phase of prosperity for the normal condition of capitalism, instead of focusing on its underlying contradictions. Socialism was not just a moral crusade, but still a matter of economic necessity, as his earlier defence of the Erfurt programme, *The Class Struggle* (1892), had attested. Repeating what Marx had written long before about the logic of capitalism, he insisted that its fundamental tendency to chronic over-production, cartels notwithstanding, had not been resolved and would lead to recurring crises. The concentration of capital too had progressed visibly, as the formation of powerful cartels, in the coal and steel as well as the sugar and dairy industries among others, demonstrated. Surviving small businesses remained subordinate to these new forms of monopoly, while joint stock companies merely put the money of small shareholders at the disposal of centralised and concentrated capital. The middle classes, he admitted, were 'not dying out'; yet it was a new class, not of independent artisans or traders, but largely of white collar professionals, dependent upon and sharing the views of the capitalists. At the same time, the ranks of the proletariat were also growing, with the division between it and the bourgeoisie increasing inexorably, if incrementally. In all, the breakdown of capitalism remained inevitable, albeit at some still unspecified time in the future. Then it would be the task of the Party to rouse the proletariat to revolution, and begin the construction of socialism.[14]

If Kautsky's critique of Revisionism was rather hackneyed and pedestrian, Luxemburg's was a more original attempt to apply Marxism to analyse the current state of capitalism, and, according to Bernstein himself, methodologically superior. First published as a series of articles in the *Leipziger Volkszeitung* (Leipzig People's Paper) in September 1898 and April 1899, it was issued as a separate pamphlet, *Reform or Revolution*, in 1900. Like Kautsky, Luxemburg was bent on demonstrating that capitalism was destined to collapse under the weight of its own contradictions. She rejected out of hand Bernstein's arguments in support of capitalist stability. The growing availability of credit had stimulated growth in production, but had not eliminated its volatility. Rather than balancing the demand for goods with their supply, at the first signs of over-production credit dried up, so provoking a fall in demand and thus exacerbating the problem of under-consumption. Cartelised industries had flourished too, but only at the expense of those sectors of the economy where competition still reigned. As cartels expanded to dominate more sectors of the economy, competition between them would intensify; profits would be squeezed; and ultimately the anarchy of production typical of capitalism, not its regulation, would be re-created at a more intensified level. Moreover, despite the survival of small businesses, which kept springing up in new branches of industry, cartels continued to accelerate 'the concentration of production, technical progress, etc.', in other words the socialisation of production, which would serve as the foundation of the socialist economy of the future. Capitalism to date, she concluded, had survived by dint of expansion into non-capitalist areas of the world, where it was able to sell its surplus goods. But this could not continue

ad infinitum, as the cartels themselves had hastened the spread of imperialism, so speeding up the assimilation of these areas into an increasingly
global capitalist system. Once the opportunity to exploit non-capitalist
regions had been exhausted, the 'final crisis' of capitalism would be at
hand.[15] In her refutation of the economic rationale for Revisionism
offered by Bernstein, by proving at least to her own satisfaction that capitalism was destined to collapse as a result of its own contradictions,
Luxemburg had sketched out a theory of imperialism that she only fully
articulated in her major treatise, written on the eve of the First World
War, *The Accumulation of Capital* (1913).

Both Kautsky's and Luxemburg's predictions concerning the economic
breakdown of capitalism turned out to be unfounded. They proved to be
on sounder ground in challenging the politics of Revisionism. As Marx
and Engels before him, Kautsky, if not Luxemburg, accepted that an
evolutionary path to socialism was possible, notably in Britain and
Switzerland, where liberal parliamentary systems existed. Where authoritarianism persisted, they concurred that reliance on parliamentarianism
would lead into a blind alley. In Germany itself, the bureaucracy, the
military and an increasingly conservative bourgeoisie were bitterly
opposed to the onward march of democracy, let alone socialism.
Revolution remained necessary, to win in the first instance the battle for
the democratic polity demanded by socialism. In the meantime, the Party
must support the workers in their fight for piecemeal reforms to ameliorate the worst excesses of capitalist exploitation, while reminding them
that reform *per se* should not be mistaken for the gradual evolution of
socialism. The ultimate purpose of everyday economic and political
struggle, Luxemburg added in a manner akin to Marx, was to raise the
consciousness of the workers and thus ready them for the final assault on
capitalism.[16]

Repeated Party Congresses, particularly those at Hanover (1899) and
Dresden (1903), overwhelmingly condemned Revisionism. They reaffirmed the Party's commitment to class struggle and the revolutionary
seizure of power, and its long-standing opposition to alliance with other
parties or participation in liberal governments. The Second International
followed the lead of the SPD. At its Paris Congress in 1900 it censured the
French Socialist Party (PSF) for permitting one of its members,
Alexandre Millerand, to enter the bourgeois government constructed by
René Waldeck-Rousseau in 1898. It accepted Kautsky's amendment that
such participation was legitimate in exceptional circumstances, when
democracy was threatened by the forces of reaction. At its Amsterdam

Congress four years later, on the behest of Jules Guesde, the Marxist leader of the French Revolutionary Socialist Party (PSDF), and Kautsky, it condemned Revisionism *in toto* in the same terms as the SPD had used at Dresden. A year later, against the better judgement of Jean Jaurès and his reformist allies, the various factions of French socialists re-united in the French Section of the Workers' International (SIFO), which adopted the anti-Revisionist platform of the International. In fact, revolutionary rhetoric did little to abate the essentially reformist practice of the trade unions, or of many socialist politicians in France, as well as in Britain, and at the regional and municipal level in Germany.[17]

The very persistence of reformism prompted Luxemburg to address the roots of this phenomenon. She did so in her article *Organisational Questions of Russian Social Democracy*, published in *Die Neue Zeit* in 1904. While nominally directed against the centralised, hierarchically disciplined party advocated by Lenin (Chapter 4), which she feared would stifle the growth of a mass revolutionary proletarian movement, the whole thrust of her critique was shaped by her concerns about German Social Democracy. In a manner analogous to Robert Michels, who later elaborated the famous 'iron law of oligarchy' in his classic work of 1911 (translated as *Political Parties*), she attributed the strength of reformism to 'the leading organs' of the party, and, one should add, of the trade unions. It was self-evident that the number of Social Democrat deputies in the *Reichstag* had risen markedly, as had union membership. These welcome advances, however, had blunted the commitment to revolution. Parliamentarianism was a classic case in point. The Social Democrat deputies, and those officials who had worked to ensure the Party's electoral victories, tended to view parliamentary struggle as an end in itself. They had carved out political careers for themselves (as had the union leaders), which were dependent on the perpetuation of the existing system, and would be jeopardised by radical action to overthrow it. Hence they were determined to contain the spontaneous revolutionary aspirations which Luxemburg assumed the mass of ordinary workers to possess. Kautsky himself came to dismiss these self-same deputies as 'time servers', who were as corrupt and degenerate as their counterparts in the French Socialist party. In a letter to Victor Adler in September 1909, he echoed Luxemburg's views that the rapid expansion of the Party and trade union apparatus had spawned a conservative, bureaucratic culture that stifled every radical initiative from below. Union and Party functionaries had become so concerned with mundane issues of organisation and negotiation that they had lost sight of the need for mass political action to overthrow the old order.[18]

While the SPD might have been a militant and vibrant movement in the 1890s, as Mary Jo Maynes recently argued, most historical studies would support the conclusions of Kautsky and Luxemburg that a conservative bureaucracy came to dominate it. What neither, especially Luxemburg, could accept was that the Party and union bureaucracies reflected the aspirations of much of the German working class more closely than they did. As long as industry in Germany expanded and prospered, as long as the power of the unions grew despite continuing employer hostility, as long as the gradual progress of Social Democracy seemed assured, the majority of German workers was satisfied with piecemeal reform.[19] Similar conclusions can be applied to the other member parties of the Second International, at least those of the more advanced and liberal North and West Europe, most notably in Britain and Sweden. For them, as much as for Bernstein, the movement was everything and they were not ready to risk it in adventurous ploys that would merely invite repression. Paradoxically, Luxemburg's fears that Lenin's organisational strictures would throttle the revolutionary consciousness of the Russian workers were not borne out. In fact, it was the lessons that she drew from the 1905 Revolution in Russia that would embroil the SPD, and the International, in yet another bitter conflict.

The mass strike and the road to power

The 1905 Revolution reinforced her belief in the spontaneous revolutionary capacities of the proletariat. With little leadership from the self-appointed intellectual vanguard, the Russian workers had engaged in a series of increasingly radical actions, culminating in a general strike in the autumn which had threatened to overthrow the autocratic order. Their example prompted her to mount a renewed onslaught on reformism and Revisionism. Speaking for the Left of the Party she demanded that the SPD should embrace the mass strike as a political weapon, lest the pursuit of incremental economic and constitutional reforms dull the consciousness of the workers. Traditionally, the SPD had looked askance at the mass strike as an anarchist, not a Marxist, weapon. Yet in the early 1900s, in face of intensified employer opposition to the union movement (lock-outs rose sharply from 1903), rising living costs and growing unemployment, a discernible current in the Party, as well as an increasing body of rank-and-file workers, had come to view organised mass action more sympathetically.

Luxemburg's appeal won her strange bedfellows. Bernstein conceded that the mass strike was justified in certain circumstances: in particular, to protect the political rights already won by the working class. Ludwig Frank, a reformist *par excellence*, also approved of it, if for different reasons. In light of its success in forcing the Austrian and Belgian governments to extend the franchise, he hoped that the threat of it would compel the Prussian government to reform its highly inegalitarian three-class voting system. This curious combination of forces explains why at its Jena Congress (September 1905) the SPD reversed the decision made by the trade union congress held in Cologne four months earlier and approved Bebel's resolution in favour of the mass political strike, as a defensive weapon to combat any threats to 'democracy'. The victory of radicalism was more apparent than real. The trade union leadership was as fearful as its counterparts in West Europe that any resort to a political strike would invite repression, and exercised its growing strength to neutralise the impact of this resolution. At a secret meeting with Party leaders in February 1906 the latter agreed to do all in their power to prevent any mass strike erupting. This agreement was endorsed by the following Party Congress, at Mannheim in September 1906.[20] For Luxemburg, this retreat confirmed her prognosis concerning the suffocating influence of the Party and union bureaucracies.

However, the debate on the mass strike rumbled on and widened the split in the Party. It resurfaced four years later, in early 1910, in response to large demonstrations provoked by the Prussian government's refusal to introduce universal suffrage, and many strikes protesting against rising prices and taxes. Luxemburg and her supporters again called on the workers to transform these demonstrations into mass political strikes, initially to win the suffrage issue, and ultimately to mount a revolutionary assault against the existing Imperial order. On this occasion Kautsky, who hitherto had supported Luxemburg and her fellow radicals in their attacks on reformism and Revisionism, clearly distanced himself from them. In an essay (*The Mass Strike*), he accepted that this strategy had been 'very well suited' to Russia in 1905. Nevertheless, conditions were different in the West, especially in Germany. There the government was much more securely based, supported by a powerful army and bourgeoisie, and the majority of workers themselves lacked the revolutionary élan of the Russians. To unleash a mass strike in Germany would risk a crushing defeat. He now advocated that the Party wage 'a war of attrition', taking advantage of the freedoms already secured to prepare the workers 'long in advance' for the final assault on the old order. The mass strike, or 'strategy of overthrow' as he termed it, was legitimate in two cases: most seriously, if the government threatened the political liberties already won; or, less likely, if it found itself in such 'a tight corner' that a rapid and fatal blow could be struck against it.

As Massimo Salvadori pointed out, Kautsky's reservations about the utility of the mass strike, as well his continued rejection of Revisionism, led him to adopt a centrist position. The gradual and peaceful evolution of socialism was impossible in an increasingly militarist German state. Political revolution was still necessary, though his vision of how it would be effected remained ambiguous. In *The Road to Power* (1909), he stated that it was impossible to forecast when it would occur, and whether it would involve a bloody confrontation or could be achieved by 'economic, legislative and moral pressure'. His equivocations apart, he was much clearer on its purposes. The *Reichstag* was to be given complete power to govern the country, while Prussia, where the three-class franchise ensured that power remained in the hands of an authoritarian elite, had to be fully democratised. In other words, the objective of the revolution was to win the battle for democracy, to create the democratic republic that he considered to be the only political system in which socialism could take root. No commune state for Kautsky! The desertion of the bourgeoisie and petty-bourgeoisie to the camp of reaction after the panic induced by the 1905 Revolution in Russia reinforced his conviction that the sole force for democracy was the proletariat, which should maintain its traditional opposition to any alliance with other parties. More curiously, in light of his earlier damning attack on trade union bureaucracy, he assigned to the organised union machines a key role in mobilising the workers behind strikes and demonstrations to advance the democratic cause. He calculated that the growing resistance of the employers' associations, backed up by the state, to demands over pay and conditions would convince the unions of the need to engage in political struggle *per se*. Even then he still cautioned against the indiscriminate use of the mass strike weapon, especially, as he added in a Preface of 1910, if it was a spontaneous and unorganised action.[21]

Kautsky's pronouncements were challenged from both right and left. In spite of his condemnation of political alliances, by 1913 the SPD had aligned itself with the National Liberals, the Progressives and the Centre Party to demand the introduction of a property tax throughout Germany.

It was even prepared to condone, contrary to the resolution on war and militarism adopted by the Stuttgart Congress of the Second International (August 1907), an increase in the military budget, provided this increase was funded by direct rather than indirect taxation.[22] The Left, not just in Germany but in the other parties of the Second International too, opposed any concessions to militarism. Some, notably Luxemburg, insisted that mass strike action was the only conceivable means to prevent the outbreak of war, which seemed increasingly likely in Europe. But to understand why this was the case requires us to turn to the final important issue of this chapter, namely, the growth of imperialism and the intensification of nationalist rivalries in Europe.

Nationalism and imperialism

Marx's underestimation of the power of nationalism haunted his followers. Much of the history of the twentieth century lends credence to the conclusion of the former Hungarian Communist Mihaly Vajda, that nationalism 'won ascendancy' over socialist internationalism. While 1914 revealed starkly the bankruptcy of international socialism, the appeal of nationalism to the workers of Europe had been manifest long before then. For example, during the Boer War of 1899–1902 it had been prevalent, in a highly jingoistic manner, in the ranks of the British working class. Those on the Revisionist wing of the SPD sought to explain why this was the case. In the debates of the late 1890s Bernstein had cast doubt on the old shibboleth about the workers having no country. Where the worker had 'a voice in the government and legislation of his country as a fully accredited citizen and [was] able to shape its arrangements according to his wishes', there he would develop a national consciousness. Under the liberal democratic Third Republic, he contended, the French workers clearly had acquired one. At the same time, he also denied the SPD's condemnation of colonialism as an unmitigated evil. Just as Marx in the 1850s had pointed to the progressive role of British imperialism in dragging India out of its Asiatic backwardness, so too Bernstein argued that European imperialism could act as a force for progress, especially in those regions of Africa where the slave trade and tribal war were endemic. Whatever the merits of Bernstein's arguments, they struck a chord within the Party and trade union bureaucracies, not to mention among German workers generally.[23]

The question became the centre of furious debate in 1907, in the SPD and in the Second International as a whole. It was fuelled by the intensification of imperialist rivalries among the great powers since the late nineteenth century (its most recent manifestation had been in 1906 when Britain and France thwarted Germany's attempt to impose its control over Morocco), and the consequent arms race that threatened to embroil Europe in war. In Germany itself, the catalyst was the unexpected reverse the SPD had suffered in the so-called 'Hottentot' election in January 1907, when it lost 38 seats in the *Reichstag*. The right-wing leadership attributed the losses in part to the fears engendered by the 1905 Revolution, and the advocacy of the mass strike by the Left. In no less part it condemned the unpatriotic stance of the Party, which had opposed the government's brutal repression of a rebellion in 1906 by the native Herero and Khoikhoi peoples in Germany's South-West African colony. Its response was to rally round the flag. In the spring of 1907 Gustav Noske, newly elected to the *Reichstag*, spoke for many Social Democrats when he proclaimed that it was the 'duty and obligation [of the Party] to see to it that the German people [was] not shoved up against the wall by some other nations'. Others, such as Richard Calwer and Gerhard Hildebrand, implied that Germany's future depended on the creation of a German-dominated economic bloc in Europe, akin to the vision of *Mitteleuropa* (Middle Europe) first proclaimed by Friedrich List in the 1840s. The Left of the Party, including Luxemburg, Paul Lensch, Clara Zetkin and others, were enraged, and bitterly opposed any kow-towing to nationalism and imperialism.[24]

Similar splits divided the International but on this occasion it did not bow to the demands of the majority in the SPD. On the contrary, its Stuttgart Congress adopted a resolution, radically amended by Luxemburg, Lenin and Martov, which committed it in rather vague terms to resist militarism; to use whatever means in its power to avert the outbreak of a future war; and should war break out, to use the ensuing 'economic and political crisis' to mobilise the workers of the belligerent countries to overthrow capitalism. Despite persistent attempts by the Left to commit the International, and its member parties, unequivocally to oppose war by unleashing 'a general strike and insurrection', which was the strategy proposed by the French Socialists (SIFO) in November 1912, it refused to budge and essentially clung to the Stuttgart 'line' – until the dark days of August 1914.[25] However, the issues of imperialism, nationalism and the threat of war gave rise to contributions of critical importance for the subsequent development of Marxism, in both theory and practice.

The most significant came from the pen of Rudolf Hilferding, Austrian by birth but a leading member of the SPD since 1906. His seminal work,

Finance Capital, first published in 1910, warrants careful consideration. Seen by Hilferding as a continuation of Marx's *Capital*, the bulk of it was given over to an analysis of the changes undergone by capitalist economies since Marx's time, in particular the ramifications of the further centralisation and concentration of capital. Developing rudimentary notions earlier propounded by Bernstein and Kautsky, Hilferding concluded that large cartels had become dominant within industry. Their *raison d'être* was to control output, and consequently prices, and in this way preserve profitability. A similar process had occurred in finance, where a few banks of immense wealth and power had emerged in each capitalist country. These banks had become the chief sources of capital for industry, leading to the fusion of industrial and banking capital, for which he coined the term 'finance capital'. In turn, this fusion had led to a growing degree of regulation in each capitalist economy, as it was in the interests of the banks to limit competition amongst the various cartels in which they had invested. This regulation gradually was overcoming the anarchic and contradictory nature of capitalism and leading to the 'socialisation of production'. In turn, this socialisation was creating the organisational framework upon which a planned socialist economy could be built. To realise this potential, however, the proletariat first had to 'conquer' state power, a conquest which Hilferding believed was achievable by parliamentary means. Once in power, the proletariat should seize control of the banks, and the regulatory mechanisms that they had created, and utilise them to proceed, relatively painlessly, with the construction of socialism. For Hilferding, a *Reichstag* majority and 'taking possession of the six large Berlin banks' would ensure the victory of socialism in Germany itself.

His study of finance capital logically led him to end his analysis with a brief discussion of contemporary imperialism. The recent move towards protectionism by most leading capitalist states was driven by the need to shield domestic cartels from foreign competition, and thus to allow them to levy inflated monopoly prices in their home markets. The charging of monopoly prices, however, limited the quantity of goods that they could sell domestically. Export markets were vital if they were to maintain levels of production and sustain profits. The pursuit of such markets, and of the raw materials required by industry, was one source of recent imperialist expansion. Moreover, it was reinforced by the need to export capital, to find profitable outlets for the monopoly profits that had accrued from cartelisation and protectionism. An added benefit of the export of capital was that it enabled cartels to set up production abroad and so avoid the protective barriers imposed by foreign rivals.

Whilst economically progressive, finance capitalism had dangerous political consequences, as it had given birth to a 'dictatorship of the magnates of capital'. Rallying the large landowners and petty-bourgeosie of the town and countryside behind them, these magnates had taken over the apparatus of the state in 'a direct, undisguised and palpable way'. They deployed state power for two purposes. The first was to suppress the rapidly developing workers' movement internally. How a parliamentary road to socialism was then possible within such a repressive system was never satisfactorily explained by Hilferding. The second was to pursue a predatory policy of territorial annexation, which fuelled imperialist rivalries among the advanced capitalist states. War, he conceded, would have been the inevitable outcome of such rivalries, were it not for the presence of 'countervailing forces'. In the first place, France and even Britain had invested heavily in German industry, which meant that they all had much to lose by going to war to settle their differences. The other restraining force was fear that the inevitable sufferings of war would drive the workers to revolution.[26]

Hilferding's *magnum opus* proved to be immensely influential. Most importantly, it informed Lenin's own study of imperialism during the First World War, on which he based his revised political strategy (see Chapter 5). Kautsky too endorsed Hilferding's analysis, writing a glowing review of it in a series of articles, *Finance Capital and Crises*, in *Die Neue Zeit* in 1911. Having already largely abandoned his previous view that colonial expansion had been driven by atavistic, pre-industrial elites, one most forcibly advanced in *Socialism and Colonialism* published in 1907, he now was convinced that large-scale industrial and banking capitalism was the dynamic force behind imperialism, as it sought markets for its goods. A further impetus, he added, was provided by the need of developed capitalist states to extend their agrarian hinterlands, to secure the food and raw materials vital to their survival. He also agreed with Hilferding that the rivalries amongst the new financial-capitalist elites need not necessarily result in military conflict. In an essay on 'Imperialism', mainly written before, but published ironically in *Die Neue Zeit* in September 1914, just after war had engulfed Europe, he argued that imperialist war was not inevitable. Realisation of the costs involved, conceivably, would bring the great powers to their senses. The 'economic bankruptcy' that it would entail might force them to seek a peaceable resolution of their conflicts and create an 'ultra-imperialist' federation, a United States of Europe. Whether ultra-imperialism was a central plank of his thought, or merely tangential to it, as John Kautsky has argued, it cut no ice with

Lenin, nor with Luxemburg.[27] Expanding on ideas first elaborated in her critique of Bernstein, Luxemburg returned to the attack in her *The Accumulation of Capital.* Downplaying the significance that Hilferding had attached to finance capital as the source of recent imperialist expansion and rivalries, she reiterated that they were a product of the inescapable dynamics of capitalism. Its very survival depended on its acquisition of markets in the pre-capitalist territories of the world, in the process of which it increasingly 'assimilated' them into a global capitalist economy. Once the entire world had been so transformed its collapse was assured. But even before the logic of capitalism had run its course, revolution would erupt. The costs and sufferings imposed by the burden of militarism, and war, would impel the workers to rise in revolution and cast off their shackles.

The import of these theoretical exchanges had little impact on the practice of the SPD, or the other parties of the International before 1914. For all their revolutionary rhetoric and professed internationalism most of them had become more and more reformist, and increasingly in the thrall of nationalism, as the outbreak of the First World War all too chillingly revealed. But the war itself proved to be a watershed in the history of European socialism. The ideological and political divisions that had haunted the SPD and its fraternal parties since the 1890s burst asunder. By its end the Left had broken away, to establish its own Communist Parties, as we shall see in Chapter 5.

Chapter 4: Russian Marxism

Marxism in the Russian Empire is of central importance to the history of Communism. In its Leninist variant it emerged triumphant in 1917, and shaped the subsequent fate of Communism in Europe. Lenin's interpretation of Marxism, in particular his theory of the party, was to have a baleful influence on Communist practice after 1917. The victory of Leninism has also cast a long shadow over the history of Russian Marxism itself. It is a well known axiom that it is the victors who write, or rewrite, history. Lenin and his successors certainly did so, to justify their political and theoretical farsightedness and hence their rightful claim to power. Many, perhaps too many, historians in the West have accepted their interpretation rather uncritically, although often to denigrate, not praise, Leninist theory and practice. Students new to the subject might be unsettled by this paradox: how can Leninists and their critics, on the basis of the same sources, arrive at quite different conclusions? Students of history, and other related disciplines, should remember that the 'facts' never speak for themselves, though they all are constrained by the evidence available. Mindful of this *caveat*, this chapter will re-examine how Russian Marxism evolved before the Great War and, hopefully, encourage students of the subject to be wary of received opinion. While Russian Marxism before 1917 remained a heterogeneous movement, the focus of this chapter will be to re-examine the evolution of Leninism. This task demands an analysis of the origins of Russian Marxism in the 1880s; the debates which divided it in the 1890s and early 1900s; the fundamental division which supposedly occurred at the Second Congress of the Russian Social Democratic Labour Party (RSDLP) in 1903; and the subsequent, halting development of Leninism as a distinct current within it.

Whether Lenin was a Marxist remains a moot point. Robin Blick recently polemicised that ' "Marxism–Leninism" is as absurd a concoction as Christian Satanism.' If Leninism was not Marxism, then what was it? One of Lenin's early comrades, N. Valentinov, who later split from him, provided a still influential answer. Leninism was primarily the product of Russian Jacobinism, with Nikolai Chernyshevskii its main inspiration. In his political novel *What Is To Be Done?* (1863), Chernyshevskii had posited that revolution in Russia would occur only if a disciplined and conspiratorial party of professional revolutionaries was formed to lead it. Numerous historians have concurred with Valentinov's thesis, among them the former Soviet historian Dmitri Volkogonov, who alleged that 'Lenin used Chernyshevskii to "russify" Western Marxism.' The French left-wing historian Marcel Liebman agreed that Lenin had 'russified' Marxism, but by assigning a major role in the revolution to the majority in the country, the peasantry. Other commentators have played down this notion of 'Russification'. Neil Harding, author of a two-volume intellectual biography of Lenin, maintained that while he 'modified and updated' the teachings of the master, he consistently sought to apply Marxist methodology to an investigation of economic and social conditions, first within Russia, and later, during the First World War, within the contemporary imperialist world. His political thinking was based on these investigations. The problem, Harding continued, was that Lenin's studies led him to 'two quite distinct... analyses which entailed two quite different political strategies with radically different objectives in view'.[1]

Lenin certainly thought of himself as a Marxist. In an obituary written shortly after his death in January 1924, the old People's Socialist V. Myakotin reflected that Leninism was 'a peculiar mixture of Marxism and Jacobinism which [he] had inherited from the previous generation'. But, he added, 'Lenin was firmly convinced that he... was a true follower of Marx, the most orthodox of all orthodox Marxists.' If so, the question remains: a Marxist of what ilk? The solution, as the Menshevik V. P. Akimov suggested, requires us to begin with the ideas of the 'father' of Russian Marxism, and Lenin's self-professed mentor, Plekhanov.[2]

Plekhanov and the origins of Russian Marxism

As we saw in Chapter 2, Marx's own views on Russia were synonymous with those of the Populists, who had propounded that a successful peasant revolution could establish socialism in Russia without the country first experiencing the capitalist stage of development. The Populists' dilemma was that in the 1870s the Russian peasants had not responded to the student revolutionaries who had gone 'to the people' to urge them to rise in revolution. Passive at best, at worst they had delivered the young revolutionaries into the hands of the police. This failure ruptured the Populist Land and Freedom (*Zemlia i Volia*) movement in the late 1870s. A terrorist faction, the People's Will (*Narodnaia Volia*), emerged from its ranks. Peasant passivity convinced it that it must act as a revolutionary vanguard whose duty was to overthrow the autocracy and liberate the people from oppression. As leader of the rival faction, Black Repartition (*Chernyi Peredel*), Plekhanov rejected this Jacobin strategy and clung to the traditional Populist belief that the peasants must carry out social revolution by and for themselves. As he later argued in *Our Differences* (1884), a political revolution without mass participation would lead to the dominance of a new 'privileged class'. But growing disillusion when faced with the continuing inertia of the peasant majority, which remained unmoved even by the assassination of Alexander II by members of the People's Will in March 1881, led to his abandonment of Populism, and his conversion to Marxism – or Marxism as he understood it.

In the early 1880s, intensive study of Russia's recent agrarian history led Plekhanov, in exile in Switzerland to escape autocratic persecution, to conclude that Populism had become anachronistic. Since the Great Emancipation of the serfs in 1861 capitalism had penetrated extensively into the Russian countryside. The consequence, as he repeatedly argued in *Our Differences*, was that the old village commune was disintegrating rapidly. The peasantry was fast becoming transformed into a petty-bourgeois class, hostile to socialism. Accordingly, he rejected Populist aspirations to build a new socialist order on communal foundations to follow a peculiarly 'Russian road' to socialism, as 'preposterous'. Now that Russia had embarked upon the capitalist stage of development, it must complete it before socialism was possible. His analysis was adopted by the Emancipation of Labour Group (ELG), the organisation of Russian Marxists founded in Geneva in 1883 by Plekhanov and his allies, Pavel Akselrod, Lev Deich and Vera Zasulich. Their determination to refute the fundamental tenets of Populism shaped the subsequent evolution of Russian Marxism. As Leon Trotsky later remarked in his *History of the Russian Revolution*, 'in its struggle with Populism, Russian Marxism, demonstrating the identity of the laws of development for all countries, not infrequently fell into a dogmatic mechanisation'. It became tainted with a fatalism and determinism that ultimately was absent from Marx's own thinking.

Plekhanov's contention that bourgeois capitalism was the next stage in Russia's history was to become the orthodoxy of all Russian Marxists, Lenin included, before 1905. Revolution, however, remained essential, to sweep away the reactionary autocracy. Such a bourgeois democratic revolution would permit a more rapid development of capitalism in Russia, and the formation of large and open working-class organisations. Only after this capitalist stage had been completed – its duration was unspecified – would socialist revolution be possible. In 1898 Akselrod again warned against premature attempts at establishing socialism in Russia as capitalism patently remained far too under-developed to permit it.[3]

Yet Russia's bourgeois revolution would have its own peculiarities. As Plekhanov emphasised in the *Programme of the Social Democratic Emancipation of Labour Group* (1884), the economic backwardness of the country meant that its middle class remained far too weak to take the lead in overthrowing the autocracy. For Plekhanov, the Populist apostate, the 'little peasant' could not be expected to assume this role. The only revolutionary class in Russia was the nascent industrial proletariat, whose rudimentary circles Plekhanov had come into contact with in the late 1870s. At the founding Congress of the Second International in Paris in July 1889, he declared that 'the revolutionary movement in Russia will triumph only as a *working-class movement* or else it will never triumph!' The Russian working class had been assigned the task of leading a bourgeois revolution against the autocracy, of being its hegemon, as Akselrod described it. More curiously, after this revolution the proletariat was to hand power over to the bourgeoisie. No party representing the workers could take part in a bourgeois government lest it be held responsible for introducing measures against the interests of the working class. This whole idea, that once the workers had toppled the autocracy they should leave the bourgeoisie to govern the country, was dumbfounding, as the Menshevik George Denike recalled.[4]

Plekhanov, though, was ambivalent about the political potential of the Russian working class. He frequently argued, as in the *Second Draft Programme of the Russian Social Democrats* (1885), that 'the emancipation of the workers must be the matter of the workers themselves'. So too did the leaders of the first workers' circles in Russia itself, Nikolai Chaikovskii and Mikhail Brusnev. But contrary to Marx (Chapter 2), Plekhanov harboured doubts whether in the course of their daily economic struggles the workers would acquire the political consciousness necessary to carry out the revolutionary duties assigned to them. Leadership of the revolution was to be the prerogative of the Marxist intelligentsia, who alone understood the laws of historical development. Armed with this knowledge its mission was to impart the requisite consciousness to the working class, to explain to it the principal political demands that it should pose. Thereafter, it was the task of the workers themselves to determine how to act to achieve these ends. His continued emphasis on mass worker participation enabled him to deny the charge of Jacobinism levelled against him by S. N. Prokopovich in the late 1890s, that a self-appointed intellectual elite could substitute itself for the working class in carrying out the revolution. Nevertheless, his elevation of the role of the intelligentsia was to leave its imprint on Russian Marxism. This is not to imply, as Harding did, that Plekhanov was merely a prototypical Leninist, the chief architect of the vanguard party. As the old Menshevik Lidiia Dan much later pointed out, unlike Lenin, Plekhanov had little interest in organisational detail, in the building of the party as such.[5]

The essence of Plekhanov's analysis was incorporated in the programme adopted by the RSDLP at its founding Congress in 1898. Written by Petr Struve, it called for an immediate revolution, to supplant the autocracy with a democratic republic that would preside over the flowering of capitalism. Leadership in this revolution lay on the 'sturdy shoulders' of the Russian working class: '[t]he further east one goes in Europe, the meaner, more cowardly and politically weak the bourgeoisie becomes, and the greater are the cultural and political tasks that fall to the proletariat.' Nevertheless, as the debates then raging within Social Democratic ranks over political tactics revealed, most of its leaders still defended the leading role of the intelligentsia. Its responsibility was to guide the mass of workers onto the path of emancipation, to ensure that it put forward political rather than narrowly economic demands. It is to this controversy that we now must turn.

Agitation and the Economist controversy

Before 1895, as Richard Pipes observed, Plekhanov and his group were little known in Russia. They had no substantial links with the emerging working class, with the exception of the relatively short-lived workers' circles formed by Dmitrii Blagoev in St Petersburg in the mid-1880s. In his brief history of the Party written in 1924 the Bolshevik M. N. Liadov conceded that while Plekhanov was the 'father of Russian Marxist theory', Blagoev had established the first active Marxist circles amongst the working class. The difficulties facing the émigrés, of conducting any political work in Russia in the era of reaction following Alexander II's assassination, limited their influence. However, other recurring obstacles to the hegemony of the Marxist intelligentsia existed. Repeatedly, the embryonic workers' groups that had sprung up since the 1870s had rebuffed the overtures of intellectuals wishing to lead them. In part, as Pamela McKinsey discovered, these groups grew impatient with the perennial squabbles that bedevilled the intelligentsia. They also feared that bowing to intellectual leadership would embroil them in radical, if futile, challenges to the authorities which would simply result in lengthy imprisonment. Finally, as the worker Bolshevik Semen Kanatchikov recounted in his memoirs, many workers suspected that the intellectuals would be unreliable allies. Bourgeois or petty-bourgeois in origin, they had no real understanding of workers' lives and aspirations. They were prone to desert the revolutionary cause, often for a summer in the country if not a permanent position in industry or the government bureaucracy, where each became 'a hard taskmaster or tsarist flunkey'.[6]

Lidiia Dan's protestations notwithstanding, the workers' distrust of the intelligentsia remained a persistent problem. In the first half of the 1890s, Marxist intellectuals responded positively to the calls for teachers made by the educational circles set up by literate workers. Their objectives were rather different from those of the workers. They reckoned that the intensive education of small numbers of workers in Marxist philosophy, political economy and history would inculcate in them a political class-consciousness which they would pass on to their less enlightened fellows. Most of their worker pupils, however, proved unprepared to engage in revolutionary activities. Instead, they transformed themselves into an educated workers' elite, standing above and reluctant to participate in any spontaneous actions of the 'rabble' in the factories lest this threaten them with imprisonment. Propaganda, defined by Plekhanov as the con-veying of 'many ideas to a single person or to a few people', had failed, and therefore constrained the Marxist intellectuals to turn to the strategy known as agitation.

Agitation had first appeared in Russian Poland. It made its way to the Russian capital St Petersburg via Lithuania, where Arkadii Kremer, with the assistance of Martov, had written the seminal pamphlet *On Agitation* (1896). Its purpose was to explain the transition from small-circle propaganda to mass agitation amongst the Jewish workers of Vilnius. Propaganda, it admitted, had created an elite worker intelligentsia 'alien-ated from the [worker] mass'. This breach threatened to leave leadership of the latter in the hands of 'practical men', lacking the nous to advance political consciousness of the mass of workers. Yet most ordinary workers, it continued, would not be mobilised to pursue political goals by education alone. The struggle for everyday objectives such as better wages or improved working conditions, initially in separate 'workshops or factories', was the first stage in their acquisition of class-consciousness. Experience would reveal that such disparate struggles were futile. Only united action could bring success. Such action would lead to confrontation not just with the factory owners, but also with the autocratic state, which would eventually send in the police or army to defend the capitalists. At this point the workers would grasp that revolution was the precondition for a better life.[7]

These principles, very much in the spirit of Marx's own thinking, were embraced in the autumn of 1895 by the Marxist intellectuals in St Petersburg. A hesitant Lenin also became a convert. *On Agitation* guided the activities of the Union of Struggle for the Liberation of the Working Class, formed by Lenin and Martov in late 1895. During 1895–6 the Union issued numerous leaflets, to provide coherence to the grievances and material demands of the workers who had struck in the textile and other factories and plants of St Petersburg. The Union's success in directing these strikes invited police repression. In December 1895 most experienced Social Democrat leaders, the 'elders', were arrested, Lenin included. Younger comrades took their place and the strikes continued, ultimately to win some notable concessions, especially legislation for an eleven-and-a-half-hour maximum working day in June 1897.

Plekhanov's conviction that Russia's future lay with the workers appeared to be coming true. As he reported to the London Congress of the Second International in July 1896, the 'awakening' of the workers was not confined to St Petersburg but could be observed, on a smaller scale, in other cities and towns of the Russian Empire. The time was ripe to create a Social Democratic Party in Russia, to lead the workers in the democratic revolution. His optimism was premature. The very effectiveness of agitation in mobilising tens of thousands of workers provoked divisions within the Marxist camp. Now that a mass movement existed many intellectuals reverted to a quasi-Populist faith in the masses. Their duty was to respond to the workers' aspirations, and to abandon the mission to lead them, as the time had come for labour to emancipate itself. Equally, workers' suspicions that the machinations of the intelligentsia would lead them into foolhardy political adventures and subsequent repression resurfaced.[8]

The outcome was that the leading role claimed by Plekhanov and his intellectual followers was challenged by the current known as 'Economism'.

What precisely it was has been obscured by a too ready acceptance of the critiques of Plekhanov, and Lenin, that it urged the workers to reject political struggle for the pursuit of limited improvements in their daily lives. With more truth, John Keep judged that it was a movement which challenged the shibboleths of the 'old guard'. Contrary to Plekhanov's diatribes, it was not attributable to German Revisionism (see Chapter 3). More astutely, he concluded that its origins must be sought in the unintended consequences of agitation, as an examination of those currents tarred with the Economist brush confirms.[9]

Let us start with the Union of Russian Social Democrats (Abroad) (URSD), an émigré organisation founded in Geneva in 1894 which had subordinated itself to the leadership of Plekhanov's group. By November 1898, when its First Congress convened, its ranks had been reinforced by a group of younger Marxists who had fled Russia after their involvement in the strikes of 1896–7. Tensions with the 'elders' emerged, first revolving more around personalities than politics. Plekhanov brooked few challenges to his authority. According to Struve, and others, he was 'an intractable and even capricious man', frequently 'unpleasant', with little patience for those who questioned his judgement. He took umbrage at the request of the young URSD leaders for greater editorial autonomy over the leaflets and pamphlets that they produced. He also was reluctant to provide what Harding has described as 'popular agitational literature' for the URSD, aimed directly at the mass of workers. Tempers rose, and Plekhanov and the 'old guard' declined to support the Union's publications.[10] In response the 'youngsters' within the URSD set up a new paper, *Rabochee Delo* (The Workers' Cause), edited chiefly by A. S. Martynov. The first issue appeared in April 1899. Its final two issues, in February 1902, contained the revised programme of the URSD, which unambiguously declared that the overthrow of the autocracy, and its replacement by a democratic republic, remained the immediate task of the working class. The best way of drawing the workers into such a revolutionary struggle was, echoing *On Agitation*, through economic strikes for better working and living conditions. Strikes would lead them into confrontation with the state, at which point anti-autocratic political propaganda would strike a chord. The *Rabochedel'tsy*, as they were called, also came into conflict with the old guard on the issue of party organisation. Despite agreement on the need for a central organisation to help the working class pursue a coordinated political strategy, none the less they shared the misgivings of many workers about a centralised party dominated by the intelligentsia. To counter the 'anti-democratic tendencies' of the Plekhanovite intellectuals and to ensure that the RSDLP remained a class movement of the workers, they demanded that it be organised on democratic foundations, responsive to the aspirations of the grass roots and thus not subject to the dictates of any single (intellectual) faction. Of course, once majority decisions had been taken, they were binding on all within the Party.

The newspaper *Rabochaia Mysl'* (Workers' Thought) also challenged the intellectuals' self-appointed leading role. First published in 1897 by a group of St Petersburg workers, after their arrest it was continued by émigré intellectuals. It too subscribed to the essential precepts of *On Agitation*. Looking back on the strike wave of 1896–7, its editor K. M. Takhtarev repeated that what had begun as individual strikes in separate factories surprisingly quickly had developed into more organised and coordinated action. Eventually the strikers had put forward common demands, which clearly heralded the emergence of a general movement seeking better legal protection for the workers. This struggle, however, could not be foisted on them at the behest of an intellectual vanguard. It had to be conducted by the workers themselves, on the basis of demands consciously and independently elaborated and understood by them. Furthermore, in Russian conditions, any attempts by the workers to wring improvements out of their employers sooner or later would face repression at the hands of the state. Slowly but surely this repression again would lead the workers into political conflict with the autocracy. Nor did *Rabochaia Mysl'* advocate the total abandonment of political struggle in favour of seeking amelioration of economic grievances. Yet its publication, and editorial endorsement, of an article by Bernstein advocating an evolutionary, peaceful approach to politics roused the ire of the 'old guard'.[11]

For a period Economism was the dominant strand of Social Democracy at the grass roots in Russia. For the majority of workers, according to Kanatchikov, economic questions were of paramount concern. Their involvement in industrial conflicts, however, had politicised them, as became evident in the strike movement that had revived in many cities across Russia from the spring of 1901. Frequently the police had intervened to put down this movement, so underlining the unity between the government and the industrialists. State coercion, rather than the proselytising of the intellectual leadership, had persuaded many workers of the need for political struggle, with revolutionary slogans such as 'Down with the Autocracy' increasingly prominent in the striking workers' proclamations. Even Lenin conceded, with reservations, that this was the case, in his famous tract *What Is To Be Done?*

Hindsight bears out Kanatchikov's admission that Economism was not as misconceived as its critics maintained. The intolerance of the autocracy, and of much of the emerging industrial bourgeoisie, precluded the possibility of reformism or Revisionism sinking deep roots into Russian soil. Workers' organisations, even after the formal legalisation of trade unions following the abortive revolution of 1905, faced constant harassment and closure. As the Menshevik trade unionist V. Sher concluded with much regret on the eve of the First World War, the absence of any significant concessions by the bourgeoisie or the government had driven the workers onto the path of revolution, without the need of leadership from the intellectual vanguard. Russia was not Britain, nor even Germany. It was not even Finland, then under Russian rule, where the Bolshevik Vladimir Smirnov bemoaned that the greater tolerance of the autocracy had tempered worker radicalism.

The very nature of Economism, and its appeal, however, have been obscured far too much by its spurious association with the beliefs of Elena Kuskova and her husband Sergei Prokopovich, who were to desert Social Democracy for the liberal Constitutional Democratic (Kadet) Party in the 1900s. In early 1899 Kuskova produced her *Credo*. A surprisingly short document considering its later infamy, it began with an explanation of the growth of Revisionism in the West. According to Kuskova, its first source was the dissipation of the energies of the more advanced workers in ultimately futile political campaigns; the second was the emergence of a mass of lumpen-proletarians, whose horizons did not transcend mundane material gains. Hence, aspirations to involve them in revolutionary struggle had given way to the pursuit of piecemeal reforms that might bring about an immediate improvement in their lives. In Russia itself, the working class was too weak and disorganised, and too subject to a 'wall of political oppression', to play an independent revolutionary role. Consequently, the only feasible strategy open to it, difficult as it still was, was the path of gradual reform. Russian Marxists, therefore, must jettison their belief in the hegemony of the proletariat in the democratic revolution. Instead, they must devote themselves to assisting the workers in their economic struggle, and supporting the Liberals in their opposition to the autocracy.

The *Credo* was refused publication in both *Rabochee Delo* and *Rabochaia Mysl'*. As Akimov pointed out, every Russian Social Democratic organisation rejected it, while the URSD had published the first public condemnation of it. However, the fact that Kuskova and Prokopovich at the time were members of the URSD and were perceived to wield considerable influence over the editors of *Rabochaia Mysl'* provided the 'old guard' with a stick with which to beat their younger opponents. In *What Is To Be Done?*, Lenin gleefully trumpeted that it 'was such an excellent weapon against Economism that, had there been no *Credo*, it would have been worth inventing one'.

The Second Party Congress and after

Lenin had been among the first to react to the Economist challenge. In August 1899, he composed a *Protest* against the *Credo*, which he prevailed upon 16 fellow exiles in Siberia to sign. Published in *Rabochee Delo*, it rejected Kuskova's pessimism concerning revolutionary prospects in Russia as mistaken, and reaffirmed the need for a disciplined vanguard party to lead the workers in the struggle against the autocracy. Plekhanov unsurprisingly followed suit, as did the supposedly more temperate Akselrod, in future to be a vociferous champion of a mass, democratic workers' party. He too had no truck with economic strikes, which he felt had become the major stumbling block to the organisation of an independent revolutionary workers' party. Oddly, he agreed with Kuskova that most Russian workers were ignorant and barbaric, and thus unable 'to raise themselves, completely independently and without any outside assistance, to the heights of conscious revolutionary strength'. Such assistance, of course, could only come from the intelligentsia. These arguments may strike many readers as familiar, as soon they were repeated by Lenin. To combat Economism the 'elders' resolved to rebuild the Party, stillborn after its First Congress. The means to do so was to be a new paper, *Iskra* (The Spark), to be published abroad and smuggled into Russia. Its role was twofold. First, it would disseminate the principles upon which a truly revolutionary party should be constituted. Secondly, it would act as the fulcrum around which the disparate local party committees that had sprung up in Russia could be united. Lenin himself, released from Siberia in early 1900, went to Geneva, where he became a member of its editorial board, together with Plekhanov, Akselrod, Martov, A. N. Potresov and Zasulich. During his work on *Iskra* he developed his rudimentary ideas on organisation, first articulated in late 1897 in *The Tasks of the Russian Social-Democrats*. The outcome was *What Is to Be Done?*

A lengthy and repetitive work, as many of Lenin's polemics were, its purpose was to justify the need for intellectual leadership in the revolution.

The workers, Lenin granted, had the spontaneous ability to undertake economic struggle. However, this would lead not to the development of a revolutionary consciousness, as the Economists believed, but to what he derisively termed a 'trade union consciousness'. The workers would see the need to form unions, whose task would be to extract material concessions from the industrialists and to demand protective legislation from the government. Even the involvement of these unions in overt political action would not mean that they had transcended 'bourgeois politics'. There could be no genuine class consciousness and thus no revolutionary movement '[w]ithout a revolutionary theory', a message which he hammered home again and again. But theory, he continued, more in the vein of Plekhanov than Marx, could only be brought to the working class from without, by the self-appointed vanguard of revolutionary-minded intellectuals. To succeed in this task the vanguard had to organise itself into a disciplined, centralised and conspiratorial party. Any attempt to create a mass party run on broadly democratic lines, he realistically insisted, could not hope to resist penetration and subsequent suppression by the Tsarist secret police. Less obviously, only an elite and disciplined party would be able to protect itself against the risk of ideological degeneration that would be posed by the mass influx of Russia's still politically backward workers. Most Russian Social Democrats, Lidiia Dan confirmed, agreed with Lenin that the creation of a mass party on the model of the SPD was impossible in Russian conditions. Her husband Fedor Dan was even more revealing. In his *The Origins of Bolshevism* he acknowledged that during the Economist controversy Lenin simply had articulated ideas on party organisation common to all who had gathered around *Iskra*. Martov also had argued for a highly centralised party in which discipline and ideological conformity were strictly enforced, as the only means to protect it from 'Bernsteinism'. Any reservations that they might have harboured about the potentially 'hyper-centralist' implications of Lenin's thinking, to employ Fedor Dan's retrospective description, remained muted at the time.

This consensus on the question of party organisation makes the split that occurred at the Second Congress of the RSDLP in July 1903 all the more puzzling. Then Lenin and Martov clashed over seemingly trivial differences concerning the definition of Party membership. Lenin proposed that this right be restricted to 'one who accepts the Party's programme and supports the Party both financially and by personal participation in one of the Party organisations'. Martov's formulation proclaimed that '[a]nyone who accepts the party's programme, supports the party by material means, and renders it regular personal assistance under the guidance of one of its organisations is to be considered a member'. Initially, Martov's proposal was approved by 28 votes to 22, with one abstention. However, a critical number of Martov's supporters deserted before the Congress ended. The five members of the *Bund* left in disgust when the '*Iskra*ites' refused to grant it autonomous power to organise the Jewish proletariat in the Empire. The representatives of URSD, Akimov and Martynov, did likewise when the Congress approved the dissolution of the Union. Lenin was now left with a bare majority (in Russian, *bol'shinstvo*). He appropriated the term 'Bolsheviks' (the 'majoritarians') for his faction, despite the fact that until 1917 he frequently found himself in the minority.

The difference between Lenin's and Martov's proposals at first sight seems to be slight, and insufficient to account for the split. The explanation suggested by Valentinov, that the dictatorial tendencies in Lenin's ideas were foreseen clearly by future Mensheviks (the 'minoritarians') wedded to the creation of a mass democratic party, was farfetched. Such an interpretation of the history of the Party arguably was much more of a post-1917 construct, and one coloured by the authoritarian fate of the October Revolution (Chapter 6). At the time most participants felt that the reasons for the split were, as Lidiia Dan recollected, unclear.[12] Few saw it as a simple clash between democratic and dictatorial conceptions of the Party, although at the Second Congress E. Y. Levin (Egorov) did point out that Martov's position alone left the door open for democracy within the Party. Lenin himself attacked it for its 'elasticity'. If endorsed, it would make the Party vulnerable to the entry of politically backward elements, which would threaten its ideological integrity and hence its ability to act as the vanguard alone capable of leading the vast bulk of the workers in revolution. Nevertheless, he did accept that the dispute over the rules for membership was not a matter of life and death that would cause the Party to perish.

Despite the splits that occurred at the Second Congress, to claim, as Lenin did in May 1920 in his *'Left-Wing' Communism, an Infantile Disorder,* that '[a]s a current of political thought and as a political party, Bolshevism has existed since 1903', was to distort the history of Russian Marxism. A precarious unity persisted within the RSDLP for many years after 1903, notwithstanding repeated bitter attacks on Lenin. In November 1903 Plekhanov unexpectedly condemned Lenin as 'a Robespierre' and switched his allegiance to the Menshevik wing of the Party. In 1904, in *Our Political Tasks*, Leon Trotsky prophetically warned of the despotic potential in Lenin's ideas: 'the party organisation is substituted for the party, the Central Committee is substituted for the party organisation, and finally a "dictator" is substituted for the Central Committee'. This prophecy (ignored by Trotsky himself in 1917) only came true much later, in the 1920s, when Stalin used, perhaps abused, Lenin's conception of the Party to promote his personal power (Chapter 6). On the other hand, in 1904 both Akselrod and Lenin, in his *One Step Forward, Two Steps Back*, were able to agree that no major issue of principle or tactics divided Russian Social Democrats. In practice, too, there was little difference between the Bolshevik and Menshevik wings of the Party, with Martov and Dan still convinced that a centralised, disciplined and underground party was necessary to lead the workers in revolution. In his memoirs, P. A. Garvi, a leading Menshevik trade unionist, acknowledged that before 1905 the Mensheviks' supposed commitment to constructing the Party on democratic foundations was little more than rhetoric, as their own scattered organisations were based entirely on the principle of co-option. They had little working-class support in Russia, and ironically remained much more a body of professional intellectual revolutionaries than the Bolsheviks. Moreover, most Mensheviks attached so little significance to the rules for Party membership that their Second All-Russian Conference in November 1905 in essence accepted the criteria that Lenin had promulgated at the Second Congress. At this Conference the Mensheviks also coined the term 'democratic centralism', to explain how they envisioned the Party should operate. While all Party members had the right to participate in the election of its leading organs the decisions subsequently taken by them would be binding on all lower-level organisations. At the time, they expressed no concerns that this concept could transform the Party into a hierarchical, and highly authoritarian, body.

Paradoxically, in 1904 when Akselrod re-emphasised the critical importance of the role of the intelligentsia in awakening the 'uncultivated' Russian proletariat from its 'immemorial slumbers', Lenin, now in the minority, changed tack. In *One Step Forward* he now dismissed many of the much-vaunted intellectuals as political dilettantes, unable to accept disciplinary strictures. He repeatedly demanded that more workers must be attracted into the Party, as only they, imbued with a sense of common purpose based upon their experience of factory life, would provide the foundation for the restoration of Party discipline. His reasoning was akin to his then ally, Aleksandr Bogdanov, who consistently claimed that the proletariat alone, not the inherently individualistic intelligentsia, possessed the collectivism required to lead the revolutionary struggle.

Furthermore, during the 1905 Revolution, Lenin, not the Mensheviks, so Denike admitted, proposed to open the Party to those workers who had become radicalised in its course. As Robert Service, author of a three-volume biography of Lenin, argued, he had two reasons for doing so. He hoped that a mass influx of workers would goad the professional revolutionaries who controlled the local committees in Russia from their inertia, and also restore his majority within them. Intellectuals, at least those of a like mind with him, were not discounted completely, as their role was to ensure that grassroots radicalism was channelled in the direction of a revolutionary political consciousness.[13]

Other areas of dispute, ones which proved to be more fundamental than that of Party organisation, developed to reinforce the gulf between Lenin and the Mensheviks, as Denike intimated. Evident in embryonic form before 1905, they came to prominence in the wake of the abortive revolution of that year, when the self-appointed vanguard had trailed in the wake of the workers. The latter, not the intellectuals, had been in the forefront of the movement that had brought the autocracy to its knees, and themselves had created the soviets (councils), through which they coordinated their strike and other political actions. The Party itself recognised their worth as agencies of revolutionary mobilisation only belatedly, at its Fifth (London) Congress in May 1907. In the meantime, different lessons had been drawn from 1905 by Lenin and his Menshevik opponents which widened the gulf between them.

The lessons of 1905 and deepening divisions

During and after 1905 both the Bolsheviks and Mensheviks reaffirmed that bourgeois–democratic revolution was the immediate task facing the Russian working class. References by Lenin in 1905, in his *Two Tactics of Social Democracy in the Democratic Revolution*, and in the Menshevik resolution of April on armed uprising, to the possibility of proceeding to the socialist stage should events in Russia spark off revolution in West Europe, were fleeting. The exception was Trotsky, who subscribed to a more voluntarist reading of Marxism than that of his fellows. The élan shown by the workers in 1905 led him to elaborate on ideas to which he had been introduced by Alexander Helphand (Parvus) a year earlier. The outcome was *Results and Prospects*, written in 1906, in which he first laid out his theory of permanent revolution. Trotsky accepted the 'orthodoxy' that the Russian bourgeoisie was too weak and dependent upon the autocracy to lead a revolution against it. Modern, large-scale industry had developed little, thanks to its efforts. In the main it had been created with the support of the state, to provide it with the economic foundations of military power. In turn, an urban proletariat had developed, which while still relatively small was concentrated in key industrial centres. This concentration had given it political power beyond its numbers, as the paralysis of the country by striking railway workers in the autumn of 1905 had demonstrated. It alone was capable of over-throwing the autocracy, although to do so it would have to win over the peasants to its side. Otherwise, as 1905 had also revealed, Russia's peas-ant army would intervene to crush it. Once in power, the proletariat would find it impossible to carry out merely bourgeois democratic reforms but would be driven to introduce socialist measures (here Trotsky provided one answer to the dilemma that had dumbfounded Denike). In consequence, it would come into conflict with the bour-geoisie and, more critically, the vast and backward peasant majority, which would resist the agrarian collectivisation demanded by socialism. The only way in which the workers' revolution in Russia could consoli-date itself would be if its success precipitated socialist revolution in Europe and victorious workers' governments there came to the aid of their beleaguered Russian comrades.

Bolsheviks and Mensheviks alike rejected permanent revolution out of hand, but agreed on little else. The question of potential allies for the working class became a major bone of contention. In face of widespread worker scepticism, during 1904 the Mensheviks had attempted to estab-lish an alliance with the liberal bourgeoisie, overwhelmingly drawn from Russia's professional strata, in the hope of cajoling it to mount a more radical assault on the autocracy. The failure of 1905, and in particular, the crushing of the Bolshevik-inspired rising in Moscow in December, convinced them of the futility of armed insurrection. Instead they sought to exploit the political concessions extorted from Nicholas II in his October Manifesto of 1905, especially the creation of a State *Duma*, a rep-resentative but far from democratic parliamentary assembly with limited legislative powers. They were prepared to participate in the elections to the *Duma* and, in union with the Liberals, to work within it to consolidate the tenuous liberties – of assembly and union organisation – that the working class had won as a result of 1905. In effect, they were abandon-ing the principle of proletarian hegemony in the democratic revolution, as Akselrod disclosed at the Fourth (so-called Unity) Party Congress, held in Stockholm in April 1906. He avowed that the political conditions currently prevailing demanded cooperation between the proletariat and the bourgeoisie if further advances were to be made. To Lenin, Menshevik prostration before the Liberals was arrant nonsense. According to Struve, he hated the bourgeoisie from the very depths of his soul, dismissing it as nothing but an utterly reactionary force. Its desertion of the 1905 Revolution in face of the radical demands posed by the St Petersburg Soviet, most notably for the 8-hour day, and acceptance of the constitutional crumbs from the table of the autocracy reinforced his canker, as well as his conviction that the proletariat must look elsewhere for revolutionary allies.[14] This fundamental disagreement was not resolved by the Unity Congress, at which the Mensheviks had a majority. As Martov remarked in a letter to Plekhanov in November 1906, the RSDLP remained riven with factions. Little did he know that factionalism would intensify, with conflict on the question of cooperation with the Liberals in the newly formed Kadet Party increasing in its bitterness. In addition, new areas of discord arose over how to exploit the precarious freedoms for organisation that existed after 1905; over participation, or not, in the State *Duma*; over the peasants' role in the revolution; and over policy with respect to the national minorities in the Empire.

Let us continue with the conflict concerning any possible alliance with the Liberals. After abandoning their boycott of the *Duma* elections when those in March 1906 resulted in a majority for the most left-wing parties standing, the Mensheviks advocated a *rapprochement* with the Kadets. To Lenin's disgust, the Party Conference held in Tammerfors in November 1906 supported the idea of local agreements with other revolutionary or democratic parties, including the Kadets, to thwart the victory of more reactionary parties. A minority of Mensheviks were prepared to go further. Fearful that a renewed revolutionary offensive would simply provoke an intensification of autocratic reaction, Akselrod in particular now urged the Party to concentrate on exploiting existing legal opportunities to create a mass party on the lines of others in Europe, such as the SPD. Participation in *Duma* electoral campaigns was one means of involving the workers in politics. The newly legalised trade unions were seen as another vehicle for organising the workers, although they were to be placed under the guidance of the Party. In response, Lenin accused the Mensheviks *carte blanche* of Liquidationism, of rejecting underground illegal activities in favour of an essentially reformist strategy. Plekhanov too entered the fray on Lenin's side, deeming Liquidationism to be but a new variant of Economism, as did Bogdanov and the Bolshevik Left.

Liquidationism has been as much misconstrued as Economism before it. At the Unity Congress and after, the majority of Mensheviks consistently upheld the existence of an illegal, underground party. In 1910, at the height of ever fiercer attacks on all worker organisations, Fedor Dan still insisted on the need to defend the modest constitutional concessions extracted from Nicholas II; to utilise the limited freedom of the press available; and to take part in *Duma* politics. All these would help to raise the workers' consciousness. Nevertheless, he continued, an underground organisation was indispensable, to lead the workers in the future revolution for democracy – although he denounced the 'fighting squads' that had been set up by the more extreme Bolsheviks to engage in bank robberies ('expropriations') to fund their factional activities. Whilst agreeing in theory with Dan that a vanguard party remained necessary to provide political leadership for the workers, Potresov wryly questioned how it was possible to liquidate an organisation that in fact no longer existed in Russia. In face of increased repression, beginning with Stolypin's coup of June 1907 when he dissolved the Second *Duma* and arbitrarily revised the electoral law to ensure a conservative majority in it, and of a deepening economic recession, the Party, as well as most trade unions, had simply disintegrated.

All this cut no ice with Lenin, who never ceased to denounce the Mensheviks as Liquidationists. Yet he too found himself under attack from 'the other Bolsheviks' on his Left, as Robert Williams has described them, led by Bogdanov and Leonid Krasin, fellow members of the secret Bolshevik Centre set up after they failed to gain a majority at the Unity Congress. Having bowed to the majority in favour of boycotting the elections to the first *Duma*, at the Bolshevik Conference in Tammerfors in December 1905, Lenin soon shifted his ground. At the Unity Congress he supported the Mensheviks' resolution in favour of independent Social Democratic participation in the elections still to be held in the Caucasus. In his little pamphlet of August 1906, *On the Boycott*, he justified this strategy as a means of pursuing revolutionary agitation. All he succeeded in doing was to alienate the Bolshevik Left, whose confidence in a renewed revolutionary upsurge was unshaken even after the dissolution of the First *Duma*. It vehemently contended that any participation in elections to the *Duma*, in its eyes a patently counter-revolutionary institution, would confuse the workers into believing that the peaceful achievement of their aims was possible. Stolypin's coup merely confirmed its rejection of *Duma* politics in any shape or form. Echoing the sentiments of the few surviving worker Bolshevik organisations in Russia, as Lenin's lieutenant

Grigorii Zinoviev admitted, they renewed their demands for a boycott of the *Duma* in an era of naked reaction. This split in Bolshevik ranks persisted until 1909, by which time it had been reinforced by the conflict between Lenin and Bogdanov on the highly abstruse issue of the philosophical principles at the heart of Marxism, as well as the more practical question of control over the money 'expropriated' by Bolsheviks in a robbery from the bank in Tiflis (Tbilisi) in 1907. In June 1909, at an extended session of the editorial board of the Bolshevik paper *Proletarii* (The Proletarian), Lenin succeeded in expelling his critics on the Left and seized control of the Bolshevik faction in exile from Bogdanov.

Lenin's pragmatism regarding *Duma* politics, however, did not temper his uncompromising hostility towards the Liberals. It led him to turn towards the vast peasant majority, without whose support, as he argued in *Two Tactics*, the workers could not hope to carry out the democratic revolution against the autocracy. His advocacy of a democratic dictatorship of the proletariat and the peasantry distanced him even further from the Mensheviks. The overwhelming majority of Russian Marxists, most Bolsheviks included, did not share Lenin's appreciation of the peasantry as a revolutionary class. They inherited Plekhanov's long-standing aversion to the peasantry as ignorant and reactionary. As Boris Nicolaevsky subsequently acknowledged, the Mensheviks' disregard of the peasantry was to prove to be a fatal political mistake.[15]

Sporadic peasant rebellions since 1900 had prompted Lenin to propose including an agrarian section in the Party programme adopted by the Second Congress. In the face of considerable opposition, his proposal for the return of the land ceded by the peasants to the landlords in the Great Emancipation of 1861, the so-called 'cut-offs' (*otrezki*), was adopted. Rents too were to be lowered and the redemption dues imposed on the peasants for the land granted to them in the Emancipation were to be abolished. He sought to justify this policy in what he considered to be Marxist terms. Stripping the large landowners of the *otrezki* would cause the dissolution of their estates, and thus destroy their political power, while making independent peasant farming viable. Unlike his analysis in the 1890s when he had overestimated the extent of capitalist development in the countryside, Lenin now argued that the landowners' estates remained feudal *latifundia*. In consequence, their destruction would not be economically regressive but would foster the growth of capitalism in the Russian countryside. Whatever the merits of Lenin's position, whether such meagre proposals would have won the support of the peasants is doubtful. They desired the equal division of all the land

('Black Repartition'), which the Socialist Revolutionaries alone promised them, as Egorov had pointed out at the Second Congress.

The revolutionary upsurge in the countryside in 1905 caused the Party to reconsider its approach to the peasantry. The Third (exclusively Bolshevik) Congress, in April 1905, approved a resolution which recognised that more would have to be offered to the peasantry to attract it to the side of the proletariat, including the confiscation of all noble, state and church land. At the Unity Congress a year later Lenin revived the proposals that he had jettisoned in 1903 under pressure from Plekhanov and Akselrod. All land, including peasant smallholdings, was to be nationalised. With the exception of the few large, modern estates on which collective agriculture could be introduced, this newly nationalised land was to be partitioned amongst the peasants. Land nationalisation, Lenin now averred, would shatter once and for all the power of the landlords, the major political prop of the autocracy, and remove all obstacles to the rapid development of capitalism in agriculture. His proposition failed to win majority support, even amongst his fellow Bolsheviks, and in the end the Menshevik programme of land municipalisation was adopted: confiscated state, church and noble land was to be transferred into the hands of democratically elected local committees, which would lease it to the peasantry. Yet it was Lenin's perception of the importance of the peasantry in the making of Russia's bourgeois–democratic revolution that had compelled the Party to confront this question. Party policy remained essentially unchanged until the summer of 1917, when Lenin was to shift his ground again, on this occasion in an attempt to mobilise the peasantry in the making of a socialist revolution (see Chapter 5).

Lenin proved to be equally responsive to the aspirations of the national minorities in the Russian Empire. Initially, in his *The National Question in Our Programme* (1903), his attitude was guarded. He contended that the right of self-determination should be confined to the proletariat of each nationality, contrary to the new Party Programme, which committed it, rhetorically at least, to self-determination for nations in their entirety. The 1905 Revolution, which reached fever pitch in the non-Russian regions of the Empire, had alerted him, he later declared, to the revolutionary potential of minority nationalism. Gradually, by 1913, he had become converted to the unqualified support of self-determination for these minorities, when he succeeded in making it Bolshevik policy. He defended this policy as faithful to the spirit of the 'founding fathers', who had warned of the dangers of denying self-determination at least to the oppressed 'historic nations' of Europe (Chapter 2). In the Russian

Empire, he argued, its denial would lead to crippling divisions between the Russian proletariat and its comrades of the minority nations, who then would be prey to the chauvinistic influence of their respective national bourgeoisie. His study of contemporary imperialism, only concluded during the First World War, convinced him of the rectitude of this policy, as we shall discover in the next chapter. Compared with those left-wing Bolsheviks such as Nikolai Bukharin and Iurii Piatakov who dismissed any pandering to nationalism as contrary to the essence of proletarian internationalism, and with the Mensheviks, who adopted the more limited notion of national-cultural autonomy for minorities first proposed by the leading Austro-Marxists Otto Bauer and Karl Renner, Lenin's support of self-determination was both straightforward and more appealing, if not practised by the Soviet state after 1917.

Bolshevism ascendant

Lenin's domination of the Bolshevik faction had turned out to be a Pyrrhic victory. He had won, in Geoffrey Swain's memorable phrase, the 'struggle for control of a corpse'.[16] To Lenin's irritation most Bolsheviks who had supported him against Bogdanov still sought to overcome factionalism in the Party and restore unity within it. The efforts of the so-called Conciliators were welcomed, according to Liadov, by what survived of the Party's grass roots in Russia, which frowned on all schismatic activity and attributed it to the squabbling émigré intellectuals. Yet neither the efforts of the Conciliators nor grassroots pressure healed the fissures in the Party. Lenin himself, as his opponents at the time justifiably claimed, was grimly opposed to Party unity, unless his own influence over it was assured. At first, he sought to secure control of the Party with the assistance of the Latvian and Polish Social Democrats, whose entry into it as autonomous organisations he had supported at the Unity Congress. To his chagrin, their unwillingness blindly to support his factional intrigues and their support, instead, for the Conciliators frustrated his attempts to take the Party over by 'democratic' (or democratic centralist) means. He then turned to more underhand methods. In January 1912 he convened a Party Conference in Prague composed almost entirely of his allies; proceeded to set up a new Central Committee; and threatened to exclude all who did not subordinate themselves to its directives. In effect, Lenin had hijacked the name of the Party for his faction. The split in the ranks of the RSDLP was all but complete, despite the continuing attempts by Trotsky in particular and the renascent unions in Russia to overcome it.

Lenin's intrigues seemed to have worked, as on the eve of war in 1914 Bolshevism had become the dominant current within the reinvigorated workers' movement in Russia. This movement had begun to revive as the recession drew to an end during 1910. Composed largely of educated and increasingly self-conscious workers, not of raw peasant recruits to industry as Leopold Haimson once alleged, it rejected the injunctions of those Mensheviks such as Akselrod to confine its demands to piecemeal reforms within a modified autocratic system and so secure a coalition with the Liberals. The continued suppression of strikes, and of the resurgent union organisations, by the government, not the exhortations of Lenin, best explains its embrace of revolutionary politics. The Economists' predictions apparently had been vindicated after all. Repression, most starkly manifest in the slaughter of striking workers on the Lena gold-fields in Siberia in April 1912, confirmed in the minds of many workers that the overthrow of the autocracy remained the prerequisite for any improvement in their material conditions. Accordingly, Bolshevik insistence on the importance of an underground organisation to lead the revolution, propagated in *Pravda* (Truth), the St Petersburg daily paper published by Lenin's faction from April 1912, was broadly accepted. But the movement itself was not Leninist. The majority of workers involved in it opposed, as they always had done, the factional conflicts that so absorbed the energies of the émigré intellectuals, especially Lenin, and backed the remaining Conciliators who tenaciously sought to re-unite the Party, if on a revolutionary platform.[17]

Whether unity was still possible is a moot point, given the profound, often personal, divisions that had emerged amongst the self-proclaimed leaders of the Party. Whether the 'general' strike that erupted and gripped the country in July 1914 would have succeeded in toppling the autocracy remains doubtful too. It was limited to St Petersburg, where only a quarter of the workers took to the streets. It had little support from the Liberals in the capital. The army, in particular the city garrison, remained loyal to Nicholas II's government. Before any definitive answer could be given to this question, the First World War intervened. Neither autocratic Russia nor Imperial Germany survived it. It also caused seismic changes within both German and Russian Marxism, with enduring consequences for the subsequent history of European Communism.

Chapter 5: War and Revolution

The First World War deepened the divisions within the European Socialist movement and ultimately led to the rupture that witnessed the creation of self-proclaimed revolutionary Communist movements. The parties of the Second International, with the exception of those in Russia and Serbia, failed to act on the vague resolution adopted at its Stuttgart Congress (1907) 'to exert every effort' to prevent the outbreak of war, or even to condemn it (see Chapter 3). While the SPD and the SIFO did organise anti-war demonstrations in the weeks following the assassination of Franz Ferdinand in Sarajevo when the threat of war was rising, they finally buckled under the swell of nationalist fervour. For the radicals the failure of the International meant that it had become no more than 'a stinking corpse', to quote Luxemburg's embittered conclusion. By the end of the war a Communist regime was in power in Russia. Communist Parties sprang up elsewhere, strongest in Germany, convinced by the Russian experience that revolution alone could eliminate capitalism and the evils of war it had brought. However, despite the establishment of short-lived Soviet republics, notably in Bavaria and Hungary in the spring of 1919, outside Russia Communist revolutions miscarried. To explain this bifurcation this chapter will continue to focus primarily, if not solely, on Germany and Russia.

Responses to the war

The outbreak of war restored a precarious unity within the SPD. On 3 August, by a majority of 96 to 14, a meeting of its deputies in the

81

Reichstag followed the lead of the General Commission, the central trade union organisation, and agreed to rally behind the government. Even those critical of the decision, such as Hugo Haase of the center-left of the Party and Karl Liebknecht on the radical left, bowed to the will of the majority, which would not brook any dissent on this issue. Indeed, Haase was prevailed upon to announce the SPD's agreement to war credits in the *Reichstag* on 4 August. In effect, the SPD had abandoned its traditional opposition to the existing political system for the duration of the war and plumped for a *Burgfrieden* (civil peace) with the government. The reason why the SPD, and its counterparts across Europe, had renounced their long-professed internationalism, and any thoughts of calling a general strike to oppose war, was quite simple. Most German workers were as susceptible to the appeal of nationalism as their fellows across Europe and would not have tolerated such unpatriotic action. In addition, as Eduard David emphasised, the SPD leadership feared that overt hostility to the war would have provoked the reintroduction of the anti-socialist legislation of the Bismarck era (Chapter 3). It justified its decision by direct appeal to Marx himself, and his indictment of Russia as 'the gendarme of Europe' (Chapter 2). It was the duty of socialists to defend the freedoms that Germany enjoyed against the reactionary threat posed by Russian despotism.

With varying degrees of enthusiasm most European Socialist parties pursued a similar course. The French Socialists quickly abandoned any residual commitment to a general strike against the war, themselves entered into a *Union sacrée* (sacred union) with the government, and even despatched two of their leaders to join it, as did the Belgians. They accounted for their actions in much the same way as the SPD, as Kautsky pointed out in the autumn, insisting that they were defending democracy against German authoritarianism. In Britain the overwhelming majority of the Labour Party, if not the small Independent Labour Party, and trade unions also swung behind the Liberal government's decision for war. Not only had the power of nationalism triumphed over that of international socialism, but the patriotic unity engendered by war calmed the industrial conflict that had gripped many European states in the years immediately preceding 1914.[1]

Yet opposition to war re-emerged, most swiftly within the SPD. In September 1914 Liebknecht and Luxemburg, supported by Franz Mehring and Clara Zetkin, denounced Party policy in the Swiss press. Three months later, on 2 December, Liebknecht voted against further war credits, calling instead for 'a speedy peace, a peace without conquest...'. Few party organisations supported him, that in Stuttgart being a notable exception. During 1915 a few more SPD deputies gradually came to share Liebknecht's doubts and on 21 December, Haase, Georg Ledebour and 16 others refused to vote for war credits. Increasingly sceptical of the tacit support of the Majority Socialists for the annexationist objectives pursued by the Imperial government, during 1916 this minority, the core of a future Independent Social Democratic Party (USPD), advocated a democratic peace, and reform of the increasingly authoritarian political order in Germany itself, not revolution. Expelled by the Party on 24 March for again rejecting war credits they formed the Social Democratic Working Group (SDAG), a motley and fragile coalition. The arch Revisionist, Bernstein, disillusioned by the chauvinism of the Majority, joined it. So too did Kautsky, largely to prevent its take-over by the radical Left, which he feared might drive the party to launch a bloody and futile insurrection against the Imperial Government. On Liebknecht's initiative the radical Left had also formed the International Group on 1 January 1916 (renamed the Spartacus League in November 1916). It adhered to the *Theses on the Tasks of International Social Democracy*, written by the imprisoned Luxemburg in the spring of 1915. Based on the conclusions outlined in her *The Accumulation of Capital*, the *Theses* denounced the war as one of rival imperialisms. Now that war had precipitated the final 'catastrophe' of capitalism, the *Theses* called upon the proletariat in all belligerent countries to re-establish the international solidarity betrayed by the Second International, and rise in 'a war against war' to overthrow capitalism. Socialist revolution, not illusory schemes such as the pursuit of 'the European federation of states' (a reference to 'the United States of Europe' fleetingly proposed by Kautsky), alone could end the war. The German Left had moved close to the position advocated by Lenin and the Bolsheviks, as we shall shortly see, and jointly with them formed the core of what became known as the 'Zimmerwald Left'.[2]

The First World War witnessed similar realignments within Russian Marxism. While the small Social Democratic faction in the Imperial *Duma*, including both Mensheviks and Bolsheviks, had refused to vote for war credits, fundamental divisions were evident from its very outset. The Mensheviks were rent asunder when Potresov and Plekhanov adopted an unequivocal defencist policy, or social chauvinist, as Lenin scathingly described it. Mirroring the Majority Socialists in Germany, they contended that it was the duty of the workers to support Russia's war against the predatory designs of the imperialist German state. Analogous to the position later adopted by the Independent Socialists in Germany, Martov and the majority of Mensheviks refused to support Russia's, or any other country's, participation in the war. These so-called Internationalists urged the socialist parties of Europe to demand of their governments the speedy negotiation of a democratic peace, without annexations and indemnities, a Utopian objective in light of the xenophobic passions fuelled by the war. They entered into an uneasy coalition with Trotsky, and some dissident Bolsheviks, including S. A. Lozovskii and D. Z. Manuilskii, around the paper *Nashe Slovo* (Our Voice), published in Paris from January 1915. A few former Mensheviks, including Alexandra Kollontai, gravitated towards Lenin, who from the outset had advocated an uncompromising defeatist position. The task of Social Democrats, Lenin insisted, was neither to support their own governments nor to seek a chimerical democratic peace, but to convert the imperialist war into a civil war for socialism. To understand Lenin's defeatism, however, requires us to examine his thinking on imperialism, summarised in his famous pamphlet usually translated as *Imperialism, the Highest Stage of Capitalism*.[3]

Lenin's imperialism

While Lenin had begun his study of imperialism before 1914, the war prompted him to devote considerable time and energy to completing it. Hindsight makes it possible to isolate the two major objectives of his analysis: first, to provide an explanation for the outbreak of war; and secondly, to refute Kautsky's prognosis concerning the possibility of the creation of an United States of Europe. In the process he arrived at conclusions which confirmed, at least to his satisfaction and to that of many of his fellow Bolsheviks, that the preconditions for socialist revolution had matured.

Let us start with the war. For Lenin, it was indubitably one of rival imperialisms. He explained its outbreak by reference to what he termed the 'law of the uneven development of capitalism'. Late and rapidly developing capitalist states, such as Germany (and Japan and even the United States), had sought to carve out for themselves empires commensurate with their new economic might. However, by the end of the nineteenth century the world already had been partitioned amongst the established, now less dynamic, imperial powers, which unsurprisingly refused to cede any of their territories. Imperial Germany's pursuit of its 'place in the sun' had brought it into conflict with them, in particular with Britain. War was the inevitable outcome of this conflict. For Lenin, uneven development was an inalienable characteristic of capitalism. Capitalist powers would go on growing at vastly different rates, which meant that it was impossible to envisage a situation whereby the imperialist powers would settle their differences peacefully, as Kautsky had speculated, and create a united, ultra-imperialist state.

The massive economic and human sufferings inflicted upon the workers by the war, Lenin continued, would radicalise them and ultimately turn them against their own governments. The war had also accelerated the tendencies within capitalism analysed by Hilferding (Chapter 3). The organisation of the economy in the most evolved capitalist societies of West Europe, and the United States, that had accompanied the growth of, first, monopoly and then finance capitalism, had been accelerated by the controls imposed by the warring governments to ensure that war matériel was produced in sufficient quantities. This intervention had resulted in state capitalism, which had advanced the regulation of production to such a degree that the framework for the introduction of a planned socialist economy existed. The time was ripe, he concluded, for revolution. Differences in the details of their analysis notwithstanding, Lenin and the German Left had arrived at essentially the same conclusions. War against war and the advocacy of proletarian revolution united them.

Where Russia itself was concerned, Lenin's position was less clear. As Neil Harding conceded, he never applied his analysis of imperialism specifically to it. Contrary to much that has been written on this question, until early 1917 Lenin clung to the established orthodoxy that the forthcoming revolution in Russia would remain bourgeois–democratic (Chapter 4). From his *Theses on the War*, first promulgated in August 1914, until the autumn of 1916, in *A Caricature of Marxism*, he repeatedly rejected the ideas of those on the Left of the Party, especially Bukharin and Piatakov, that socialist revolution would sweep across the world in a single mighty wave, to embrace Russia too. On the contrary, the uneven development of capitalism dictated that socialist revolution itself would develop unevenly. Its victory in just one country was quite possible in the first instance. Moreover, in the still under-developed parts of the world, comprising 'the whole of Eastern Europe and all the colonies and semi-colonies', bourgeois–democratic revolution awaited completion. Here too, where nationalist revolutions had not yet been completed, Lenin added in support of his policy concerning subjugated nationalities, the struggle for self-determination remained legitimate (see Chapter 4).

In January 1917, on the eve of the collapse of the autocracy, he recapitu-
lated the thrust of his arguments. It remained, of course, the duty of
Russian Marxists to work for the defeat of the autocracy. Its downfall
would clear the way for the development of capitalism, the essential
prerequisite for the progress of 'our movement', that is, for socialism.[4]

War and revolution

As the war dragged on, with no immediate end in sight, the patriotic zeal
of many of Europe's workers faded away as their living and working
conditions deteriorated, and the carnage of their fellows mounted.
National unity was threatened first in Russia, where strikes broke out in
the summer of 1915. Initially seeking better economic conditions, in face
of brutal, on occasion murderous, repression they rapidly became transformed into political movements, demanding the overthrow of the autocracy and an end to the war. In Germany also, sporadic strikes at the
workplace had begun during 1915. Unrest there escalated in the summer
of 1916. On 29 June a mass strike in Berlin was held in response to the
arrest of Liebknecht for his opposition to the war. Inflation, growing food
shortages (the winter of 1916–17 was dubbed the 'turnip winter' in
honour of the workers' staple diet), the introduction of labour conscription on 2 December and the continuing slaughter on the front lines
heaped fuel on the flames of the workers' discontent. Protests elsewhere
in Europe were slower to develop, and only became widespread in 1917,
after the February Revolution in Russia.

As Leopold Haimson pointed out, mounting criticisms of the war were
encouraged by the Zimmerwald movement. In August 1915, 42 socialist
delegates, drawn from organisations in eleven countries, gathered at
Zimmerwald, in neutral Switzerland. The manifesto finally adopted, that
of the Centre rather than of Lenin and the radical Left, unequivocally
condemned the war as one of rival imperialisms, driven by 'their greed
for profit'. Socialist parties now must cease to offer any support to their
own governments and summon the workers to take up the class struggle
again, to put an end to the war. This struggle alone could achieve a
democratic and non-annexationist peace, as well as furthering 'the
sacred aims of socialism'. Eight months later, in April 1916, 43 delegates,
from organisations in eight countries, met again in the little Swiss town
of Kienthal. The resolution approved on this occasion again denounced
the war as imperialist. However, its call to arms was more explicit: the only

way to secure 'a lasting peace' was by the revolutionary overthrow of capitalism itself. While the precise impact of these resolutions remains difficult to determine, the dramatic events that shortly were to overtake Russia undoubtedly galvanised opposition across Europe.[5]

Just as Russia had been the first country to experience major strikes and anti-war protests, so too it was the first to succumb to revolution. Unrest in all quarters of Russian society, provoked by Russia's abysmal record of defeats, and deepening worker immiseration, exploded in February 1917. A combination of striking workers on the streets of the capital, renamed Petrograd in August 1914; the desertion of most of the city garrison to their side; the failure of the army High Command to despatch loyal troops quickly, to restore order; and the lack of support from the weak middle classes and even the nobility, led to the collapse of Nicholas II's government. On 3 March a new Provisional Government (PG), composed of liberal and moderate members of the State *Duma* (Aleksandr Kerensky was the sole socialist), replaced it. Russia's bourgeois–democratic revolution, so it appeared, at last had been realised.

As in 1905, the February Revolution again caught the Russian Social Democratic intelligentsia unawares. As Anatolii Lunacharskii, the future Commissar of Education (or Enlightenment), recalled, news of February had left it 'thunderstruck'. Hastily returning from emigration or internal exile it was faced with the question of what was to be done. One answer was expounded by the Menshevik–Internationalist Irakli Tsereteli, after his release from Siberian exile. Social Democrats, he urged, were to offer conditional support to the newly formed PG. The workers' and soldiers' Soviets that had sprung up largely spontaneously during the Revolution were to monitor its actions, to ensure that it carried out a programme of democratic reform, a system known as that of Dual Power. In Russia, he cautioned, capitalism remained insufficiently developed to permit the immediate transition to socialism. Any attempt to leap the bourgeois–democratic stage would be fraught with peril. The premature advance of socialist objectives would provoke widespread opposition, from the industrialists, the landlords, the elite officer corps and most of educated society, and immerse Russia in a ruinous civil war. Moreover, now that Russia had become a democracy – even Lenin called it 'the freest country in the world' in 1917 – it was the duty of socialists to defend the gains of the revolution from German militarism, until such time as a democratic, non-annexationist peace was negotiated. Tsereteli's proposals in favour of Dual Power and revolutionary defencism were adopted not just by the Mensheviks and Socialist Revolutionaries (SRs) but also by the leading Bolsheviks in Russia, Lev Kamenev and Joseph Stalin, when they arrived back in the capital from exile in Siberia. On the basis of such a commonality of views, attempts yet again were made to reunite the factions within Russian Social Democracy, as much of its rank and file desired.

The logic of Lenin's analysis, in particular his belief that only a bourgeois revolution was possible in Russia, dictated that he should have supported Tsereteli's position. But by now he had changed tack again. In his final writings in Swiss exile, his *Draft Theses* and his *Letters from Afar*, he insisted that the revolution in Russia had not ended with the fall of the autocracy and the establishment of a bourgeois–democratic government. The time now had come for the Russian proletariat, in alliance with the proletarianised and poor peasants, and the workers of the West, to move the revolution on to its socialist stage. In his celebrated *April Theses*, pronounced immediately on his return to Russia on 3 April, he declared that the struggle for socialism must begin at once. Although his *Theses* remained couched in terms of broad principles, on two issues Lenin was adamant. First, even under the PG, Russia remained an imperialist state, waging an imperialist war. Accordingly, there could be no support for revolutionary defencism. Secondly, there was to be no support for the PG, nor any 'parliamentary republic'. For Lenin there was no viable parliamentary path to socialism. His studies of the imperialist state, under-taken in the winter of 1916–17, had led him to endorse the analysis put forward by Bukharin in 1915. Under finance capitalism the state, even a democratic republic, had acquired unprecedented coercive and ideolog-ical power to quash or deflect any and all opposition to itself. This 'new Leviathan' had to be smashed before any progress towards socialism was possible. It was to be replaced by a new 'commune state' – in Russia's case, a Republic of Soviets. This was the political blueprint for socialism, he concluded, that Marx had bequeathed from his reflections on the short-lived Paris Commune of 1871 (see Chapter 2). He elaborated his vision of the post-revolutionary order later in 1917 in his famous tract *State and Revolution*. Another convoluted and repetitive work, it was a paean in praise of the capacities of ordinary workers to administer the new socialist state with little, if any, aid from the much vaunted vanguard party of *What Is To Be Done?*

The corollary of Lenin's new-found radicalism was that the Bolsheviks, then a minority, were to have no truck with 'petty-bourgeois opportunist elements', such as the Mensheviks. He berated those who had advocated unity with them. To emphasise his point he demanded that the name of the Party be changed, from Social Democratic to Communist. His dramatic *volte-face* provoked consternation in Russian Marxist ranks, the leading Bolsheviks included. The Menshevik B. O. Bogdanov derided his call for socialist revolution in a still backward, predominantly peasant Russia as 'the raving of a madman'. At the Seventh [Bolshevik] Party Conference in April, Aleksei Rykov concurred: socialism was not just unthinkable but also impossible in Russia, 'the most petty-bourgeois country in Europe'. In his history of 1917 the Menshevik–Internationalist Nikolai Sukhanov alleged that Lenin's *Theses* were profoundly un-Marxist, lacking any consideration of the economic conditions that made socialist revolution possible in Russia. In response to this barrage of criticism, Lenin eventually sought to justify in Marxist (or determinist) terms his call for socialist revolution in Russia. In the summer of 1917 he at last applied Hilferding's analysis (Chapter 3) to Russia, arguing that during the war the financial and industrial sectors of its economy had become ever more centralised and concentrated. On top of that, the autocratic state had intervened to an ever greater extent to regulate production. This process had culminated in the formation of 'state-monopoly capitalism', the basis on which a planned socialist economy could be founded.[6]

Despite the initial furore that the *Theses* provoked they quickly became the basis upon which the Bolshevik Party, as Trotsky pithily stated, was re-armed ideologically. The opposition that he initially faced within the Party was overcome through a combination of Lenin's persuasive logic, the return of radical Bolsheviks from exile, and the influx of new recruits itching for a more radical revolution to resolve their material difficulties. Lower-ranking Bolsheviks, who since February had been advocating much the same revolutionary strategy, supported him too. Astonishingly, by October Lenin, written off as a 'has been' by the Menshevik M. I. Skobelev, and discounted by the British ambassador Sir George Buchanan, who saw Kerensky as the coming man, was *de facto* leader of a new Soviet Russia.[7]

Divergent answers have been offered to account for Bolshevik victory. After the collapse of the Soviet Union, Richard Pipes (among others) resurrected the long-standing explanation that attributed it to the Party, disciplined, centralised, obedient to Lenin. According to Pipes, the October Revolution was a well-planned coup carried out by 'small, disciplined units of soldiers and workers' under Bolshevik command. The implication of this argument is that the October coup was carried out behind the backs of the majority of ordinary people, and thus was illegitimate. However popular, this picture is one-sided. First, it fails to acknowledge the absence of discipline and obedience within the Bolshevik Party in 1917, which failed to live up to the model of Lenin's *What Is to Be Done?* In March and April its leaders in Russia opposed Lenin's call to turn the revolution into one for socialism and deliberately suppressed his own views. In April, he had a mighty struggle to convert the Party to support socialist revolution in Russia. Ironically, in July he failed to control extreme elements and prevent them from mounting what he judged to be a premature rising in Petrograd, known as the July Days (3–5 July). Troops loyal to the PG launched a counter-offensive against the Bolsheviks, who were slandered as agents of Imperial Germany bent on subverting the Revolution. Many were imprisoned, and, in fear for his life, Lenin fled to Finland. There, he again revised his political programme. He abandoned his call for 'All Power to the Soviets', which would simply deliver the Revolution into the hands of the effete Mensheviks and SRs who had condoned the repression of the Bolsheviks after the July Days. In face of considerable opposition the Sixth Party Congress, in August, eventually supported his proposal. In September and October his demand that the Party act immediately to transfer power into the hands of the Soviets, newly Bolshevised in the wake of the abortive military coup launched by General Lavr Kornilov in late August, met with much hostility. His old comrades-in-arms, Kamenev and Zinoviev, publicly challenged him, declaring that any attempt to seize power would precipitate a victorious counter-revolution. Aware of the rapidly increasing support for the Bolsheviks in the urban soviets, Trotsky insisted that any move to overthrow the PG be delayed until the Second All-Russian Congress of Soviets convened in October, which would lend legitimacy to their actions. The much-vaunted discipline and unity of the Party was not the key to Bolshevik success in 1917, though their imposition after 1917 was to have profoundly dictatorial consequences (see Chapter 6).[8]

Nor was the Party primarily responsible for the radicalisation of the workers, peasants and soldiers during 1917, which is better explained by the failure of the Bolsheviks' opponents to resolve the dilemmas facing the country at that time. The first major crisis centred on war aims. Rather than seeking a democratic peace, as the Petrograd Soviet optimistically had urged, in April the foreign minister, P. N. Miliukov, had sent a note to Russia's allies reiterating the PG's commitment to prosecute the war to a victorious conclusion. In face of mass protests in Petrograd the PG was forced to ditch Miliukov, and the equally belligerent war minister, A. I. Guchkov. Furthermore, to provide it with greater credibility in the eyes of the majority of the population, the Mensheviks and SRs agreed on 5 May to become junior partners in a coalition with the Liberals, contrary to their axiom of non–participation in government during the bourgeois–democratic revolution. All this was grist to the mill of the rearmed Bolshevik Party. Lenin's charge against the PG, that it was pursuing the same imperialist objectives as the autocracy, was given substance, while the Mensheviks and SRs now could be held to be directly responsible for its actions. Their reputation was irreparably damaged by their support for the ill-conceived offensive of June, which quickly turned into a rout. Moreover, their inability to exert any influence to halt rapidly rising inflation, unemployment and food shortages in the cities, or to engineer any tangible land reform that would satisfy the peasant majority, accelerated the erosion of their grassroots support.[9]

Growing popular disillusion galvanised the more radical factions within these parties, the Menshevik Internationalists led by Martov, and the Left SRs. In the summer they renounced coalition with the Liberals, whose unwillingness to implement any meaningful economic, political and social reforms had risen markedly. They strove to establish a revolutionary democratic government, in effect a Soviet government of all the socialist parties. It alone could pressurise the Allies to enter negotiations for a democratic peace; introduce curbs on prices and excess war profits; speed up land reform; control the production and distribution of goods; and even seize those enterprises where the bourgeoisie was suspected of sabotaging production. Despite growing in strength they remained minorities. Their reluctance to split from the majority and to form a bloc with more moderate Bolsheviks, such as Kamenev and Zinoviev, condemned them to impotence.[10]

Despite the temporary setback occasioned by the July Days, Lenin's populist slogans articulated what the workers, peasants and soldiers increasingly saw to be the only solution to their problems. He promised peace; bread to the workers; and land to the peasants. Faced with widespread opposition within the Party, which feared that an egalitarian division of the land would convert the peasantry into a class of reactionary-minded property owners, in the summer of 1917 he had modified his agrarian policy again. On this occasion he bowed to peasant demands for 'Black Repartition' (Chapter 4). In sum, his responsiveness to popular demands helped to ensure that by October the Bolsheviks had majorities in the key Petrograd and Moscow soviets, and those in the towns of the Volga, the Central Industrial Region around Moscow, and the Urals.

Many of the soldiers' soviets also had swung behind the Bolsheviks, while potential peasant resistance to a Bolshevik seizure of power at the very least had been neutralised by his conversion to land division. Consequently, when the PG found itself under attack in October it had no grassroots support. Moreover, it had lost all sympathy at the highest levels of Russian society. Its failure to check the growing forces of radicalism and the apparent betrayal of General Lavr Kornilov, the beacon of order, by its head, Kerensky, cost it dearly. The officer corps, in particular, failed to come to its aid, in the mistaken belief that the Bolsheviks would not be able to survive in power long.

The impact of 1917

The events of 1917 in Russia, beginning with the collapse of the autocracy, stirred up increased opposition to the war across Europe. In France, the *Union sacrée* was challenged by a renewed wave of strikes in the spring of 1917 and finally collapsed in September 1917. Living and working conditions had declined markedly. Confidence in the ability of the government to lead the country successfully through the trials and tribulations of the war had also fallen sharply, especially after the slaughter accompanying the spring offensive launched by General Nivelle had ended in the mutiny of many French troops. In Britain a combination of war weariness, rapid inflation and growing state intervention in the economy, largely on the side of capital, to ensure production for the war was not hit, provoked a gradual escalation of industrial conflict. Here, as in much of Europe, shop stewards, especially those in factories producing armaments, were at the forefront of this militancy. In Italy, which had entered the war in 1915, growing food shortages had resulted in riots in the summer of 1917. The Austro-Hungarian Empire experienced similar waves of protest in the winter and spring of 1917–18, culminating in mass strikes in Vienna and Budapest in January 1918.[11]

In Germany itself opposition escalated dramatically, with increasing numbers of striking workers, and many white collar workers too, demanding immediate improvements in their material conditions; the abolition of labour conscription; an end to the war by means of a negotiated peace; and the introduction of democratic reforms, which was resisted most bitterly by the Conservatives in Prussia and by the military. Moreover, the Majority Socialists' justification for supporting the war had been removed at a stroke by the fall of the autocracy. Yet they continued to vote for war credits. At the same time they urged the conclusion of a negotiated peace (as did the French and other Socialists), and rather naively sought the introduction of parliamentary government in a country which in reality had been transformed into a military dictatorship under Generals Hindenburg and Ludendorff. These policies were incorporated in the resolutions adopted by the Würzburg Congress of the SPD in October 1917. In the meantime, in April, the minority had convened at Gotha. Reinforced by those opposition-minded members of the rank and file who had been expelled from the Party in January 1917, Haase and Ledebour, despite the misgivings of Bernstein and Kautsky, took the initiative in the formation of a new party, the USPD. Rejecting the pleas of the few Spartacists in its ranks that revolution was vital to overthrow the military dictatorship and secure peace, its programme reflected the aspirations of most workers for democratic reform within Germany and a non-annexationist peace.[12]

The stubborn determination of Generals Hindenburg and Ludendorff, firmly supported by the conservative elites and the proto-fascist Fatherland Party, to pursue war to a victorious conclusion, and the worsening of economic conditions within Germany, led to ever greater disillusion. Further enraged by the government's refusal to conclude a non-annexationist peace with the infant Soviet republic in Russia more and more workers, especially in the metal and war industries, responded willingly to the promptings of increasingly militant shop stewards on the shop floor to take direct action to end the war. Massive strikes gripped the country in the winter of 1917–18. They were fuelled by the Draconian peace conditions imposed upon Soviet Russia at Brest-Litovsk, which starkly revealed the expansionist ambitions of the Imperial government. Trotsky's stance during the negotiations, refusing to agree to a dictated imperialist peace whilst declaring that for Russia the war was at an end (his famous 'no war, no peace' strategy), helped to expose its predatory designs, as Ian Thatcher suggested. Whether the continuation of a 'no war, no peace' policy would have inspired Germany's increasingly disgruntled workers to rise in revolution remains less certain, as do their prospects of success. Certainly workers' councils were set up in many of Germany's major industrial cities but their revolutionary potential was contained by a combination of repression and fear of unemployment.

Nevertheless the threat that they posed to the old order drove Ludendorff to a last-ditch effort to win the war and so head off radical change. He took advantage of the withdrawal of Soviet Russia from the war after the imposition of the Brest-Litovsk treaty in March 1918 to launch a major offensive in the west. His gamble failed. With troops from the United States arriving daily in greater numbers the offensive was checked in June and the German forces were inexorably pushed back. By late September the High Command described the military position as 'hopeless'. To avoid crushing defeat and subsequent revolution, Ludendorff concluded that Germany's only salvation lay in suing for peace, on the basis of the terms laid out by Woodrow Wilson in his famous Fourteen Points. However, for such a peace to be achieved, he heeded the advice of Paul Hintze, the foreign minister, that Germany would have to be transformed into a parliamentary state. Cynically abandoning his repeated objections to such a course of action he prevailed upon the Kaiser, on 1 October, to appoint a government responsible to the *Reichstag* under Prince Max of Baden. At last Germany had become a constitutional monarchy, although Ludendorff himself was forced to resign under continuing pressure from Wilson.[13]

The German revolution

Ludendorff's machinations were all too little and too late. The revolution from above that he had sought to engineer was transformed into a revolution from below by the crazed decision of the naval staff on 28 October to send out the German fleet to engage the British navy and perish with honour in an inevitably futile battle. The Baltic Sea sailors balked at this decision. On 3 November those in Kiel set up revolutionary councils. Their example was quickly followed by sailors in the other Baltic ports, then by soldiers and workers across Germany. As well as the call for an immediate peace, the demands previously promulgated by militant shop stewards, in Berlin and beyond, that a new government based on the councils be set up, now resonated throughout the country. On 8 November, the USPD in Bavaria, led by Kurt Eisner, set up a Democratic Socialist Republic (in reality, more democratic than socialist), to be governed by a Council of Workers, Soldiers and Peasants. The events in Bavaria exacerbated the fears of the Majority Socialists, hitherto content to work within the framework of the parliamentary monarchy introduced in October, that mounting grassroots pressure would result in revolution on the Bolshevik model, and galvanised them into action. Already, on 7 November, they grudgingly had demanded the abdication of the Kaiser in order to prevent their own grassroots support from haemorrhaging away. On 9 November, terrified that the entreaties of Liebknecht and the

Spartacists for the creation of a dictatorship of the proletariat would radicalise the revolution to such an extent that violent civil war would ensue, Philipp Scheidemann, one of the two Socialist ministers in Max of Baden's Cabinet, was moved to announce to the workers on the streets of Berlin that Germany had become a People's (or Democratic) Republic. The following day Friedrich Ebert, the leader of the Majority Socialists, who professed to hate revolution 'like sin', strove to ensure that the situation did not career out of control. He accepted the offer made by General Wilhelm Groener to despatch the army to quell any revolutionary disturbances. In return, Ebert promised to restrain the soldiers' councils, whose clamour for the democratisation of the army and the election of officers threatened to destroy the power of the old officer corps. A new *Burgfrieden* between the Majority Socialists and the forces of the old Imperial order had been concluded. He also invited the USPD, whose ranks had grown greatly throughout 1917 and 1918, to join him in government. He hoped that the inclusion of the USPD in a new coalition government would act as a moderating influence over the various councils where it had garnered much of its support. By a small majority the USPD agreed to enter Ebert's Cabinet, and on 10 November the Council of People's Deputies (*Rat der Volksbeauftragten*), composed of three Majority Socialists and three Independents, was formed.[14]

Fissures, unsurprisingly, soon emerged within the new government. For Ebert and the Majority Socialists, the revolution was over. The future of Germany was to be determined by a popularly elected National Assembly. They had secured, albeit hesitantly and reluctantly, the abdication of the Kaiser; the establishment of a democratic republic; and, with the armistice on 11 November, the end to the war. At long last, a genuinely reformist, if gradual, path to socialism seemed to be open. The experience of Russia in 1917 convinced them that the main danger emanated from those forces on the Left craving a Bolshevik-type revolution, an anxiety shared by moderates within the USPD, such as Kautsky. The USPD as a whole was less sanguine. The majority in it supported the formation of a National Assembly at some future date, as Kautsky explained in a pamphlet of the same name published in December 1918. In other words, they still subscribed to his tenet that parliamentary democracy was consistent with socialism, 'a precondition to the social revolution'. But many Independent Socialists also questioned whether the reforms introduced to date had been sufficient to ensure that the country's political structure had been democratised thoroughly, and a future parliamentary road to socialism secured. Wilhelm Dittmann outlined their fears at a meeting of the Council on 28 December. '[T]he instruments of power of the old regime [had not] been destroyed,' he contended, as the bureaucracy, the judiciary, and especially the military remained dominated by authoritarian elements inherited from the Imperial regime. Others were concerned that the power of the property-owning classes, agrarian and industrial, also had been left untouched. In fact, the agreement drawn up between the industrialist Hugo Stinnes, for the employers, and Carl Legien, a leading trade unionist, on 15 November had guaranteed the inviolability of private property, in return for the industrialists' recognition of free trade unions. To safeguard democracy from counter-revolution issuing from these quarters Dittmann insisted that the old Imperial institutions be cleansed of all reactionary figures, and that key sectors of the economy be socialised, or at least subject to state control. He emphasised the continuing role that the councils of sailors, soldiers and workers had to play before the National Assembly convened. Their task was to rid the country of all vestiges of Prussian militarism and oversee the root-and-branch democratisation of the old order. To this end, the Independent Socialists, with the support of the radically inclined shop stewards, prevailed upon the Berlin Workers' and Soldiers' Council on 23 November temporarily to take power into its own hands, 'to uphold the achievements of the Revolution...as well as to ward off the counterrevolution'. Only a revolutionary minority shared the views expressed by Ernst Daumig at the All-German Congress of Workers' and Soldiers' Councils when it met on 16 December, that government by councils, not a democratic republic, was 'the natural form of organisation of modern revolution'.[15]

The outcome of this Congress suggested that in the long run the majority of German workers and soldiers would be satisfied with parliamentary rather than council (or soviet) democracy, although there was widespread support for radical motions in favour of socialisation of the economy and the democratisation of the army. However, in the interim until the National Assembly was elected, Ebert's government was to be given an essentially free hand to run the country. This outcome is somewhat puzzling. It would be facile to deny the doubts of many involved in the council movement that more was required to extirpate the country of the authoritarian forces which for decades had resisted the principle that power should reside in the hands of a popularly elected *Reichstag*. Others apparently clung to the belief, or hope, that perhaps enough had been achieved, which helps to explain the fractured response within the council movement. What is clearer is the pique of the USPD leadership.

In particular, it took umbrage at the decision of the Congress that deprived its newly elected Central Committee of Councils (*Zentralrat*) of effective supervisory power over government actions, and refused to enter it. By default the *Zentralat* fell into the hands of Ebert and the Majority Socialists. The USPD's intransigence cost it dear. Lacking any organisational leverage within the Central Committee it was unable to prevent Ebert from summoning the army to Berlin on 23–4 December to crush a spontaneous rising of sailors, who had taken to the streets simply to press for further measures of democratic reform, not to foment a Communist revolution. All it could do was to protest, with its three members of the Cabinet eventually resigning on 29 December. This second act of political ineptitude, or suicide, condemned the USPD to impotence.[16]

Dismayed by the moderation of the Majority Socialists and pusillanimity of the USPD, the Spartacists more vociferously than ever advocated a revolutionary transformation in Germany similar to that in Russia. They disavowed parliamentary democracy once and for all. The programme which they adopted on 10 November called for the destruction of the old state, its army, police and bureaucracy. They were to be replaced by a workers' and soldiers' militia and a government of elected councils. Having gathered in Berlin in late December, on 1 January 1919 they formed themselves into the German Communist Party (KPD). In her final speech, delivered to the founding congress of the KPD, Luxemburg endorsed the 10 November programme, but typically reiterated that it was one that could only be realised by mass revolutionary action, not by a vanguard party. Mindful of her repeated warnings that organisational centralisation and hierarchy had led to reformism, the KPD refused to impose disciplinary strictures from above on its followers. The consequences of this decision were disastrous. Notwithstanding the misgivings of Luxemburg and her fellow leaders, the KPD had no command structure capable of preventing its supporters taking to the streets in January 1919 when incited to do so by a faction of revolutionary shop stewards in Berlin. Luxemburg's antipathy to the old order is not in question, nor her belief in revolution as vital to its overthrow. Yet her foreboding that the revolutionary assault was premature, especially as the council movement remained riven with doubts whether such action was needed, transpired to be well judged. The Spartacist rising was inchoate, largely confined to Berlin, and lacked sufficient strength to overthrow Ebert's government. It was crushed mercilessly, but not by divisions of the regular army, which had proved reluctant to move against ordinary workers. To their shame, the Majority Socialists had condoned the formation of paramilitary units led by rabid right-wing officers from the old regime, the infamous *Freikorps*. On Gustav Noske's behest they were let loose upon the Communists. In the process, Liebknecht, Luxemburg and hundreds of others were brutally murdered.

Communist Revolution in Germany had been averted, but not without further peradventures. The failure of the new coalition government, comprising the SPD, the Catholic Centre and Democratic parties, which had been formed after the elections to the National Assembly on 18 January, to introduce radical political or economic change, sparked off another wave of ill-organised and ill-coordinated Communist risings across Germany in the spring of 1919. All of them were ruthlessly put down by the *Freikorps*. On 9 April the Communists established a Soviet Republic in Bavaria, but it proved to be short-lived. Within weeks it had been overthrown, once more by the *Freikorps*, again with the blessing of Noske, now the minister of defence. The parting of the ways between Social Democracy and Communism, evident in embryonic form before 1914, was now complete. The German Communists were permanently estranged from the perfidious Social Democrats, who had shown no compunction in condoning their slaughter.[17]

Revolution in Russia, Germany and the West

Before considering how Communism evolved after 1917 let us pause to reflect upon the distinct outcomes of the revolutions in Russia and Germany, and in Central and West Europe more generally. While there is some weight to the argument that the splintering of the Socialist movement across Europe, not just in Germany, hampered a concerted, radical assault on the old order, the Russian Socialists had been seriously divided too. Socialist disunity thus is patently insufficient to account for the failure of Communist revolution in Central and West Europe. Other factors, some transitory, some much deeper rooted, militated against it. One immediate and striking difference between Russia and the rest of Europe concerned the war. When Lenin and the Bolsheviks struck for power, Russia was still at war, if barely so. The Bolsheviks' promise of peace, ultimately delivered at enormous cost, struck a deep chord among the war-weary masses. The war, which arguably was the major source of unrest amongst the workers and latterly the increasingly mutinous armed forces in Germany, ended as its Revolution began. There, as in the other belligerent states of Europe, most workers, and soldiers, desired demobilisation, the restoration of order and peace, a return to 'normality', albeit one in which their economic and political demands were satisfied. Moreover, reformism had sunk deep roots within the socialist movements in Central and West Europe before 1914. Workers there, unlike their Russian counterparts, had participated actively in electoral politics in the decades preceding the Great War, with marked success. Hence it was unsurprising that in 1918–19 the majority of workers heeded the views of their moderate leaders that further progress could be achieved through parliament. In Germany itself authoritarianism apparently had been replaced by a democratic polity, while in Britain universal male suffrage had been introduced. Moreover, the preparedness of the post-war regimes to compel the employers to honour collective bargaining agreements, and to satisfy to some extent the demands of the workers for shorter hours and improved welfare legislation, reinforced the widespread belief in reformism. The Russian proletariat, on the other hand, had little experience of, or faith in, parliamentary practices and so remained much more willing to back revolutionary solutions.[18]

Furthermore, the class structure of most Central and West European societies was unlike that of Russia. They possessed, to varying degrees, stronger and more organised middle classes, small producers and traders and white collar professionals as well as the *haute bourgeosie*, who were opposed to socialism and its potential threat to their property. Consequently, any attempt to carry out a Communist revolution there was likely to precipitate a bloody and brutal civil war in which there was no guarantee that the workers, even had they supported it, would emerge victorious. In Russia, the middle class was small and ill-organised. It was incapable of offering much effective resistance to the growing radicalism of the masses in 1917, although it did rally behind the reactionary landlords and White Generals who frantically tried to oust the Bolsheviks after October. In addition, as Hobsbawm pointed out, the terror associated with the Civil War in Russia and the revulsion engendered by the rapidly emerging Bolshevik dictatorship, which ruthlessly suppressed even its socialist opponents, reinforced the commitment of the socialist parties and most ordinary workers in much of the rest of Europe to parliamentary politics. Moreover, the peasantry in West Europe was unlike its Russian counterpart. Large in numbers, it was a class of smallholders which had considerably more to lose than its chains. At the very least it was wary of radical proletarian revolution, and any threats to its property that it posed. Hungary was a clear case in point, where the short-lived Soviet Republic set up by Bela Kun in March 1919 elevated collectivisation above land redistribution. In turn, the peasants deserted the revolution and swung behind those who did promise a measure of land division. The situation was quite different in Russia, as it was Lenin and his often reluctant fellow Communists who had promised and in fact given the peasants hungry for the land what they had long desired. Besides, the fact that the war ended before the German and other European armies had disintegrated totally under its strains had other critical ramifications. It did not mean that the armies across Europe had become forces of conservatism and order. In Germany particularly, but even in Britain and France, many ordinary soldiers were sympathetic to the aspirations of striking or insurgent workers, and could not be set against them willy-nilly. Paramilitary organisations were another question, as disaffected soldiers, and officers, could be mobilised to counter the threat of Bolshevik revolution – the *Freikorps* in Germany, and those who later joined the Fascists in Italy. In Russia, the PG under Kerensky, as we have seen, could not mobilise any support, either from rank-and-file troops or from the officer corps.[19]

In sum, it is difficult to attribute the failure of the KPD, or any other revolutionary movement in West and Central Europe, to carry out a revolution of the Bolshevik type to the absence of a Leninist vanguard party. The emphasis on such a party as the key to Bolshevik victory in Russia has been much exaggerated. John Kautsky aptly concluded that Communist revolution failed in Germany as the preconditions for it were lacking. Karl Radek's oft-quoted conclusion that revolution fitted Germany like a saddle fitted a cow remains apt. It is a conclusion, it must be added, that applied to much of the rest of Europe as well. Conversely, reformism and the possibility of a parliamentary road to socialism had the weakest of roots in Russia, as we saw in the preceding chapter.

PART III
Communism in the Soviet Union

Chapter 6: The Rise of Stalinism

The vision of an egalitarian and self-governing society, the commune state, briefly espoused by Lenin in 1917 rapidly faded from view. Instead, a murderous authoritarian state ultimately emerged from the ashes of the old autocratic order. By the end of the 1930s, it had been culpable for the deaths of millions of its citizens. Why was it that Communism in its Soviet guise followed such a tragic course? Was it the product of a philosophy whose logic was monstrous, as Peter Baldwin has remarked of Nazism, or of a philosophy which could be given a monstrous interpretation? Since the collapse of the Soviet Union the old Cold War axiom, which stressed the 'monstrous' and dictatorial imperatives inherent within Marxism, has received renewed emphasis. Martin Malia depicted the Soviet Union as an 'ideocratic regime', driven by Marx's injunctions to suppress 'private property, profit and the market', which inexorably led to Stalinist totalitarianism Andrzej Walicki agreed. While purporting not 'to diminish, let alone ignore, the role of nonideological, historical and social, factors in the formation of the Soviet system', none the less 'the part played by ideological factors was relatively independent and for a long time of decisive importance'. The pursuit of Marx's 'kingdom of freedom', which demanded the elimination of 'the "blind forces" of the market', was the fundamental source of Soviet totalitarianism.[1] A related school contends that the chief source of Soviet totalitarianism was not Marxism *per se* but Leninism. This leaves open the question discussed in Chapter 4 of whether Leninism was a form of Marxism. David Lovell thoughtfully concluded that Leninism was one possible 'progeny' of Marxism, albeit one-sided and profoundly illiberal. Lenin's own contribution, in particular his conception of the Party as the infallible 'representative of the historical working-class interest', provided the decisive 'theoretical foundations for Soviet authoritarianism'.

Robert Service, who wrote a three-volume biography of Lenin, robustly expanded on this theme. Admitting that had Lenin lived 'several Stalinist horrors would have been avoided', he continued that Lenin's basic ideas, 'of dictatorship, the one-party state, violence in pursuit of political goals, massive state economic direction, cultural persecution, militant atheism, ideological monopoly, forcible maintenance of a multinational state', were simply taken to their logical extremes by Stalin. Stalinism was the product of the Party and the system that Lenin built.[2] Other historians, notably Stephen Cohen, Graeme Gill and Moshe Lewin, have contested any simple continuity between Stalinism and Leninism. Cohen rather typically condemned Stalinism as a unique system, characterised by its 'excess, extraordinary extremism'. Nikita Khrushchev similarly drew a sharp dividing line between Lenin and Stalin, as did the well-known dissident historian Roy Medvedev. They argued, in a rather blinkered manner, that Stalin had driven the Revolution from its rightful democratic Leninist path, in the process erecting his own 'cult of the personality', which was primarily responsible for the country's sufferings.[3]

Yet other historians deny the culpability of Marxism, or Leninism, for the dictatorial evolution of Soviet Communism. That doughty old cold warrior Richard Pipes has attributed it to the influence of Russia's 'patrimonial' political culture. What Pipes understood by patrimony was the system whereby the autocracy had acquired the absolute right to control the country's people, land and resources, unchecked by any institution, or even by a system of law. After 1917 the Bolsheviks laid claim to this tradition of unlimited power and raised to new levels of efficiency and terror the police state instituted by the autocracy. While legitimating their seizure and retention of power by reference to 'Marxist slogans', their actions corresponded little to 'Marxist doctrine'. For Robert Tucker, the Tsarist legacy of economic backwardness best explained Stalinism. The imperative behind it was 'the quest for military power in support of the state's external ambitions' ... The rapid industrial revolution that this quest demanded drove the Party-state ruthlessly to deploy its power to carry it out, regardless of the human costs involved. A similar line of reasoning led Edward Carr and Theodore von Laue to emphasise the isolation of the Soviet Union in a world dominated by more advanced and potentially hostile capitalist powers as the fundamental source of Stalinism.[4]

The contention of this chapter, however, is that the ideological presumptions of *Russian* Marxism remain essential to understanding

Soviet Communism. In his *Memoirs of a Revolutionary*, Victor Serge, a former anarchist who joined the Party in 1919, recognised this all too clearly. Whilst accepting that events had influenced the forging of the Communist autocracy, he maintained that circumstances alone could not account for it. Due heed also had to be paid to what he termed 'Lenin's "proletarian Jacobinism" ', the belief '[t]hat the Party is the repository of truth, and any form of thinking which differs from it is dangerous or reactionary error. Here lies the spiritual source of its intolerance.' But other ideological elements must be considered too, especially the anti-peasantism that had marked Russian Marxism from its birth. As James Millar aptly remarked, 'the Bolsheviks were city boys. ... They didn't understand the peasants [and] they didn't like the peasants ...'. In their minds socialism could not be built in a peasant society, which had to be transformed by the spread of industrialism throughout the country. Moreover, Stephen Kotkin added that 'the bedrock proposition' of the Bolsheviks was 'that, whatever socialism might be, it could not be capitalism'. The market system symptomatic of capitalism would have to be superseded by a planned economy.[5] Proper attention must be paid to these presumptions, for in times of crisis they were triggered by and shaped Communist responses. But to pursue this argument, it is essential to reconstruct historically the interaction of circumstances and ideas that ultimately gave rise to Stalinism.

The formative years: October 1917 to March 1921

Having come to power the Bolsheviks could now proceed, to use Trotsky's memorable phrase, 'to construct the socialist order'. Their problem was, like Marx before them, that they had no detailed plan for doing so, as Lenin himself admitted shortly after October. Yet they did possess certain principles on which they believed a socialist society should be built. The old state was to be smashed and replaced by a commune (or soviet) state (Chapter 5). The banks and large industries were to be nationalised; agriculture was to be collectivised, which remained official Party policy despite Lenin's promise of all land to the peasants in the summer of 1917; production and distribution of all goods was no longer to be subject to the vagaries of the market but was to be planned; and universal labour conscription, under the auspices of the various organs of workers' control, was mooted.[6] However, in the early months of Soviet power their policies did not slavishly follow these principles. Industry was not systematically nationalised, while land division rather than the collectivisation of agriculture was sanctioned by the Decree on Land of 26 October 1917 and ratified by the Land Socialisation Law of February 1918.

In the spring and summer of 1918 a series of menacing developments impelled them to change tack radically. The isolation of the revolution, which had not spread to the West, particularly to Germany, meant that the new regime inherited the problem of war. Convinced that if it was not ended quickly the infant Soviet republic would be crushed by German imperialism, Lenin resolved upon a separate peace with Germany. The largely unopposed German advance in February 1918 enabled him to overcome widespread opposition, in the Party and beyond, and peace was concluded at Brest-Litovsk on 3 March. It was ratified by the Seventh Party Congress a few days later when the Party formally changed its name to Communist. It cost Soviet Russia dear in territory, stripping it of one-third of its grain-producing area, two-fifths of its industry, and nine-tenths of its easily exploitable coal reserves. In consequence, it was imperilled by 'the bony hand of hunger', to quote the sardonic words of the Left Communist critic G. A. Usievich.[7] Furthermore, these losses accelerated the economic decline gripping the country. Industry was threatened with a standstill, largely because of fuel, material and food shortages. Agriculture was in no better condition. Politically, land division might have neutralised potential peasant opposition to Communist power. Economically, it had destroyed the large estates, previously providing an estimated 70 per cent of the grain required to feed the towns, which were replaced by a much less productive system of small-scale, peasant farming. It had also strengthened the ranks of propertied peasants, who had no incentive to surrender grain surpluses in their hands to the state. There were few industrial goods on offer, while rampant inflation rendered paper money increasingly worthless. The selfishness of the peasants, as Lenin warned in the late spring, was threatening to starve the Revolution to death.[8]

Moreover, the Brest peace had not removed the military threats facing the regime. In April, Japanese forces had penetrated into Siberia, while in the late spring, civil war on an intensified and broadened scale was sparked off by a clash between the Czechoslovak legions, departing Russia via Siberia for the Western front, and the regional Soviet authorities in the Urals. Soviet Russia was encircled by 18 anti-Communist regimes, many aided by the capitalist powers of the West. Meanwhile, in the territory under Communist control, dissatisfaction was growing.

Unemployment mushroomed and much of the suffering working class criticised the Communists' failure to provide it with the bread and economic security promised in 1917. In the countryside dictatorial measures to extract food from the peasantry led it to compare the 'good Bolsheviks' (who had given it the land) with the 'bad Communists' (who then took its grain)! Political opposition grew commensurately, which was reflected in elections to the Soviets and the newly formed independent workers' assemblies, where support for the Mensheviks and SRs revived markedly.

Political opposition was the simplest problem to deal with: it was suppressed. All parties critical of the Communists were expelled from the Soviets by July, and in the case of their erstwhile allies the Left SRs, after the bloody repression of alleged counter-revolutionary risings. Within nine months of the October Revolution a one-party dictatorship had been established. Worse was to follow. On 30 August, after an attempt on Lenin's life and the murder of Mosei Uritskii, head of the Petrograd *Cheka*, a policy of 'Red Terror' was introduced. The arbitrary powers of the secret police rose rapidly. Even then some voices predicted the growth of a capricious and despotic police state, notably the Left SR leader Maria Spiridonova, then imprisoned in the Kremlin – though it was only some twenty years later that many Communists fell victim to their own secret police.[9] Thermidor, one might argue, had overtaken the Revolution within a year.

To combat the growing military threats, Trotsky, then Commissar of War, replaced volunteer militia forces with a new conscript Red Army, conventionally organised and disciplined, and led by officers of the old Imperial Army. To be effective, however, it had to be supplied with food and munitions. To this end, grain requisitioning, first introduced in the late spring, was intensified. Detachments of workers, and of secret police, were sent to the countryside to extract grain, by force if necessary, from the rich peasants (the so-called *kulaks*), though in practice, from all the peasants. Short-lived committees of poor peasants (*kombedy*) were set up to assist these detachments, with the added task of fomenting class war in the countryside against the *kulaks*. Efforts, half-hearted and ephemeral, at establishing collective farms were also introduced. The grain so procured was distributed by the Commissariat of Food according to its own scale of priorities: to the army and to key industrial workers, the military and social pillars of the regime; and but little to the rest of the population. Large-scale industry itself was nationalised on 28 June, a policy extended to embrace virtually all small industries by 1920. Similarly, all industrial products were distributed by the state. Traditional, authoritarian methods of labour discipline replaced workers' control, which Lenin and increasing numbers of Communists exaggeratedly held to be responsible for industrial decline. Centrally appointed directors, often former capitalists or their managers (*spetsy*), were put in charge of industry to restore production. On Trotsky's urging, workers increasingly were subject to compulsory labour service, and sent by the state to where they were deemed necessary. His call for the general militarisation of labour was endorsed in 1920.

This economic system was dubbed 'War Communism' by Lenin in April 1921, although at the time, Serge reminded us, it simply had been called Communism. In a lengthy essay, *The Tax in Kind*, Lenin argued that it had been 'a temporary measure', dictated by 'war and ruin'. The market, if we overlook the pervasive black market that enabled much of the population to survive, had been replaced by growing state control over the production and distribution of goods. The rudiments of a planned economy seemingly had been laid too, although as Lev Kritsman admitted in his seminal work on the period, *The Heroic Period of the Russian Revolution*, 'there was no real single centre for organising the economy'. At first sight it was consistent with Marxist principles, that socialism demanded the root-and-branch abolition of the market, castigated by Osinskii as 'the seedbed of contagion from which the embryos of capitalism continually issue forth'.[10] No Communist then would have disagreed.

War Communism's apparent correspondence with Marxist preconceptions has led many commentators to insist that it was determined in the final analysis by Marxist doctrine, an argument recently advanced by Stephen Louw. Weight is added to such explanations when one considers that Trotsky and particularly Bukharin had written lengthy tracts in defence of it. At its height in 1920, in his famous *Economics of the Transformation Period*, Bukharin argued that in the transition to socialism commodities, value and price, the odious features of the capitalist market system, had to be abolished. They were to be replaced by the 'collective' and 'conscious' regulation of the economy by the proletarian state. Several years later, in *The Heroic Period*, Kritsman repeated the thrust of Bukharin's argument, averring that 'so-called "War Communism"... cannot be represented as something – fundamentally – imposed upon the revolution from without'. In practice as well as in theory, the Communists proved extremely reluctant to abandon it even when the Civil War was over. New material from the Tenth Party Conference, held

in May 1921, confirms that Lenin faced bitter opposition when he proposed to replace it with the New Economic Policy (NEP).[11]

Appeals to ideological arguments, however, are less persuasive than
they first appear. Let us start with some specifics. As Lars Lih recently
pointed out, the central feature of War Communism, grain requisitioning, was little more than a continuation of the attempts to establish a state
grain monopoly introduced during the war by the Tsarist and Provisional
Governments to cope with the ever worsening problems of food shortages.
The 'abolition' of money itself was more the product of hyper-inflation
than of ideology. In the *ABC of Communism* (1920), in Lih's opinion 'the
most complete and systematic compendium of Marxist–Leninist theory
produced until that time', Evgenii Preobazhenskii, regarded as the architect of such a policy, categorically affirmed that commodity production
and money remained 'inevitable' in what could only be a lengthy transition to Communism. Moreover, the commitment of many Communists to
War Communism was caused, so the Soviet historian M. N. Pokrovskii
wrote in his *Seven Years of Proletarian Dictatorship* (1923), by a misplaced
euphoria that against all expectations its construction had brought the
regime very close to socialism, even without the victory of proletarian
revolution in the West.[12] Besides, in these years the Soviet Communists
did not possess a monolithic vision of what socialist construction
entailed. Two distinct visions existed, as James McClelland and Thomas
Remington have argued. The first was the 'Utopian', or 'democratic',
current. This current posited that the vital precondition for socialism was
a cultural revolution, in the course of which the 'popular participation'
of the workers in government and economic administration would lead
them to acquire 'a truly proletarian class consciousness'. This libertarian
vision, embraced by Lenin in *State and Revolution*, was submerged by the
economic and military crises of the Civil War period, which led to the
ascendancy of the 'revolutionary heroic' or 'technocratic' current. For
this current, the essential prerequisite of socialism was the 'scientifically
planned transformation of society', or the 'massive build-up [industriali-
sation] of the economy'. It was to be achieved, so Lenin, Trotsky and
Bukharin agreed, by the state, the dictatorship of the proletariat, mobilising the human and material resources at Russia's disposal. This latter
current was embodied in War Communism, when workers' democracy
gave way to state control of the economy.[13] Arguably, it also was one
source of inspiration for Stalin's subsequent programme of state-
sponsored rapid industrialisation.

The retreat to the New Economic Policy (NEP)

But there was no straight line, ideological or otherwise, from the Civil War to Stalinism. The euphoria evoked by War Communism about leaping quickly to the Communist future clashed with Soviet realities. In the winter of 1920–21 the economy was on the point of collapse. Industrial production had plummeted to one-seventh of its 1913 levels. Agriculture was in an equally parlous condition, with urban Russia and considerable parts of the countryside threatened with hunger, and in some areas even famine. With fear of a return of the old order removed by Communist victory in the Civil War, widespread opposition erupted across Russia. In many towns and cities striking workers protested against food shortages, the material privileges enjoyed by the Party and state elite, labour militarisation and the suppression of democratic liberties. Peasant resistance to grain requisitioning exploded into open rebellion, most violently in Tambov province, West Siberia, and parts of the Ukraine. The 'flower of Bolshevism', the sailors of the naval base of Kronstadt, rose in revolt against Draconian Communist policies. They demanded the elimination of the Communist dictatorship; the democracy and egalitarianism promised in 1917; and the abolition of grain requisitioning and labour conscription.

In these perilous circumstances, Lenin ultimately imposed the NEP upon a sullen Party. It was an economic retreat, a concession to the hated peasants – David Riazanov bitterly dubbed it the 'peasant Brest-Litovsk'. Grain requisitioning was abolished and replaced by fixed taxes on the peasants' production. Centralised food distribution by the state ended, with any surpluses in peasant hands able to be sold legally. But inducements were needed if the peasants were to produce, and sell, more grain, desperately needed to feed the towns and drought-stricken regions of the country. To improve incentives other steps back were made. While the 'commanding heights' of the economy remained nationalised, small-scale industry and trade were returned to private hands, in the hope that privatisation would stimulate increased production and availability of the consumer goods demanded by the peasants. A mixed economy had been established, with capitalism, free trade and the odious market restored across much of the economy. Modest concessions were made to the workers. Labour conscription was ended, and the trade unions were given a limited, and temporary, degree of independence from the state. However, there was to be no return to the workers' democracy of the early months of the Revolution.

Economic liberalisation was not accompanied by any political liberalisation. The idea that the era of the NEP was a 'golden era' of political
and cultural freedom and tolerance is misconceived, as Nadezhda
Mandel'shtam stressed in her memoirs. On the contrary, the Party dictatorship was immeasurably strengthened. First, all surviving opposition
(strikers in the cities, insurgents in the countryside, the Kronstadt rebels,
Mensheviks and SRs) was subject to repression, often brutal. Some were
shot; others arrested or sent to the camps recently established in the
north of the country; while the fortunate few, including Lenin's old
comrade, the ailing Martov, were permitted to emigrate. In 1922 the first
show trials were held, of the SRs and Left SRs, an ominous indication of
what was to follow. The Communists had no truck with pluralism of any
sort. This enduring pattern of Communist politics was moulded by a
combination of Leninist ideology and circumstances. While Lenin had
first advanced his theory of the vanguard party in 1902 (see Chapter 4),
in 1917 he downplayed it, instead often extolling the spontaneous capacities of the workers, and even the peasants, to effect socialist revolution
in Russia. His affair with grassroots democracy was but a brief flirtation.
His distrust of spontaneity grew from the spring of 1918. No doubt, the
Civil War influenced his perceptions. It had taken a heavy toll on Russia's
small proletariat. Many workers died, at the front or from disease. Those
more fortunate were promoted into the state and Party bureaucracies.
Yet others had fled the hunger and unemployment of the towns for the
countryside, where family ties often survived. Soviet Russia's cities and
towns experienced substantial de-urbanisation, the worst hit being
Moscow and Petrograd.[14] Much of the surviving working class had been
alienated by Communist policies. In these circumstances, Lenin's
rejection of workers' democracy became increasingly unequivocal.
During the debate on the trade unions in the winter of 1920–21, he
declared that 'every worker did not know how to run the state ...'. The
illiteracy, the lack of culture of the workers precluded this.

Lenin elaborated on his problem in his last major writings, especially
Better Fewer, but Better (1923), when he bewailed that 'we [the Russians]
lack[ed] sufficient civilisation to enable us to pass straight on to socialism'.
His solution was to emphasise again the leading role of the Party. Its task
was to substitute itself for the 'missing' working class and deploy state
power to create the material and cultural conditions necessary for socialism.
In *Our Revolution* (1923) he insisted that it was possible to seize power
first and '*then*, with aid of the workers' and peasants' [i.e. Party] government and the Soviet system', create the prerequisites of socialism. He had

all but abandoned the determinism of the Second International for a more voluntarist interpretation of Marxism. Most Soviet Communists supported him. Trotsky and Bukharin certainly did. They accepted the need for Party dictatorship over the workers until such time as, in theory, they became sufficiently numerous and class conscious to build socialism themselves.[15] Old Marx would have turned in his grave!

Equally, the crisis of 1921 changed the very nature of the Party dictatorship in significant ways. Hitherto, debate within it had been relatively open. Since 1918, factions on the Left had repeatedly criticised the authoritarian implications of the policies of Lenin and the majority, without ever offering a feasible democratic programme of their own. Now the Party found itself subject to repression, with free debate within it silenced. The Tenth Party Congress approved Lenin's resolution, *On Party Unity*, to ban factions which opposed the policy of the majority, on the rather farfetched grounds that splits would open the door to counter-revolution. Any recalcitrants were subject to expulsion. Democratic [*sic*] centralism had triumphed. Whether Lenin expected this ban to persist for long is a moot point. Robert Tucker has suggested that he looked forward to renewed conflict within the Party as a sign of its health.[16] But whatever Lenin's intentions may have been, a fateful precedent had been set. Loyalty to the 'general line' of the Party, the triumph of *partiinost'*, now took precedence above all else. Addressing the Leningrad party organisation in July 1926 (Petrograd had changed its name to Leningrad in 1924), the supposedly 'liberal' Bukharin defended the Party's monopoly of power, denying any place in it for 'independent and autonomous groups, factions, organised currents, etc.' So much for Bukharinism as the precursor of 'socialism with a human face'.

Often it is difficult for Western readers to comprehend these concepts, especially *partiinost'*. One illuminating answer had come not from Lenin himself but from the Left Communist opposition of 1918. Seeking a solution to the bureaucratic degeneration already evident in the infant Soviet republic, Vladimir Sorin insisted on the revitalisation of the soviets. As institutions of the 'broad working masses', he assumed that they possessed greater revolutionary élan than the officials employed by them. Yet the soviets could be relied upon only so far as they did 'not degenerate ... in a petty-bourgeois direction'. Since they represented 'the petty-bourgeois peasantry' as well as the proletariat they were susceptible to corruptive and demoralising influences that might dilute their socialist zeal. The only reliable bastion of proletarian interests was the Party, '*in every case and everywhere superior to the soviets*'. The task assigned to the

Party was to ensure that the soviets 'implemented an undeviating proletarian line in foreign and domestic policy' – somehow defined! Other left-wing Communists were dissatisfied with Sorin's solution. Bukharin, Osinskii and Radek harboured grave reservations about the health of the Party itself. No longer was it solely the Party of the proletariat. Its growth during 1917 had led to its degeneration into a 'national party', permeated by alien peasant influences. Its proletarian character had been diluted too by the increasing exodus of old Party workers to take up positions within the state administration after October.

If the Party was to act in defence of 'undeviating' socialist policies, then it had to be cleansed, or purged, of all non-proletarian elements. The problem was to determine who these elements were. Social origin or former occupation were deemed to be insufficient. The Left Communists' proposed solution was to define 'proletarian' by reference to support for their own policy prescriptions, and 'non-proletarian' by opposition to them. The majority within the Party, not the workers themselves, would establish what this 'proletarian' or 'general line' in fact was. Any dissenting minority thus could be accused of being non-proletarian, or at least of suffering from 'false consciousness', and in the interests of building socialism must recant or be purged from the Party. However alien and undemocratic the concept might seem, *partiinost'*, the spirit of loyalty to the 'general line', permeated the Party, with fatal consequences. The major intra-party oppositions after 1918 could not rise above it. Their unwillingness to solicit popular support outside the Party was one factor which condemned them to defeat, with Trotsky's belated appeal in 1923 to the ordinary workers he had earlier dragooned falling unsurprisingly on deaf ears.[17]

The psychology associated with this concept was exposed in the infamous conversation that took place in Paris in early 1928 between the Menshevik émigré Nikolai Valentinov, and Iurii Piatakov, recently expelled from the Party for his opposition to the 'general line'. Explaining to Valentinov why he had recanted in order to re-join it, he insisted, quite plausibly given his well-known asceticism, that he had not been driven 'by the base desire to get back the material wealth, advantages, privileges, etc. ... lost on our expulsion from it'. The Party, he continued, was a phenomenon unprecedented in history. It was infallible, as proven in its ability to carry out the well-nigh impossible, such as winning the Civil War and surviving economic collapse and famine. Its infallibility demanded that all personal convictions condemned by it be surrendered. If the price of re-entering its ranks meant the sacrifice of 'dignity, self-respect and everything else besides', of accepting that white was black, then this price must be paid! A similar faith in the Party, reinforced when necessary by torture, led many of those accused in the great show trials between 1936 and 1938 to confess to various invented crimes against the regime.

The ultimate beneficiary of Lenin's disciplinary strictures was Joseph Stalin, who used, or abused, them to quell his own rivals. But increased discipline in the Party remains insufficient to explain Stalin's rise to power. He was also an extremely adept politician, exploiting his various key roles in the Party and state machines, in particular his position as General Secretary of the Party, to appoint his own supporters to key local and regional posts. Accordingly, he ensured that his men (there were few women) dominated all the major institutions of the Party and state, from the grass roots upward. He had created what Robert Daniels elegantly identified as the 'circular flow of power'. Those at the local and regional level, dependent upon Stalin's patronage for their positions, repaid his favour by ensuring only those loyal to him were returned to the major central bodies, such as the Central Committee of the Party – and used their own power of patronage to construct their own cliques. Moreover, many who had been promoted within the Party-state machine were no longer revolutionary idealists. Their formative experience, to borrow Sheila Fitzpatrick's somewhat plaintive coinage, had been the life and death struggle of the Civil War. Mark von Hagen developed this idea, to argue persuasively that the militarisation of Soviet political culture had been the result. The attitudes which had brought victory, obedience, discipline, the suppression of all dissent and opposition, dominated the Party even after the Civil War had been won. Ideas of democracy found little resonance in its ranks. The legacy of Russia's autocratic political culture made itself felt too. Officials from the old Tsarist bureaucracy continued to staff much of the state bureaucracy. From the outset, the new regime had found their services to be indispensable as it lacked sufficient educated cadres of its own to replace them. Accustomed to giving and receiving orders, they too were contemptuous of democracy. The growth of authoritarianism, of kowtowing to the 'general line', was compounded by these factors.[18]

The Great Debate

It would be wrong to think, however, that the Party was transformed into a monolith overnight. Conflict persisted within it throughout the 1920s.

In the New Course debate of 1923, Trotsky and the Left Opposition criticised the drift to bureaucratic authoritarianism evident in the Party and state apparatus. Yet arguably the most significant debate centred on whether the NEP constituted a viable long-term strategy for the construction of socialism, and not just a temporary retreat dictated by circumstances. The success of the NEP in significantly increasing production, 'great results' according to Pokrovskii, had converted many in the Party to supporting it. Their confidence was reinforced when the tensions that had emerged in 1923, termed the 'scissors crisis' by Trotsky, were resolved successfully. Primitive technique notwithstanding, agrarian recovery had far outstripped that of industry. The price of grain fell while manufactured goods remained three times as expensive compared with 1913. In this situation, the peasants' reluctance to market their grain surpluses to purchase such costly goods threatened to stymie the still weak industrial recovery. The state responded by further concessions to the peasants. The price of manufactured goods was lowered to entice them to market their grain. The scissors closed and all seemed set fair for further steady recovery and growth. The Left of the Party, and much of a reviving working class, denounced these concessions as encouraging the growth of a peasant capitalism, blocking rapid industrial development and delaying the introduction of a planned socialist economy.

The ground was set for the Great Debate of the mid-1920s. It focused essentially on means, not ends. All Communists accepted the need for industrialisation and, in the long run, the elimination of the market. Even Bukharin, the principal defender of the NEP, agreed in his [1926] critique of the economic programme of the Left Opposition, ' "in the final analysis" everything is "subordinated" to the development of large-scale industry, for *this* is the basis of socialism, its leading principle, etc.' Internally, the Communists could never feel secure as long as the peasantry comprised the vast bulk of the population. Industrialisation alone would create the urban proletariat which, ostensibly, would serve as the social base for Soviet power. It also would provide the equipment necessary for the successful collectivisation of agriculture and the elimination of agrarian backwardness. Internationally, continuing isolation meant that they remained vulnerable to the greater military power of the advanced capitalist countries. In a letter to Molotov in July 1925 Stalin wrote that unless the country's military industries were built up, then its potential capitalist foes could crush 'us with their bare hands'.[19] The problem was finding the means to do so, as the absence of aid or investment from abroad meant that the Communists were faced with the task of building an industrial economy on the resources of the Soviet Union alone – to construct socialism in one country, to use the term Stalin had borrowed from Bukharin.

For Bukharin, the NEP no longer was simply a retreat but offered a serious, if gradual, solution to the country's backwardness. In the long run, he argued, the accumulation of capital necessary for industrialisation could be realised only on the basis of rapidly growing agrarian prosperity: hence his call to the peasants to 'enrich themselves'. In the first place, taxation of a burgeoning rich peasantry would provide one source of capital for investment in state industry. Secondly, it would lead to the growth of peasant savings in the State bank, which also could be mobilised for industrial investment. Thirdly, it would expand demand for the goods of state industries, whose increased sales would reduce their fixed costs of production and so raise their efficiency. Consequently, profits would rise, which could be reinvested to promote further industrial growth. Fourthly, it would provide the food necessary to sustain a growing industrial workforce. The remaining surpluses of grain in the hands of the state could be exported, to pay for the import of the capital equipment for continuing industrial development. Admittedly, industrialisation would proceed slowly, 'at the pace of a tortoise' as Trotsky caustically remarked. Initially, it would be concentrated in the light industries, to satisfy peasant demand for goods. Bukharin explicitly cautioned against too rapid investment in heavy industry, which would create a shortage of consumer goods, deter the peasants from marketing their grain, and destroy what the NEP promised to achieve.

The Left of the Party had grave doubts about Bukharin's strategy. His most articulate and cogent critic was Preobrazhenskii. He cajoled the regime to pursue a faster rate of industrial development. To achieve this he harked back to the idea first formulated by Vladimir Smirnov, not Bukharin as is commonly supposed, namely, primitive socialist accumulation. The country's capital stock, he argued, had been depleted severely during the Civil War. Accordingly, in the medium to long term, existing consumer industries, even if restored to producing at full capacity, would be unable to satisfy future peasant demand. In turn, the prices of consumer goods would rise markedly, threatening a renewal of the scissors crisis of 1923, with the only beneficiaries being the private traders (NEPmen), who would make greater profits from selling scarce goods. Hence, the development of heavy industry capable of producing new plant and equipment was the first priority. In the absence of foreign loans and investment, of which he was wary in any case, this development could be achieved only by curtailing personal consumption in the short term. Increased taxation of the peasantry, higher prices for industrial goods, and wage cuts for the workers were required to achieve this end. The resources thus acquired by the state would be used to finance basic capital reconstruction in heavy industry in the first instance. Whether his plan would have worked, at least without coercion, is doubtful, as in the short term it promised to reduce peasant income and the availability of cheap consumer goods and thus to reproduce the scissors crisis.[20]

In the mid-1920s, when the NEP appeared to be working successfully, Bukharin's strategy was endorsed by the majority in the Party. By 1926 agriculture had more or less recovered to its 1913 level, while industrial production too was approaching its pre-war, if not peak 1916, levels. Yet all was not as well as it seemed. The longer-term impact of land division made itself felt. NEP agriculture was conducted overwhelmingly by small peasant farmers, employing primitive techniques. Productivity on the land, therefore, was low and the grain surplus available to feed the towns and for export to pay for the import of vital capital equipment remained well below its pre-war level, falling from one-fifth in 1927 to only one-twentieth in 1928 according to Stalin. Industrial recovery too had been uneven. The output of basic heavy industry, iron and steel, remained at about three-quarters of its pre-war level, while the defence industries had barely regained their 1913 levels. Consumer-goods industries in general were producing less in 1926 than they had been in 1913. This shortfall, combined with the continued inefficiency of much of state industry, and exploitation of the scarcity of goods by the NEPmen, resulted in the cost of industrial goods sought by the peasants remaining relatively high. Another worrying feature was that the industrial recovery that had taken place had failed to halt a marked growth in unemployment in the cities and towns. Successes of the NEP notwithstanding, the historian's benefit of hindsight suggests that in relative terms the Soviet Union lagged further behind its capitalist rivals, both in absolute production and in the development of modern industries, than the Russian Empire had in 1913.

The Great Transformation

The Soviet government lacked this hindsight and continued essentially to support the economic gradualism advocated by Bukharin, until the grain crisis of 1927. There were two main elements underlying it. What

James Hughes has described as a 'bumper grain harvest' led to a sharp decline in prices. At the same time, consumer goods became scarcer, in part the result of increased investment in heavy industry in 1926, and in part through the curious decision to reduce their prices in the spring of 1927. The scissors re-opened and the amount of marketed grain in 1927 decreased by half as peasant incentives to produce and market grain fell. Quite rationally, the peasants concentrated on other products, such as livestock and dairy produce, for which much higher prices could be obtained. The mounting grain shortage threatened to deprive urban Russia, and the army, of food, and the state of vital export earnings, and so jeopardise industrial development. The sense of crisis was heightened by international developments when, in the spring of 1927, the Conservative government in Britain broke off diplomatic relations with the Soviet Union. By the end of the year the Communists in China had suffered a crushing defeat. While Stalin himself may have exaggerated the danger of renewed conflict to dish his rivals, the 'war scare' focused the attention of the Party leadership on the isolation and vulnerability of the Soviet Union in a hostile capitalist world. The only solution, as the Fifteenth Party Congress in December 1927 decreed, was to accelerate 'most rapidly' the development of heavy industry, 'to strengthen ... the defence capacity of the USSR'. On numerous occasions in the next few years Stalin insisted that the country must break the cycle of backwardness that had plagued it since the seventeenth century. In February 1931, he reflected that Russia had suffered continual defeats because of its backwardness. Its current security demanded that this be overcome, and quickly: 'We are fifty or a hundred years behind the advanced countries. We must make good this distance in ten years. Either we do it, or we shall be crushed.'[21]

Whether a modified NEP strategy would have allowed continued agrarian and industrial growth is a highly contentious question. James Millar suggested that increased taxes on the peasants would have pressured them to produce and market more grain to sustain their income, while Holland Hunter claimed that an increase in grain prices would have had the same effect. In the world of theoretical economics, where all other things are always equal, these arguments might be valid, as Alec Nove conceded. But, he swiftly added, other things were *not* equal. Here we need to consider again the ideological propensities of the Communists. The grain crisis triggered their anti-peasantism, both at the highest levels and at the grass roots. Virulent opposition to any further concessions to the peasants became widespread. The peasants, it seemed to many

Communists, had been the main beneficiaries of the Revolution. They had acquired the land that they had long sought and had profited most from the NEP. In the Party the feeling grew that they were holding the regime to ransom, as they had in 1918 and 1923. Many ordinary workers shared these views. Ten years after 1917 they had gained little. Unemployment remained widespread, affecting an estimated 10 per cent of the workforce; conditions of work were onerous and the urban standard of living low; and discipline was Draconian, imposed by the old bourgeois *spetsy* who were still in positions of authority. It was all a far cry from the heady days of workers' control in 1917 and 1918. The solution was to proceed with the construction of socialism that Trotsky had promised on the morrow of October. But socialism was synonymous with industrialism, and planning, in the eyes of most Communists. They had never become reconciled to the (partial) restoration of the market under the NEP. All it appeared to have done was to create another crisis. The time had come, as the Fifteenth Party Congress resolved, for 'the anarchy of the market' to be overcome.

There is little doubt that Stalin was in full agreement. He was in no mood for retreat. He was ready to confront and overcome, by force if necessary, the obstacles to rapid industrialisation posed by the NEP framework and a recalcitrant peasantry. A straw in the wind was the decision of the Fifteenth Congress to promote the collectivisation of agriculture, albeit at a *gradual* pace. The assault on the peasantry swiftly accelerated. Steeled in his resolve after his tour of Siberia in January 1928, a region renowned for the strength of its independent small farmers, he became gravely alarmed at the strength of the rich peasants (*kulaks*) and their ability to withhold grain from the state. His response was to encourage forcible procurement policies on the lines of War Communism, halted temporarily in July in face of opposition from Bukharin and the moderate Right of the Party.[22] Yet resort to coercion evoked much sympathy in the lower ranks of the Party, especially those schooled in the Civil War, who had few scruples about the use of force: against the peasants; against those in the Party and state bureaucracy who advocated caution and concessions; against non-Party *spetsy*, of bourgeois or intellectual origins. Recent recruits to the Party, often poorly educated, unfamiliar with sophisticated policy debate and used to 'obeying orders', also weighed in on the side of coercion.

Unsurprisingly, Stalinist policies exacerbated the grain supply crisis, at a time when drought and early frosts had led to poor harvests in the Ukraine and north Caucasus in 1928. But his commitment to rapid industrialisation, unequivocally reaffirmed in November 1928, precluded any grain imports to resolve the growing food shortages as this would have jeopardised the purchase of vital capital equipment. Stalin's solution to this problem was to extend the so-called 'Uralo-Siberian method', the imposition of procurement quotas at low prices upon the villages, throughout the country. In addition, the Sixteenth Party Conference in April 1929 endorsed the general collectivisation of agriculture, despite the lack of the machinery required for its success. The assault on the peasantry intensified in the autumn of 1929 when Molotov, acting as Stalin's mouthpiece, announced the policy of de-kulakisation at a plenary session of the Central Committee (CC). Its objective was the elimination of the *kulaks* as a class, who in December, on Stalin's *diktat*, were excluded from the new collectives. In effect, war had been declared on the peasantry. It continued for several years, with ebbs and flows, most famously in March 1930 when mass peasant resistance and fear of huge grain deficits forced Stalin to retreat, for a time. By December 1934, 70 per cent of the peasants had been driven into the new collectives, a figure that had risen to 90 per cent by 1936.[23]

Economically, the Great Transformation (*velikii perelom*) was a disaster. Collectivisation had calamitous consequences in the short term, as most peasants consumed, or destroyed, their grain reserves and livestock rather than surrender them to the Communists. Overall agricultural production fell by about a quarter between 1928 and 1932, barely recovering to its 1927 level by 1939. The human costs were catastrophic too, as millions of peasants died, either shot for opposing collectivisation or, the majority, some 5 million to 6 million according to some estimates, victims of the famine of 1932–3. More than a million others were deported, either to the rapidly growing labour camps of the infamous *Gulag*, or to resettle in remote and barren regions of the country. In the long term, collective agriculture was far less productive than the Communists had reckoned, in part because of inadequate investment, in part through the continuing passive resistance of the peasants, who refused to work efficiently. Yet counter-factual arguments, positing that a continuation of the NEP would have yielded a gradual yet more productive transformation of agriculture, miss the point. The regime now had imposed its control, brutal and repressive, over the countryside and was in a position to extract the resources that it required from the peasants by exacting quotas from the new collective farms. The peasants themselves had a much clearer grasp of the reality of the situation than later academic commentators. For them the initials of the Party, VKP (*Vserossiiskaia*

Kommunisticheskaia Partiia), signified their second serfdom (*Vtoroe Krepostnoe Pravo*).

Crash industrialisation, the bastard offspring of the revolutionary heroic tradition of the Civil War years, was more successful, but not universally so. Massive advances were made between 1928 and 1940 in the construction of heavy industry, as well as of basic infrastructure such as power plants and canals, often built by slave labour. Mining output quadrupled, oil production tripled, the generation of electrical power rose ninefold, while iron and steel production quadrupled. The growth of the consumer-goods industries lagged well behind, sacrificed to the military–industrial imperatives of Stalinism. The creation of a planned economy, more accurately a bureaucratically commanded one, caused at least as many problems as it was supposed to solve. The production targets set were often unrealistic, resulting in the *ad hoc* and costly diversion of resources from other purposes to try to meet them. Bureaucratic command itself led to a plethora of scarcely believable economic practices. In his seminal study *The Great Retreat*, Nicholas Timasheff pointed out that '15 per cent of coal output ... [was] lost en route from the mines to the furnaces'. He also recounted how the Krym preserve trust sold a trainload of tomatoes to its Minsk counterpart, which sold it on to the Gomel trust, which then sold it back to the Krym trade office! He concluded, with some wonder, that the anarchy of the market had simply been replaced by the 'anarchy of the plan'![24]

Anarchic or not, the command economy had enduring socio-political repercussions. It spawned a 'new class', a vastly inflated bureaucracy with dictatorial power over society. In the long run, it proved to be highly resistant to any reforms which threatened its position, and concomitant privileges. This bureaucracy was new in another sense too, as it was drawn from the ranks of newly, sometimes barely, educated workers, the so-called *vydvizhentsy*, who replaced the old bourgeois *spetsy*, whose services until then the Communists had found to be indispensable. Since the spring of 1928 when over 50 engineers in the Shakhty mines in the Donbass became scapegoats for the failings of industry, accused and convicted of economic 'wrecking', the *spetsy* had been subject to intensified persecution. This campaign was unleashed from above, by a regime increasingly eager to place its own 'proletarian' cadres in their positions. It gained support from below, as many workers exploited it to oust the hated *spetsy* and obtain promotion themselves. In a paradoxical sense the Great Transformation engineered a cultural revolution of sorts, if not that envisioned by the Utopian current of the Civil War years.[25]

The Great Terror

The revolutionary transformation wrought by Stalin also had immediate political repercussions at the highest levels of the Party which left an indelible mark on Soviet Communism. In 1930 Sergei Syrtsov and Beso Lominadze, till then supporters of Stalin, openly criticised the mass repression that forced collectivisation in particular had entailed. For their pains they were removed from the Central Committee. In the autumn of 1932 Mikhail Riutin denounced the dictatorship of terror instituted by Stalin; demanded the removal of Stalin and his entourage from power, together with the imposition of severe limits upon the power of the secret police; called for a slower rate of industrialisation; and sought curbs on the pace of collectivization, which had placed excessive burdens and strains on the entire population. His fate was a ten-year sentence in the Gulag. Accounts based on circumstantial evidence that Stalin flew into a fury when his call for Riutin's execution was rejected by the Politburo remain unproved. Many Communists in the Ukraine, where the famine of 1932–3 had been most cruelly felt, also were aghast at the costs of collectivisation. They feared that it would alienate the peasants to such an extent that ultimately it would undermine the power of the Party, and of the army – an anxiety echoed by General Iona Yakir. At the Seventeenth Party Congress, 'the Congress of Victors', in January 1934, again unconfirmed circumstantial evidence suggests that a substantial body of Communists lobbied, in vain, for Sergei Kirov, head of the Leningrad party organisation and mystifyingly seen since as a 'moderate' Stalinist, to replace Stalin as General Secretary.[26]

By the end of the year, Kirov was dead, shot on 1 December by Leonid Nikolaev. Stalin's alleged role in engineering Kirov's assassination, not just to remove his most popular potential rival but also to provide himself with a pretext to purge all his opponents, real or imagined, has never been substantiated. Recent evidence from the former Soviet archives indicates that Nikolaev acted independently, vexed by the fact that Kirov was having an affair with his wife. That Stalin took advantage of the shock of the Kirov affair to move against those who had formerly opposed him remains plausible. Kamenev and Zinoviev, the first in a long line of victims, were arrested (but not yet executed) in January 1935. However, critics of Stalin's power and policies were not silenced by this action. Many in the Party viewed what Timasheff called the 'Great Retreat', when the egalitarianism, iconoclasm and internationalism of the Revolution gave way to careerism, cultural conservatism and nationalism, even some toleration of religious Orthodoxy, as a betrayal of socialism. There was disquiet too about his foreign policy, when in 1934 the promotion of international revolution was subordinated to the creation of Popular Fronts, alliances of Communists, socialists and liberals, to prevent the emergence of further fascist regimes in Europe (Chapter 8). This disquiet grew in the summer of 1936 when his cautious strategy failed to prevent the authoritarian forces led by General Francisco Franco launching a civil war against the popularly elected Spanish Republican government. To curb potential challenges to his power, Stalin acted with ever greater brutality, and unleashed the Great Terror. In August the first show trial took place, with the main defendants, Kamenev and Zinoviev, bizarrely charged with treason and sabotage and sentenced to death. Thereafter, the terror spiralled upwards. Genrikh Iagoda, head of the secret police, was replaced by Nikolai Ezhov in September, apparently because Iagoda had opposed the execution of old Bolsheviks. Under Ezhov a brutal campaign to eliminate all former oppositionists, and Iagoda's supporters within the secret police, was unleashed. A second show trial was held in January 1937, with Piatakov and Radek among the major accused; 15 per cent of the officer corps of the Red Army, not the 25 to 50 per cent once thought, were arrested in June 1937 and many senior commanders were executed, falsely charged with conspiring to oust Stalin; and in March 1938 Bukharin himself was shot after the third and final show trial. At lower levels many who had been expelled from the Party met a similar fate.[27]

Stalin's culpability for the Terror is beyond dispute. To attribute his actions to Marxist ideology is exaggerated. As Tony Benn sagely remarked, '[i]t would be as wrong to blame him [Marx] for Stalin's tyranny as it would be to lay the blame for the Spanish Inquisition on the teachings of Jesus'. Equally, to emphasise Stalin's alleged paranoia is also too simplistic. Opposition did exist, but its problem was that it remained inchoate and ineffectual. To argue that he acted in a 'traditional' Russian manner and modelled his actions on those of Ivan the Terrible, who had launched his own terror against his real or potential rivals, as Robert Tucker contended, is certainly an intriguing thought. Yet there is little evidence to support the notion that in the late 1930s Stalin consciously modelled himself on Ivan. Echoing the explanation of Stalin's lieutenant, V. M. Molotov, Oleg Khlevnyuk recently suggested that he acted to remove all potential 'fifth columnists' in light of an expected war with Germany. While we can agree on his culpability, we are still unclear as to all his motives.[28]

While Stalin launched and personally oversaw the implementation of much of the Terror, as it unfolded it developed into a more complex political and social phenomenon. A growing body of evidence indicates that many Party functionaries at the regional and local level took advantage of the regime of arbitrariness established by Stalin to rid themselves of their own opponents. Ordinary Soviet citizens, in the towns and in the countryside, also became implicated. Many workers and peasants denounced their fellows, and in numerous instances their immediate superiors, to the authorities. Their reasons for doing so are not yet fully understood: to achieve promotion; to exact retribution on those who had abused their power and made the daily life of their fellows hell; or even to demonstrate their vigilance against suspected 'wreckers', for the sake of a (misconceived) sense of loyalty to the regime. These elements help us to grasp better the momentum and scale of terror in these years. They also explain Stalin's decision to end it. Plagued by increasing worries that it had slipped from his control, he gradually took steps to halt it before it damaged the economy, and the security, of the country beyond repair.[29]

The most obvious impact of the Terror was the human cost involved. Recent archival evidence marshalled by Arch Getty and Oleg Naumov suggests that in 1937–8 close on 700,000 executions took place. According to the calculations made by the Russian historian V. N. Zemskov, in 1938 almost one million were incarcerated in the dreaded camps of the Gulag, where almost 10 per cent died, while nearly 900,000 others were held in prison or corrective labour colonies. These figures, of course, may have to be revised in light of material released from the archives in the future. What the Terror also did was to consolidate Stalin's personal rule. All vestigial opposition to him had been eliminated and from top to bottom the Party was staffed by his appointees. The circular flow of power was absolute.[30]

Stalinism in focus

What Stalinism was is a question that has generated much heat, but often less light. It has been variously characterised as: a form of state capitalism in which the Party-state bureaucracy had become transformed into a new ruling class (Chapter 7); a degenerate workers' state which could either develop towards socialism or regress back to capitalism, as Trotsky argued in *The Revolution Betrayed*; or a modernised, more brutally efficient autocracy, as Pipes implied. This question will continue to provoke much debate, but adds little to an understanding of the historical evolution of Soviet Communism. Whatever Soviet Communism became under Stalin it should not be confused with socialism, despite Kotkin's powerfully argued thesis that many ordinary Soviet citizens did believe they were building a new socialist civilisation in the 1930s. However one defines socialism the extension of individual and civil freedoms is central to it. Democracy, as Bernstein, Kautsky and Marx himself had repeatedly averred, was the *sine qua non* of socialist society, and notably absent in Soviet Russia from the middle of 1918. Whether the demise of democracy and the emergence of a barbarous dictatorship was the product of Marxism or of circumstances continues to divide historians. There is little doubt that the Soviet Communists thought of themselves as Marxists, and certainly they subscribed to the master's belief that any advance towards socialism ultimately demanded the abolition of the market and its replacement by a planned economy. Moreover, from Marxism, at least in its Leninist variant, they acquired the theory of the vanguard party, whose supposed infallibility justified one-party – perhaps more accurately one-faction – dictatorship. But the again fashionable concentration on ideology, be it Marxism or Marxism–Leninism, as the primary cause of the horrors that befell the Soviet Union after 1917 is simplistic. It is eerily reminiscent of what Arthur Marwick once disparaged as 'ball of string' history: Stalin's actions were determined by Leninism, while Lenin himself had merely elaborated upon the axioms enshrined in Marxism.

As I have been at pains to explain in all that has gone before, such an approach is quite unhistorical. Marxism came to mean different things in different settings: hence the concentration on historical context. In the case of Russia, any regime that had come to power after the collapse of the autocracy would have inherited the same dilemmas as the Communists did. Independence and security in the increasingly competitive world of the twentieth century did not come cheaply. The sheer survival of a still backward country, as Russia was, would have demanded modernisation, and rapid modernisation at that. For the Soviet Union, a self-professed socialist island isolated in a hostile capitalist world, this need was doubly necessary. Stalinism succeeded in this task, despite the terrible costs. Victory in the Second World War, as Stalin claimed in his well-known pre-election speech of 9 February 1946, justified crash collectivisation and industrialisation, even the Terror, which allegedly had removed opponents intent on sabotaging these policies. In the 1970s Rudolf Bahro, a dissident East German Marxist, developed this argument to its logical, if extreme, conclusion. Stalinism in all its manifestations really was necessary, as it alone provided the country with the means to defend itself against subjugation, and cruel exploitation, by the advanced imperialist West, Nazi Germany in particular. What Soviet Communism had engineered was not a socialist revolution, but rather a nationalist, or anti-imperialist, revolution that by building up the country's industrial and military might had ensured its independence.[31] The complex, even confused, character of the Revolution had not been lost on the early Soviet Communists themselves, as Kritsman recognised in *The Heroic Period*. Insisting that October was a genuine proletarian, and socialist, revolution, nevertheless he conceded that one of its consequences was to have liberated Russia from its servitude to Western imperialism.

Chapter 7: Late Stalinism to Gorbachev

While authoritarian one-party rule and the command economy remained in place when Mikhail Gorbachev was elected General Secretary in March 1985, in other respects Soviet Communism had changed much after Stalin's death in March 1953. Overt terror gave way to more sophisticated methods of control. Extensive surveillance over the population and the actuality, or fear, of imprisonment for any actions against the regime, persisted. Yet the threat of repression was accompanied by material concessions, whose purpose was to prevent opposition growing amongst the majority of ordinary citizens. By the 1980s, however, the command economy was stagnating and thus losing its capacity to generate the continued growth necessary to sustain the latter strategy.

Late Stalinism

The paucity of reliable sources has resulted in the period of late Stalinism (1945–53) remaining something of an enigma. Access to the archives has grown since 1991 but many key documents are still classified, or rumoured to have been destroyed. Dependable memoir accounts of the period have been few too. This lack of detailed knowledge has meant that the totalitarian model that dominated thinking about Stalinism in the West for at least two decades after the Second World War has been revived, and gained credence in Russia itself after the collapse of Communism in 1991. The model posits that after the Terror of the late 1930s Stalin, or Stalin and a monolithic Politburo under his strict control, had absolute power over the entire economy, polity and society, a power buttressed by the secret police, censorship, and terror. This power was exercised to carry out the prescriptions of Marxist–Leninist ideology. Stalin's personal dictates, allegedly fuelled by his increasing paranoia, or his 'sickly, suspicious nature', to quote Khrushchev, determined the entire course of events. By the later 1960s, however, the totalitarian explanation had become subject to serious challenge. Many commentators dismissed it as little more than a political weapon of the Cold War. Stalinism was equated with Nazism (hence Adler and Patterson's coinage of the term 'Red Fascism'), in order to justify the military costs of containing a Soviet Union seen as being as bent on expansion as its totalitarian Nazi counterpart.[1] Detailed studies undertaken in the 1970s and 1980s, by William McCagg, Timothy Dunmore and Werner Hahn, provided additional grounds for questioning the validity of totalitarian theory. Without minimising Stalin's own power, they questioned whether his domination was as 'total' as it had been on the morrow of the Great Terror, and raised doubts. His actions, they averred, were constrained by the rivalries amongst his putative successors, most notably Andrei Zhdanov and the party revivalist faction, and Georgii Malenkov and Lavrentii Beria, the leaders of an opposing statist faction. They suggested not that Stalin was simply a prisoner of either faction, but that he secured his power by the time-honoured strategy of dictators, of divide and rule. Most recently, Yoram Gorlizki suggested that after 1945 the system of government became 'routinised', with control over the economy assigned to a Council of Ministers. Stalin remained the dominant figure in the Politburo, where he exercised what has been described as patrimonial power. In essence, he intervened on occasion to impose his own will on the Council, and on the state bureaucracy generally. His will would be done, but he was not the omniscient, all-seeing figure who determined every facet of policy, as depicted in the totalitarian model.[2] The available evidence makes no conclusive answer to the question of the nature of late Stalinism feasible at present. This problem, combined with the fact that little of permanence was added to the theory and practice of Soviet Communism in this period, means that it need not detain us much further.

What is incontrovertible is that late Stalinism dashed the hopes of the Soviet people for a continuation of the limited economic and political relaxation introduced during the Great Patriotic War. Contrary to Stalin's promise in his speech of 9 February 1946 that 'special attention [would] be devoted to extending the production of consumer goods, to raising the living standard of the working people', the heavy and defence industries continued to take priority. The onset of the Cold War indisputably influenced the concentration of resources on them, as well as on the development of nuclear weapons. Dunmore added that the power of the bureaucracies within these sectors traditionally favoured by Stalinism had risen markedly during the war, the result of their vital contribution to the production of the matériel required to win it. With the backing of Malenkov they exercised their clout to ensure that their own particular interests were satisfied, at the expense of the consumer orientated industries.

The anti-peasant mentality that had characterised Stalinism also resurfaced. The meagre concessions granted to the peasants during the war were rescinded. In particular, permission for the peasants within the collectives to hold and cultivate larger individual plots, whose production had helped save the country from starvation, was swiftly rescinded. Renewed emphasis was placed upon collective agriculture, so much so that the relatively successful link (*zveno*) system, whereby small groups of up to ten peasants had worked allotted portions of collective land, also was abandoned. The official justification, that such a small-scale system frustrated the efficient application of mechanisation in farming, had some merit. The unspoken reason was that the Party had insufficient cadres in the countryside to control the peasants organised in small links rather than large, if much less efficient, brigades. The pattern of the 1930s was repeated. The countryside suffered grievously as again it was exploited ruthlessly, if not as murderously. Delivery quotas from the collective farms, and from the peasants' truncated individual plots, were increased; the prices paid for them were reduced; and payments for the use of equipment held by the state-owned Machine Tractor Stations (MTSs) established during collectivisation rose. These impositions, combined with the drought of 1946 and the poor harvest of 1947, plunged the peasants into a state of hunger and dire poverty.[3]

Culturally and politically, Stalin and his acolytes sought to re-establish their authority over a society shaken by the trauma of war, when some of the harsh controls imposed during the 1930s had been loosened in order to mobilise the energies of the people to defeat the Nazi invader. Stalin's *Concordat* with the Russian Orthodox Church in September 1943 had been a classic case in point. With Stalin's support, Zhdanov, who had become the leader of the party revivalist faction in May 1945, assumed control of this campaign. His tasks included the restoration of greater Party control over the army, whose prestige had grown enormously during the war (political commissars were reinstated to achieve this end), and of the increasingly powerful economic bureaucracies allied with Malenkov. Moreover, as Cold War tensions rose he also launched a swingeing attack on all Western, or cosmopolitan, influences on Soviet culture, in which writers and artists were maliciously denounced, if not shot, for their alleged deviations in the direction of apolitical or bourgeois philistinism. The clampdown was intensified by the fear that the many Soviet soldiers who had come into contact with their Allied counterparts would realise that conditions in the socialist motherland were far inferior to those that prevailed in the capitalist West, and thus provoke a more general questioning of the system. On their return, many were transported to the camps to prevent them acting as a source of ideological 'contamination', as were ex-prisoners of war. The elevation of Great Russian nationalism to a position of ideological dominance accompanied these repressive measures, so completing the transformation begun by Stalin in the 1930s. Seen from this perspective, the Iron Curtain that descended upon Europe soon after the end of the war was designed, as Isaac Deutscher pointed out many decades ago in his classic biography of Stalin, in large part to exclude all corrosive Western influences from the Soviet Union, and its new satellites in East Europe.[4]

This campaign, known as the 'Zhdanovshchina', in fact peaked after Zhdanov's own death in August 1948. In early 1949 an even more vicious assault on 'nationless (or bourgeois) cosmopolitanism' was unleashed, in which Soviet Jews were singled out as an especially pernicious influence. East Europe, too, as we shall see in Chapter 9, was subject to rigid Stalinisation, counter to Zhdanov's preparedness to tolerate national paths to socialism (polycentrism). Purges, on a more limited scale than the 1930s, marked this era too. In 1949 about five hundred of Zhdanov's supporters, most prominently Nikolai Voznesenskii and Alexei Kuznetsov, who had succeeded in promoting their allies from the Leningrad party organisation to key positions across the country, were arrested and executed. Precisely who initiated this so-called 'Leningrad Affair' is still unclear. Stalin undoubtedly assented to it, presumably to ensure that he kept control over the revived Party. But the cogs behind it seem to have been the previously demoted Malenkov, now restored as Secretary of the Central Committee, and Beria, who were intent on eliminating any possibility that Zhdanov's followers in the party revivalist faction would succeed the ageing Stalin. What conceivably persuaded Stalin to support their scheming, as David Brandenberger concluded, was his hostility to the Leningraders' demand to re-create an autonomous

Russian party organisation, which had been disbanded in the 1920s. Such an organisation undoubtedly would have been a potentially powerful and independent force. Its defence of narrowly Russian interests might also have jeopardised those of the other national minorities, and so provoked a backlash threatening to the longer-term stability of the Soviet Union.[5] Almost immediately afterwards, Stalin recalled Khrushchev to take charge of the Moscow party organisations, to act as a check, according to Khrushchev himself, on the Beria–Malenkov bloc. Later, in November 1951, he took more direct measures against his over-mighty lieutenant, Beria, when his fellow Mingrelians in the Georgian party were arrested for their supposed promotion of a nationalist conspiracy. Towards the end of his life, in January 1953, Stalin finally concocted the 'Doctors' Plot'. He accused a group of Kremlin doctors, largely Jewish, of conspiring to murder leading members of the Politburo and the army. This 'plot' apparently was to have been a pretext for a new wave of terror, to eliminate his real or potential rivals throughout the Party-state elites. The particular target again was Beria, whose secret police were accused of a lack of vigilance in uncovering the plot. The death of the old *vozhd'* (leader) on 5 March 1953 removed this threat, once and for all, as the future was to reveal.[6]

Khrushchev and de-Stalinisation

Despite the sufferings that Stalin had inflicted on the Soviet people, his death occasioned widespread outpourings of grief. Over fifty years later, Mikhail Gorbachev confessed to having shared such feelings. Malenkov, chosen to deliver the Central Committee's report at the Nineteenth Party Congress in 1952, appeared to be Stalin's anointed heir. However, immediately he was forced by his rivals, wary of the concentration of too much power in the hands of one individual, to choose between heading the Party or the state. He surrendered leadership of the Party to Khrushchev and retained his position as Chairman of the Council of Ministers (Prime Minister), so repeating the error made by Kamenev and Zinoviev some 30 years earlier in abandoning control of the Party to Stalin. A collective leadership had emerged, the major danger to which was Beria. His control of the Ministry of Internal Affairs (MVD), and its vast secret police empire, provided him with the potential means to establish himself as the new dictator, while he sought to win popularity for himself by advocating a series of concessions to the non-Russian minorities and the peasants.

The new leadership moved rapidly to eliminate this threat. With the support of the army, which had suffered grievously at the hands of the secret police in the 1930s, he was arrested on 26 June and executed on 24 December. The secret police itself was stripped of its ministerial status, renamed the Committee of State Security (KGB), and placed under the direct control of the Central Committee, to guarantee that it never again could be unleashed against the ruling elite. The beginnings of a new era, free of mass terror, had dawned.

Beria's fall served another useful political purpose for the new leadership. Rather than attack Stalin directly for the crimes of the past, which would undermine the credibility of the Party that he had led for so long and possibly provoke opposition to its claim to power, Beria became the scapegoat, so Khrushchev admitted. At its July Plenum the Central Committee attributed all the ills of the Stalin era to him, the evil genius behind the throne, a conclusion later mistakenly endorsed by Svetlana Alliueva, Stalin's daughter, in her *Twenty Letters to a Friend*. Khrushchev's subsequent judgement was more accurate: 'Beria didn't create Stalin, Stalin created Beria.'[7]

Other significant changes followed soon after Beria's arrest, which set a pattern that was to persist until the Gorbachev era. Democratisation and an end to one-party rule were not contemplated, although the heavy-handed repression of 'cosmopolitan' influences in the cultural world was replaced by a 'thaw' which continued, with ebbs and flows, until the mid-1960s. Instead of political liberalisation, the new Premier, Malenkov, introduced a 'New Course' in economic policy. Its objective was to raise the standard of living of the population, in the hope that material improvements would buy popular support for the existing system and thus secure the elite in power. In a speech in August 1953 he announced major concessions to the peasants, yet ones that stopped well short of dismantling collective agriculture: markedly higher prices for the quotas compulsorily procured from the collective farms; a reduction in compulsory deliveries of produce from their private plots; and lower taxes. At the same time, food prices were lowered, which benefited the urban population but saddled the state with increasingly costly, and ultimately unsustainable, subsidies. While not challenging the fundamental structures of the command economy created by Stalin his proposals to increase the production of much-desired consumer goods provoked major disagreements. To justify the diversion of resources from the traditional heavy and defence industries necessary to realise this end he also pursued 'peaceful co-existence' with the West.

Khrushchev spearheaded the opposition to Malenkov's proposals. On the one hand, he honestly disagreed with them. He accepted the satisfaction of popular aspirations for a better standard of living as a laudable objective. Yet its attainment demanded the speedy resolution of the agricultural problems that had bedevilled the country since the crash collectivisation. The heart of his solution did not threaten the principle of collective agriculture. Instead, with an extravagance that became typical of him, he insisted that mass investment to open up vast areas, some thirty million hectares of hitherto uncultivated 'virgin lands' in Kazakhstan and Siberia, was the best and quickest method of eliminating grain shortages and thus of improving the supply of food. His control of the Party machine enabled him to gain the approval of the Central Committee for this project when it met in February–March 1954. The immediate returns from Khrushchev's grandiose scheme were gratifyingly high, with wheat production much increased. In the longer term it absorbed billions of roubles and valuable machinery that could have been more productively utilised elsewhere, and eventually turned some of the virgin lands into arid dust-bowls. On the other hand, his assault on Malenkov was part of a calculated, if cynical, strategy to boost his own power. By attacking the diversion of investment to the consumer industries and defending traditional Stalinist priorities Khrushchev won the support of the forces of conservatism: the bureaucrats who controlled the heavy industries; the military; and old hardline Stalinists, notably Viacheslav Molotov and Dmitrii Shepilov, the editor of *Pravda*, who vociferously opposed Malenkov's proposed concessions to consumerism. His political machinations succeeded. In February 1955 Malenkov was forced to resign as Prime Minister, to be replaced by Nikolai Bulganin, a friend and ally of Khrushchev since the 1930s. Yet unlike Stalin's own opponents, and Beria before him, Malenkov was neither imprisoned nor executed. A watershed had been reached in the history of Soviet Communism.[8]

Khrushchev had emerged as the *primus inter pares*, but with powerful potential rivals. Ironically, within a year of donning the mantle of defender of the Stalinist faith he had appropriated Malenkov's 'New Course' for himself, wholeheartedly embracing the need to satisfy the material aspirations of the Soviet people and advocating peaceful coexistence. He also shook the world by his unexpected condemnation of Stalin, in what proved to be a not so Secret Speech delivered to the concluding, and unscheduled, session of the Twentieth Party Congress on the night of 24–5 February 1956. His motives for doing so were complex. One major reason, as Stephen Cohen has emphasised, was to contain mounting pressure from below. After 1953 a steadily rising trickle of prisoners had been released from the Gulag. Their return precipitated growing demands from the families of those still in captivity, and of those already dead, for their release or rehabilitation, and condemnation of the system that had put them there. Power politics arguably also played a part. His denunciation tacitly implicated his rivals, Malenkov, Molotov and others, who had been very close to Stalin and directly involved in the Terror of the late 1930s. This strategy was not without some personal risk as Khrushchev too had been a participant in and beneficiary of the purges.

Astounding as it was, Khrushchev's Speech did not amount to a root-and-branch assault on Stalinism, as a variety of observers remarked at the time. Both the old Menshevik émigré Boris Nicolaevsky, and the leader of the Italian Communist Party (PCI), Palmiro Togliatti, pointed out that it offered no serious or systematic analysis of the ideological and political roots of the Stalinist system, nor any criticisms against its fundamentals. Crash collectivisation and the human devastation that it had wrought, the creation of the command economy, and the one-party dictatorship were not questioned. Nor did it say anything about the atrocities inflicted on ordinary citizens, or about the mass deportation of 'disloyal' national minorities, Chechens, Crimean Tatars, Volga Germans and others, during and after the Second World War. In essence, Khrushchev confined himself to a condemnation of the unwarranted assaults inflicted upon the Party, the murder or imprisonment of its innocent members after 1934. Moreover, prominent 'enemies of the people', such as Bukharin and the Soviet 'anti-Christ', Trotsky, were not exonerated. Yet, unlike the July 1953 Plenum, he did not scapegoat Beria. He held Stalin to be directly culpable for the Terror, simplistically attributing it to the flaws in his personality, his intolerance of any criticisms or opposition, even his 'paranoia'. Yet with Stalin's death the 'cult of the personality' that he had created had ended. The way forward was now open, to restore the democratic [sic] norms that had operated under Lenin.

Whatever the motivations of, and limitations to, Khrushchev's Speech, the simple fact that it had been delivered served another purpose. His attack on the arbitrary terror unleashed by Stalin satisfied the needs of the Party and state bureaucracies, the main victims of the Great Terror, for the security to enjoy the privileges that accompanied their power. Indeed, it would not be stretching the point too far to argue that Khrushchev had consolidated what the dissident Yugoslavian Communist Milovan Djilas had termed *The New Class*, the title of his seminal work first published in 1957. Anticipating Bahro's influential analysis of the 1970s (see Chapter 6), Djilas contended that the October Revolution had not brought about a classless, socialist society. Its achievement had been the modernisation of a country backward not just economically, but also culturally and socially. The driving force behind this rapid and dramatic transformation had been the authoritarian state machine, perfected by Stalin. This machine, Djilas continued, was not some impersonal or supra-human entity, but one composed of bureaucrats. The heart of it initially had been the Party. But as the heroic periods of the revolution, encompassing October 1917, the Civil War and Stalin's Great Leap Forward in the late 1920s and early 1930s, had passed, the Party had lost its dynamic character. Echoing Timasheff, he asserted that it had been transformed into a conservative oligarchy, or a new bureaucratic class. Its *raison d'être* was to preserve its power, and associated privileges, which had been imperilled by the capricious nature of the Stalinist Terror. By denouncing terror, Khrushchev in effect had removed this danger to it and rationalised its rule. In this sense, he was the epitome of the 'new class'. Strength is added to this line of argument by the fact that his subsequent threat to its hegemony was the cause of his fall in October 1964, as we shall see shortly.

Partial as its denunciation of Stalin was, the impact of the Speech nevertheless was sensational. Millions of prisoners were released during 1956 and 1957 (the precise number is still a matter of debate), though without a full pardon or compensation for their incarceration and suffering. They became a continuing source of pressure for a much more far-reaching denunciation of Stalinism, and reform of the Soviet system, than Khrushchev had contemplated. Many intellectuals too, and some radical voices at the middle and lower levels of the Party itself, pushed to extend the boundaries of the 'thaw' in cultural and even political life ever further. Its high point came several years later, in 1962, with the publication of Aleksandr Solzhenitsyn's famous labour camp novella, *One Day in the Life of Ivan Denisovich*, in the literary journal *Novyi mir* (New World). In Stalin's native Georgia, on the contrary, the Speech provoked counter-demonstrations in defence of him that were only put down by force, including the deployment of tanks against civilians. Finally, and most dramatically, Communist power in parts of East Europe was shaken to its roots, most so in Hungary and, to a lesser extent, Poland (Chapter 9).

While the Speech had encouraged those designated by Cohen the 'friends of reform', it also provoked a conservative backlash from its foes within the Soviet Union, especially amongst those horror stricken in particular by its influence on the revolutionary events in Hungary later in the year.[9] Die-hard Stalinists in the Party Presidium (as the Politburo had been renamed in 1952) such as Molotov, Lazar Kaganovich and Shepilov and the previously more reform-minded Malenkov, became increasingly alarmed at the potentially destabilising consequences of de-Stalinisation. They feared that it would impel critics of the system to mount ever greater challenges to it. They also were troubled by the general thrust of Khrushchev's policies. His enthusiastic promotion of consumerism, his scheme for economic decentralisation and his growing emphasis on peaceful co-existence drove his opponents in the late spring of 1957 to form what became known as the Anti-Party Group, to unseat him from the leadership of the Party. Utilising the circular flow of power (see Chapter 6), Khrushchev deftly fended off the intrigues of this group. Insisting that only the Central Committee (CC), composed of regional and local leaders largely dependent upon him for patronage, not the Presidium, could remove him, he called a special plenary session of it on 29 June 1957. Convened with the assistance of Marshal Zhukov and the military, which flew the CC delegates to Moscow, it unsurprisingly rejected the demand of the Anti-Party Group for his removal. Having secured his own position, Khrushchev did not eliminate his rivals as Stalin would have done. Their fate was expulsion from the Presidium and the CC. Malenkov, for example, was consigned to run a power station in Kazakhstan, and Kaganovich a cement factory in the Urals, humiliating demotions, no doubt, but not lethal. His conduct reaffirmed that Terror had been removed as a characteristic of Soviet Communism, although less murderous forms of repression remained pervasive.

The imprint of the Khrushchev era on the Stalinist economic system was to prove less permanent. Its major innovation was the decentralisation of decision-making power from the central economic ministries into the hands of 104 regional economic councils (*Sovnarkhozy*). At the time, however, only the most far-sighted would have argued the case for fundamental reform, as the stagnation that was to overtake the Soviet Union was not yet evident. On the contrary, in some areas it seemed to be in advance of the West, launching *Sputnik*, the first non-manned satellite, and then Iurii Gagarin, the first man in space. So why did Khrushchev tinker with the system? Politics more than economics determined his policy.[10] The ministerial bureaucracies, anxious at the direction of Khrushchev's policies, had thrown their weight behind his critics in the Presidium. Hence dismantling them would deal a severe blow to this opposition. At the same time, economic decentralisation would bestow greater power on his own constituency, the regional and local party leaders. Admittedly, there was also an economic logic behind this decision, as decentralisation, it was thought, would extirpate the absurd inefficiencies of the over-centralised command economy described by Timasheff, mentioned in the previous chapter, such as sending coals to Newcastle – or the Urals – and back again. Equally, the destruction of the old ministries would remove the obstacles that they hitherto had put in the way of a greater emphasis on the development of light industry, and consumerism. In practice, the *sovnarkhoz* period turned out to be an economic disaster. The ills of hyper-centralisation were replaced by those of rampant regional autarky, with the regional authorities hoarding goods and resources much needed elsewhere.

In fact, the measures to which Khrushchev resorted to prevent stagnation setting in were not economic, but political. George Breslauer has described them as a form of populism designed to goad the bureaucracy into operating efficiently and honestly. They included the widespread recruitment of technical specialists into the Party; greater trade union supervision over the actions of the managerial class; greater control over state officials by those elected to the soviets; and the encouragement of rank and file criticism of any malfeasance on the part of the Party apparatus.[11] In effect, Khrushchev was sponsoring a massive campaign of whistle-blowing: of popular exposure of the failings of the Party and state bureaucracies. While it stopped significantly short of genuine liberalisation, it did confound the expectations of the bureaucracy for a quiet life in which to enjoy its privileges. Predictably, most of the 'new class' bitterly resented Khrushchev's threat to its security and increasingly rallied behind the foes of change. Aware of the possibility of a renewed threat to his position, fuelled by problems in agriculture, and subsequent price rises on foodstuffs, as his 'Virgin Lands' project ran aground in the late 1950s, and by the growing rift with Communist China, he went on the attack at the Twenty-Second Party Congress, in October 1961. Still not offering a root-and-branch critique of the origins and consequences of Stalinism, nevertheless he publicly revealed more about the horrors of the Stalin era, including the scale of the camp system, and implied that collectivisation had been implemented with excessive force. He also directly waded into his major rivals, explicitly naming Molotov, Malenkov and Kaganovich as active accomplices in the Terror. He had them ejected from the Party – and at the same time removed Stalin's body from the Lenin mausoleum in Red Square.

Buoyed up by his victory at the Congress, Khrushchev pressed on with his populist policies, with fatal consequences. The Party apparatus became his main target. The rules of the Party were revised to ensure that one-third of the members of all committees had to retire at every 'election'. In effect, committee members were now restricted to two terms of office, and a subsequent and inevitable loss of power and privilege. The 'new class' in the Soviet Union, as the exiled lawyer Konstantin Simis explained, was quite different from elite groups in the West. It owned no property itself. Whatever material benefits it enjoyed accompanied the member's position and would have to be surrendered if this position was lost. Intended to facilitate the removal of unreconstructed Stalinists from power and to prevent the perpetuation of often corrupt local and regional Party cliques, Khrushchev's reforms now were challenging his own power base. He then proceeded to split the regional (*oblast'*) committees into separate agricultural and industrial sections. Apart from the administrative confusion this caused, it eroded the power of the regional secretaries who had saved him in 1957 and converted them into irreconcilable enemies. By 1964 Khrushchev had turned the bulk of the Party and state bureaucracy against himself. It exploited his policy failures and the consequent sharp decline in his popularity, to oust him – failures such as: the bloodily repressed riots in the town of Novocherkassk in June 1962, provoked by the rise in food prices that he had imposed; his public climb-down in face of the opposition of the United States to the basing of Soviet missiles in Cuba; the disastrous harvest of 1963, which had forced the Soviet Union to import grain and fodder for the first time in its history, but too late to prevent the mass slaughter of livestock; the chaos and confusion in industry occasioned by the *Sovnarkhoz* reform; and his threat to cut back on military spending. The 'palace coup', orchestrated by Leonid Brezhnev, took place on 13 October 1964, when Khrushchev was voted out of office at a meeting of the Presidium. The 'new class' had secured its continuing supremacy, in jeopardy from his increasingly erratic administrative interventions. Yet Khrushchev's own mark on Soviet Communism remained evident, as he was simply pensioned off, not shot, and lived to write his memoirs.[12]

In retrospect, some elements of Khrushchev's policies foreshadowed those later introduced by Gorbachev. Khrushchev's populism has been compared to the *glasnost'* of the first years of the Gorbachev era, both being designed to expose bureaucratic shortcomings. Terror had also abated, and arbitrary imprisonment now was the exception rather than the rule. Moreover, the promise of consumerism had become a central feature of Soviet Communism, as the post-Stalin leadership strove to deflect political opposition by raising the standard of living of ordinary

Soviet citizens ('goulash Communism' as it became known in Hungary) and so lend some legitimacy, or simply stability, to the system. Yet unlike Gorbachev, Khrushchev never contemplated democratisation, in the sense of accepting any degree of political pluralism. Nor did he seek to emancipate the institutions of the state from Party control, as Christopher Read commented. What he had done was to get rid of the worst excesses of Stalinism. Religion was the notable exception, which was subject to increased persecution, as Khrushchev ordered the mass closure of churches. Yet little was done, as Alexander Yakovlev, a leading architect of the reforms of the Gorbachev years, pointed out, to remove the fundamentals of the system that Stalin had created.[13] What the long-term impact of his reforms, 'hare-brained' as some of them were, might have been is a matter of idle speculation. His successors swiftly undid them, and ushered in a period of conservatism, or neo-Stalinism, in the opinion of some.

Brezhnev and the stagnation of Soviet Communism

Another short-lived period of collective leadership followed Khrushchev's fall. Brezhnev became First Secretary of the Party, Alexei Kosygin was the new Premier and Nikolai Podgornyi the new President of the Supreme Soviet. Like his predecessors, Brezhnev, the Party leader, rose to become the dominant figure, albeit with considerable constraints on his personal power. To describe this period in the history of Soviet Communism simply as one of stagnation, as Gorbachev and many others were wont to do, is one-sided. It masks a number of achievements. Till the late 1970s the command economy, in-built inefficiencies notwithstanding, retained sufficient dynamism to enable Brezhnev to preside over what Cohen has called the golden age of Soviet consumerism. At the same time the Soviet Union built up its nuclear arsenal to the level of a 'rough parity' with the United States. As the dissident historian Roy Medvedev remarked, the very success of consumerism led to the 1970s proving to be the most stable and tranquil decade in Soviet history.[14]

Substantial resources were devoted to raising the standard of living of ordinary people. Agriculture was the major beneficiary. The prices paid for produce, and thus peasant incomes, were raised. The consumer remained protected by ever greater state subsidies to keep retail prices fixed, to avoid another Novocherkassk. Massive sums, some 25 per cent of overall state investment, were funnelled into attempts to modernise argiculture, though much was wasted as the potential advantages of increased mechanisation and electrification were vitiated by the lack of spare parts and the unreliability of the electricity supply in parts of the countryside. Furthermore, the continuing neglect of the necessary infrastructure, resulting in inadequate storage depots, processing plants, and rail and road links, led to much that was produced rotting in the fields before it could reach the cities, where shortages were still common. Despite the funds that it received, agriculture continued to be the Achilles' heel of the Soviet economy, with output rising by only one-third between 1965 and 1980 while the numbers living in towns and cities with a population of over 100,000 rose by over 20 million between 1970 and 1980. Consequently, the regime had to continue to import grain and other foodstuffs to sustain improvements in supply. They were paid for by exports of gas, gold and oil, whose prices by fortune rose substantially in the 1970s. Besides, the countryside itself remained a backwater, culturally and materially, with many villages still lacking running water and proper sewage. Labour shortages arose too as rural youth fled the countryside to the towns and cities in the 1970s, with almost 16 million migrating.[15]

Much of the urban population, at least in the major cities, experienced a perceptible rise in its standard of living. The range and quantity of food and consumer goods available did improve, especially in the large cities, although not sufficiently to keep pace with the rise in workers' incomes, which resulted in persisting shortages. The housing programme begun under Khrushchev accelerated markedly. Contrary to Solzhenitsyn's warped critique in his report on *The State of the Nation* in 1983, millions of families were freed from the constraints of communal living and provided with flats of their own, often of low quality, but at the most nominal of costs. They also enjoyed, for all their deficiencies in quality, comprehensive social welfare benefits, including free education and medicine, and virtually free utilities, and what many now look back on as an age of law and order.

The major failure of the Brezhnev era was to address the problem of the reduction in growth rates, first evident at the end of the 1950s, and a major cause of concern by the early 1980s. By then, growth in national income was at best 3.5 per cent, according to official figures, at worst less than 1.0 per cent, according to the calculations of G. Khanin. Given the annual population growth of 1 per cent, plus the accelerating drain of resources to the military as the second Cold War intensified from the late 1970s, this meant that little, if anything, was left to raise the general standard of living. Moreover, outside of Moscow, Leningrad and the republican capitals, shortages of food, especially meat and dairy produce, now were the norm, which led to the introduction of rationing. Other basic necessities, ranging from shoes to toothbrushes, could not be found. In part, this decline in growth can be attributed to the fact that the advantages of backwardness that the Soviet Union had previously enjoyed had been exhausted. Its vast reserves of labour and easily exploited mineral and energy resources had been used up by then, in a process of extensive growth that had seen the building up of basic heavy industries. If growth was to be sustained in the long run it was necessary for another economic revolution to take place. The Soviet Union needed to shift onto a path of intensive development that would enable it to expand into areas of modern technology, such as electronics, chemicals and precision engineering, as well as producing the range of good quality consumer goods the population hungered for.[16]

However, the very structures of the Stalinist command economy precluded such a transformation. The managers and workforce of any enterprise continued to be rewarded for meeting targets, measured in terms of the physical quantity of production, set by the centre. This system of success indicators had many deleterious consequences. For example, it obstructed innovation from below, lest plan targets not be met or bonuses paid; it drove enterprise managements deliberately to conceal their productive potential in order to be given lower ('soft') targets; it led to the hoarding of scarce resources, labour and material supplies, to ensure that targets could be met; and it meant that enterprises had no incentive either to cut costs or to ensure that the range and quality of the goods they made satisfied consumer demand, as any losses incurred were met out of the state budget. The greatly over-staffed economic bureaucracies had no interest in radically reforming a system, however inefficient and wasteful it was, that gave them power and privilege. Nor had much of the labour force, which at least enjoyed job security, rising pay and, outside of the military industries, little pressure imposed upon them to work diligently. After Khrushchev's fall the *Sovnarkhoz* experiment, and the narrow, self-centred localism it had engendered, was abandoned, to be replaced by the old system of central ministerial control.

Nevertheless, in the autumn of 1965, Kosygin, who had some grasp that the inadequacies of the centralised, command system would frustrate the increased consumerism promised to the population, introduced a series of modest, if complicated, reforms designed to overcome some of the them. Drawing upon ideas initially put forward by the economist Evsei Liberman, he aspired to devolve greater decision-making power to the level of the enterprise by reducing the number of centrally imposed targets. Enterprise success now was to be measured not by the crude criterion of gross output but by sales and profits, in an attempt to stimulate management to raise efficiency. As an added incentive, 20 per cent of profits achieved were to be available to the enterprise for reinvestment or distribution amongst the workforce. Acidly described by Alec Nove as 'the reform that never was', it never threatened the fundamentals of the Stalinist order. Half-hearted as Kosygin's measures were, they foundered in face of stifling opposition from the bureaucrats themselves, who exaggerated the threat that the measures posed to their power, as Gorbachev later lamented. All Kosygin achieved was to ratchet up wages, as workers naturally insisted that any enterprise profits be passed on to them rather than reinvested. In turn, this rise in earnings raised demand for food and scarce consumer goods, whose prices remained fixed after the Novocherkassk riot. The Prague Spring (Chapter 9), which had promised to introduce a form of market socialism, hardened entrenched resistance to all meaningful attempts to restructure the command economy. The notable, and partial, exception was the Shchekino experiment, named after the chemical plant where it was first introduced in 1967. It was designed to shake out surplus labour, and so raise productivity; management was empowered to sack workers, and use 50 per cent of the wages so saved to reward the surviving workers. Although remarkably successful it was not applied generally across the Soviet economy, partly since the stability of the regime was dependent upon it providing employment for all, and partly since the central bureaucracy again opposed it.[17]

The prerequisite for substantive economic change, it seemed, was political reform. Sadly, stagnation did typify the politics of the Brezhnev era. Khrushchev's attempts to mobilise popular opinion to overcome bureaucratic inertia and lethargy were swiftly cut short. So too were his challenges to the power of the local and regional cliques, which under Brezhnev were allowed to entrench themselves in power more firmly than ever before. Gorbachev mournfully reflected on this phenomenon in his *Memoirs*, averring that the consolidation of the corrupt cliques, most pronounced in the Central Asian Republics but prevalent also across the entire Soviet Union, was the political *leitmotif* of the time. De-Stalinisation was halted lest it become the focus of more radical challenges to the ruling elite, in the form of demands for genuine liberalisation. The rehabilitation of Stalin's victims, and the release of the relatively few remaining political prisoners, also ceased. Yet the efforts of the neo-Stalinist faction within the Party to rehabilitate Stalin himself, and re-impose an overtly brutal dictatorship, did not come to fruition. As Richard Sakwa commented, the dissident movement that had emerged under Khrushchev played an important role in constraining neo-Stalinism, and might well have won the passive support of many Party and state bureaucrats too.[18] In face of dissident opposition the Brezhnev regime concluded that any attempt to restore Stalinist 'norms' would be likely to undermine rather than underpin the stability of the regime. Yet it did clamp down on vocal opponents of the system, the 'other-thinkers', with marked success.

The 'other-thinkers', the dissidents, were very small in number. Drawn largely from intellectual and professional ranks, artists, writers, scientists, academics, and minority nationalists, they had become vociferous during the 'thaw' of the Khrushchev years. Some became more politicised in response to the increasing intolerance of the Brezhnev regime. As early as 1966 the writers Andrei Siniavskii and Iulii Daniel had been imprisoned for the publication of their work abroad. The crackdown after the Prague Spring virtually destroyed the dissident movement, which crumbled in the early 1970s. Many of its leaders were silenced by imprisonment, either in the camps (Vladimir Bukovskii) or, even more horrifically, in psychiatric hospitals (Zhores Medvedev briefly, and ex-general Petr Grigorenko), or were forcibly exiled (Solzhenitsyn). The fundamental political divisions that bedevilled the movement also contributed to its weakness. For example, the faction associated with Roy Medvedev, probably the least numerous of the three, believed that a return to Leninism would set the regime on the correct path to democratic socialism. Andrei Sakharov, the Nobel prize-winning nuclear physicist, abandoned this belief in the 1970s and insisted that the only solution was to introduce Western liberalism – in effect, political pluralism – to the Soviet Union. Solzhenitsyn rejected Western ideas of democracy totally. He sought salvation in the restoration of the particular religious, and Slavophile, traditions and values that he believed had inspired Russia before the Revolution, which prompted Siniavskii to condemn him as an authoritarian nationalist. Its most critical weakness, however, was its lack of mass support. As Andrei Amalrik observed in the 1960s, and the Ukrainian nationalist Leonid Pliushch bemoaned in the mid-1970s, few peasants or workers, or members of the national minorities themselves, supported the few surviving dissidents.[19]

Why this was the case demands further exploration. It would be far too simplistic to ascribe this lack of support for the dissidents to the chasm found between intellectuals and workers evident in many societies, not just the Soviet Union. A crucial part of the explanation for the political passivity of the peasants and workers lay in the regime's continuing embrace of the consumerist and welfarist objectives set down by Khrushchev. This had resulted in the gradual, but real, improvement in living standards during the 1960s and 1970s, as Pliushch himself conceded. Another part, of course, was the power of the secret police (KGB), at least 700,000 strong at the end of the Brezhnev era, and its equally numerous army of informers. In consequence, 'self-policing', enforced by the threat of denunciation by colleagues or neighbours, was also evident, although the increasing availability of separate flats did enable families, and exceptionally close and trusted friends, to discuss the shortcomings of the system in private. However, for the bulk of ordinary citizens criticism of or opposition to the regime no longer necessarily resulted in prison or a stretch in the camps. Rather, the state exercised another range of sanctions at its disposal, including its control of the deployment of labour and access to promotion and education, to contain potential opposition and ensure the acquiescence of the majority. It created a sophisticated system of divide and rule, or organised consensus, which the émigré dissident Viktor Zaslavsky identified as a central feature of the Brezhnev era. For instance, many workers, especially the semi-skilled, welcomed the conservatism of the Brezhnev regime, its opposition to major economic reform which threatened to raise the intensity of work or cause unemployment. Many skilled workers were drawn into military industries, so-called closed enterprises, where pay and conditions were good, even if surveillance by the secret police was much tighter. The skilled were also separated from their semi- and unskilled counterparts by the fact that most of them resided in 'closed cities', including Moscow, Leningrad, and the capitals of the national republics, where a residence permit (*propiska*) was required. In these cities access to material goods, educational opportunities, half decent housing and other social and cultural amenities was much better than in the smaller 'open cities', or the still benighted countryside. To avert too much resentment growing amongst those confined to the latter, a controlled pattern of migration was permitted to the closed cities, or commuter towns close to them. As well as keeping the working class divided, the threat of expulsion (often for one's family as well as oneself) from the closed cities and the relative privileges that they offered was a major disincentive to any political activity directed against the regime.[20]

Potential opposition from the minority nationalities was also deflected with some subtlety. Many national republics benefited from the transfer of resources from the Russia Republic. The standard of living in many of them, the Baltic Republics of Estonia, Latvia and Lithuania, and the Caucasian Republics of Armenia and Georgia, was considerably higher than that of the Russian Republic. In turn, many ordinary Russian citizens resented the privileged treatment of these republics and were vulnerable to the Great Russian chauvinism espoused by conservatives within the Party, most prominently the leading ideologue of the Brezhnev era, Mikhail Suslov. Morever, Communists within the national minorities were promoted to administer their own republics, albeit under the watchful eye of Russians in key positions within the national Party and state bureaucracies, and the secret police. Academic and professional elites, the potential leaders of nationalist movements, were neutralised by being given sinecures. For example, republican universities and academies of science provided positions, and accompanying privileges, for the indigenous intellectuals, however mediocre some of them were, while quotas were set for positions for native technocrats within the republican state and economic administration. With upward mobility guaranteed to them they were unlikely to act as the fulcrum of nationalist opposition, and any remaining recalcitrants could be dealt with by the secret police.[21]

The problem was that the price of securing stability was high. By 1980 the Brezhnev era was one of economic and political stagnation, and all-pervasive corruption. Yet when Brezhnev finally died in November 1982, after years of ill-health and a lack of firm leadership, few, if any, predicted that within ten years the Soviet Union would collapse. Despite growing signs of economic slowdown, which was compounded by heightened defence burdens caused by military intervention in Afghanistan and the outbreak of the second Cold War, no major internal threats to the system were yet evident. While the dissident movement may have provided the inspiration for many of the reforms subsequently instituted by Gorbachev and his key advisers, so Sakwa contended, critical voices within the Party still remained mute.[22] The dissidents themselves had become subject to ever greater oppression by the KGB, with Soviet Jewry the main victim. As the astronomer Konstantin Liubarskii, then in exile in West Germany, argued, the crackdown was a response primarily to fears of the impact of growing food shortages and the reintroduction of food rationing on the attitudes of the bulk of ordinary citizens, whose resentment was fuelled by the all too blatant privileges enjoyed by the ruling elite. Isolated strikes had flared up, for example, in the Togliattigrad car plant in May 1980. Incipient nationalist unrest, especially in the Baltic Republics, the

Caucasus and the West Ukraine, also had caused much concern within the ruling elite. But all in all no major challenges, no mass protests were yet visible.

The Interregnum: the Andropov and Chernenko years

The ills that had befallen the country were a phenomenon well known to the new General Secretary, Iurii Andropov. In charge of the KGB since 1967 he had been privy to its reports indicating the levels of corruption, pilfering, alcoholism and absenteeism endemic throughout the Soviet Union, from top to bottom. He was less aware, it seems, of the gravity or causes of economic stagnation, and the Soviet Union's technological inferiority *vis-à-vis* the West. His response was a series of puritanical campaigns to eliminate these evils, in order to restore the probity and discipline that he reckoned could lead to an accleration (*uskorenie*) in the rate of economic growth. Hindsight indicates that Andropov's measures were insufficient to revitalise the system, a conclusion that he dimly grasped in arguing for a shift from the extensive to intensive development of the economy.[23] Whether he ultimately would have been forced to grasp the nettle and institute fundamental reforms, had he not died early, is a moot point – Gorbachev suggested not. It was left to the sociologist Tatiana Zaslavskaia, a member of the research institute of the Academy of Sciences located in Novosibirsk in Siberia, to offer a more realistic explanation for the malaise that she perceived to have afflicted the country increasingly since the 1970s.

Her now famous Novosibirsk Report, first presented in April 1983, rooted it firmly in the nature of the socio-economic system, which had remained essentially unreformed since first established by Stalin in the 1930s. Echoing the terms first used by Marx and Engels (Chapter 2) she argued that 'the system of production relations' had lagged far behind 'the level of development of the productive forces'. She conceded that the command economy had enabled the basic industrialisation of the country to be completed, when the abundance of easily exploited natural resources and of labour had allowed rapid extensive development. Now that that phase was over, its flaws had become the main source of stagnation. While paying lip service to Andropov's discipline campaign she dismissed it as futile, as it did not address the ills of the command economy that was at the root of stagnation. More radical reform was required to rejuvenate the economy, and bring about the shift from 'administrative methods of management ... to economic methods of regulating production'. She posited, in rather Aesopean language, that the reintroduction of market relations, a form of market socialism, was the only solution. Such reform, she admitted, would encounter widespread opposition. The functionaries employed in the vast ministerial bureaucracies would resist the threat posed to their positions, and accompanying privileges. Many long-standing enterprise managers too would be reluctant to embrace market reform, and the new challenges and uncertainties it would entail. Finally, numerous ordinary workers, long accustomed to shirking, and engaged in pilfering and theft, would be equally hostile to change.[24] Zaslavskaia's analysis, and her proposed solution, were not adopted by Andropov, nor by his successor, Konstantin Chernenko, an old crony of Brezhnev and very much a part of the old corruption. It was only under Gorbachev, and even then not immediately, that her proposals were considered seriously. But we must defer Gorbachev, and his reforms, to the final chapter.

PART IV
Communism in Europe

Chapter 8: Communism in West Europe since the First World War

Communism in West Europe, as Eric Hobsbawm aptly concluded, was 'the history of revolutionary parties in countries without insurrectionary prospects'.[1] That was the principal reason for the failure of the Communist Parties of West Europe to emulate the success of their Russian counterparts in coming to power, as we have seen in Chapter 5. Their Bolshevisation in the inter-war period, and their increasing, if not absolute, subordination to strategies dictated by Moscow, merely added to their impotence. Moreover, on the few occasions when Western Communists openly challenged the existing capitalist order, notably in Italy in the early 1920s, and in Germany in the early 1920s and again in the depths of the Depression in the early 1930s, they were crushed by the coercive forces at the disposal of the ruling elites, both the army and the paramilitary organisations of the Fascists and the Nazis. After Stalin's death the continuing inability of the Communist Parties of the West to acquire any significant purchase on power led, eventually, to the emergence of Eurocommunism, in an attempt to free themselves from the blind alley of opposition politics. A rather amorphous doctrine that made most headway in Italy and Spain, and to a much lesser extent in France, it too ended in disappointment.

While the aspirations of the Western Communists ultimately came to naught, at the theoretical level Marxism in the West proved to be highly inventive and vibrant, if, as Perry Anderson remarked, all too often 'divorce[d] ... from political practice'.[2] Motivated by Communist defeats after the Great War, by the bureaucratic and tyrannical degeneration that

151

overtook the Soviet Union, and the belated publication of Marx's early philosophical writings, most Western Marxist thinkers paid little attention to the hitherto much studied areas of economics and to a lesser extent politics. They focused instead on the neglected questions of culture, ideology and philosophy. Admittedly, Western Marxism never developed into a unified doctrine (a proper treatment of it requires a book in itself), yet it offered varying explanations for the West's resistance to Communist revolution. For example, the founders of the Frankfurt School, Theodor Adorno and Max Horkheimer, posited that in modern capitalist societies the ever increasing bureaucratic control of both the economy and polity; the growth of increasingly fragmented and mind-numbing tasks associated with the technology of mass production; and the expansion of a stultifying popular mass culture, which provided the enjoyment denied in the workplace, all had so dulled the consciousness of 'the masses' that they had become incapable of revolutionary thought, let alone action. The Frankfurt School also borrowed insights derived from Freudian psychoanalysis. From this, they suggested that many workers harboured an unconscious craving for authority, which helped account for their inability in the end to resist the rise of fascist dictators.[3] In a related, if somewhat different vein, the Italian Marxist Antonio Gramsci elaborated a concept of hegemony. It focused on the cultural and ideological mechanisms deployed by the dominant bourgeoisie to gain the consent of the subaltern classes to the existing economic and socio-political order. In so doing, as Donald Sassoon wryly observed, he became the 'theorist of the defeat of the working class movement in Europe' in the inter-war period.[4]

To avoid another potted history of West European Communism this chapter will focus on three key themes. First, its dismal record in the inter-war era will be re-examined in light of recent scholarship which has reaffirmed that in some instances Western Communists were as culpable for their own defeats as was Moscow's meddling in their affairs. Secondly, Gramsci's theoretical work, mostly written in prison, and in a highly Aesopean language which he professed he was 'not sure others [would] be able to understand', warrants special attention, for two reasons. He was unusual amongst Western Marxists in that he sought to use his reflections on the failures of Italian Communism in the 1920s to construct a more realistic and effective political strategy for the future.[5] In addition, his legacy has been appropriated, perhaps misappropriated, to underpin the later theory and practice of Eurocommunism. Finally, the post-1945 period, which began promisingly with the brief incorporation of the

French, Italian and other Communists in coalition governments, and ended with the dashing of the hopes nurtured by Eurocommunism, merits consideration.

Western Communism in the era of the Comintern

As we saw in Chapter 5, by 1917 many Bolsheviks had concluded that the development of imperialism, and the carnage and sufferings of the war that it had precipitated, had brought the world to the verge of revolution – socialist revolution in the advanced countries of the West and bourgeois–democratic or anti-colonial revolutions elsewhere. As the old European empires disintegrated at the end of the war, the Soviet Communists convened the founding congress of the Third, or Communist, International, the Comintern, in Moscow in March 1919. Its purpose was to gather under its wing all revolutionary factions or parties, to provide them with the leadership to exploit the potential for revolution then thought to be present across Europe. The treacherous 'social patriots' of the old Second International, those who had elevated defence of the nation above their commitment to international revolution, were excluded.[6] Were revolution to be successful in Europe, Soviet Russia itself would be rescued from its dangerous isolation in a hostile capitalist world.

At first a rather inchoate body, lacking any fixed rules and regulations, the Comintern was soon transformed into a stereotypical Leninist organisation. At the root of this transformation was the failure of the short-lived Soviet republics set up in Hungary, Bavaria and Slovakia in the spring of 1919 to consolidate themselves in power. Their collapse, as well as the continued absence of Communist revolutions in Germany and the rest of Europe, prompted Lenin in particular to seek to explain why this was the case. Unable, or unwilling, to comprehend the appeal of reformism for many workers in the more advanced capitalist countries, Lenin and his fellow Soviet Communists mistakenly attributed the miscarriage of revolution to the lack of theoretically equipped and disciplined vanguard parties in the West. The solution, spelled out unequivocally by Lenin in 'Left-Wing' Communism: An Infantile Disorder, written in April 1920 for the forthcoming Second Comintern Congress, was 'absolute centralisation and rigorous discipline'. He insisted that Bolshevism was of international, not simply Russian, significance. Accordingly, he argued for the creation of parties on the Bolshevik model elsewhere, which alone could lead the proletariat of Europe towards revolution. When the Second Congress convened in the summer of 1920 it was presented with the infamous Twenty-One Conditions for membership, drafted by Zinoviev, the first President of the Comintern. Ostensibly designed to eliminate its infiltration and contamination by reformists, and their alleged centrist allies, the second condition ruled that member organisations first had to purge themselves of all such elements and fashion themselves, according to the twelfth condition, along the democratic centralist lines of the Russian Communist Party. The sixteenth condition also made the decisions taken by the Executive Committee of the Comintern (ECCI) binding on all member parties, which in effect transferred a great measure of control over their practices to the Soviet Communists.

Apart from Lenin's own designs there were a number of other reasons that underlay this development. First, the Soviet Communists alone had seized and retained power, which bestowed considerable prestige and authority on them. Secondly, until revolution did spread, Moscow was the only safe location for the ECCI. As the statutes adopted by the Second Congress affirmed, the consequence was that the Russian Communist Party would bear the main responsibility for the work of the ECCI. Finally, the fact that the Soviet government financed, in part or whole, its fraternal parties gave it additional leverage over them.[7] Yet increasing Soviet control of the Comintern did not live up to Lenin's expectations that it would result in the formation of large and re-armed Communist Parties capable of carrying out successful revolutions. Rather than marginalising the 'traitors' of the Second International the Communists found that their growing Bolshevisation had cut them off from sympathetic 'fellow travellers', and left them representing a minority of the working classes across Europe.

However, recent research, in particular that of Kevin McDermott and Jeremy Agnew, has confirmed that the newly founded Communist Parties of Europe were not, as they often have been depicted, just pawns in the hands of Moscow. While the Twenty-One Conditions were a Bolshevik construct, moulded by the Bolsheviks' formative experience of operating under a highly repressive autocratic regime and thus ill-suited to the more liberal political systems of West Europe, only two of the 200 delegates present at the Second Congress voted against them. Many German Communists, who had formed the largest party outside the Soviet Union, willingly accepted Moscow's strictures, with critics such as Paul Levi and Clara Zetkin in the minority. The latter despised the Weimar Republic, in which the forces of the old authoritarian Imperial order remained entrenched. They equally intransigently rejected any collaboration with the Social Democrats who had set the paramilitary *Freikorps* against them in 1919. As Eric Weitz has shown, the commitment of the KPD to revolution was sustained throughout the 1920s by its conversion largely into a party of the unemployed, whose street demonstrations, repeatedly, were put down by the police, often at the behest of local Social Democratic officials. One notable instance, as Hobsbawm recalled in his memoirs, occurred in Berlin as late as May Day 1929 when some thirty Communists were killed.[8] A similar current existed within the Italian Communist Party (PCI), constituted when it broke from the Italian Socialist Party (PSI) in January 1921. Amadeo Bordiga, the leader of the new party, would have no truck with parliamentarianism, or collaboration with the reformists, and shared Lenin's predisposition for strict discipline and unity. Gramsci's views at the time were similar and he did little to resist the subsequent Bolshevisation of the party after he had replaced Bordiga as leader in 1924. In Spain, too, the fledgling Communist Party (PCE) turned itself into a highly bureaucratised and intractable revolutionary organisation, with little popular appeal. In the French and Czechoslovakian parties, particularly strong Leninist, ultimately Stalinist, factions became dominant and zealously abetted their own Bolshevisation.[9]

Clear testimony that militant factions, arguably more dogmatic than the Bolsheviks themselves, existed within the Communist Parties of Europe surfaced in the spring of 1921. Many in the German, Italian and Spanish parties, and the newly formed French party, the product of its split from the SIFO in December 1920, rejected the Comintern's new directive to jettison the immediate promotion of revolution in favour of the formation of United Fronts with the denigrated socialists. In part, Moscow's *volte-face* was the product of the Soviet Communists' grudging, at times inconsistent, realisation that revolutionary prospects had ebbed in Europe. A series of disappointments had prompted this shift. First, the Polish workers had refused, unsurprisingly, to rise in support of the Red Army advancing on Warsaw in the summer of 1920. Secondly, in the winter of 1920–21 the Italian workers had been unable to convert their occupation of the factories in the northern cities (the factory council movement) into a revolutionary seizure of power. Last but by no means the least, the bloody suppression of the 'March action' in Germany in 1921, an insurrection that had been launched primarily on the Comintern's initiative, albeit enthusiastically supported by Ruth Fischer and other radical German Communists, was a major influence behind this change in strategy. In part also, it was motivated by the introduction of the NEP within Soviet Russia itself (Chapter 6). The economic recovery from the devastation caused by war and civil war that was one of its purposes would be greatly assisted, so Lenin and others concluded, by the normalisation of commercial relations with the capitalist world. Such normalisation demanded the cessation of Soviet attempts to foment revolution abroad. A split, between Soviet state interests and those of promoting European revolution, had emerged. In turn the Comintern became transformed from the agency of world revolution into one expected to support whatever Moscow decreed best served the priorities of the Soviet Union.[10]

Consequently, Moscow sought to tighten its control over the Communist Parties of Europe. Its will to do so was fortified by the continuing refusal of the Czech and French parties to accept the requirements of a united-front strategy. Rather than working within the existing trade unions, with the ultimate objective of suborning their members into their own ranks, they defied Moscow and set up their own union organisations, with little success. Moreover, the disastrous failure in 1923 of the October insurrection in Germany – much the responsibility of Moscow, chiefly Trotsky and Zinoviev, but with the enthusiastic backing of the Left in the KPD – led to an exercise in 'buck-passing'. Those German Communists initially sceptical of the prospects of success, Heinrich Brandler and his followers, were purged. Within two years, the radicals, led by Ruth Fischer, suffered a similar fate. At the root of this purge was their opposition to the moderate line urged by Stalin and his clique, as well as their support for the Left Opposition in the Soviet party, now led by Kamenev, Zinoviev and Trotsky. Imposed moderation brought little gain to Communists across Europe, who in the relative calm and prosperity of Europe in the mid- to late 1920s lost ground, not least in those societies where parliamentarianism and reformism still offered a way forward for the majority of workers.[11]

Yet within a few years, the left-wing 'diehards' were in the ascendant again, as the Soviet leadership dramatically changed tack. The ideological inspiration behind this change, it is now clear, came from the supposed arch-moderate Bukharin. From late 1926 he predicted that the period of capitalist recovery after the Great War was drawing to a close. A revolutionary crisis was imminent for which the Communist Parties of Europe must prepare themselves. Bukharin's theoretical predictions, however, are insufficient to account for Moscow's turnabout. The crushing of the Chinese Communists and the rupture in relations with Britain in the spring of 1927 were taken as portents of a renewed capitalist offensive, which revolution alone could avert. Equally, many German, Czech, French and surviving Italian Communists were eager to supplant the united-front strategy with more overtly revolutionary tactics. So began, with Stalin's sanction, what has become known as the Third Period in the Comintern's history. Communists across Europe now reverted to the uncompromising promotion of revolution and again castigated the socialists, or 'social fascists' to quote the pejorative term ever more frequently employed to describe them, as nothing but the props of capitalism and the major enemy to be overcome.[12]

The Wall Street Crash of October 1929 and the ensuing Great Depression appeared to confirm the prognosis upon which the politics of the Third Period was based, as capitalism was about to experience the greatest slump in its history. But revolutionary Communism was not to profit from the Crash. Mass unemployment engendered fear and passivity in much of the European working class, rather than the will to rise in revolution. In Germany most of all, where the prospects for revolution seemed to be the greatest, many Communists in a fit of what has been described as 'suicidal idiocy' enthusiastically took to the streets. Their actions simply strengthened the appeal of Hitler and the Nazi party, as the bourgeoisie and *Mittelstand* (middle classes) increasingly rallied to it as the only viable bulwark against a Communist take-over. They were as culpable as Moscow in underestimating the threat posed by Nazism, and their 'political insanity' eased Hitler's path to power. Whether the creation of a political bloc with the socialists then would have been viable cannot be answered with any certainty. A decade of grassroots hostility made this improbable, and the KPD attacked the socialists with as much enthusiasm as the Nazis. Whether the creation of such a political bloc would have been capable of thwarting the rise of Nazism is also doubtful. Trotsky's repeated suggestions that the potential for Communist revolution existed in Germany in the early 1930s were fanciful, given the forces ranged against it: the Nazi paramilitary organisations; the police; and the army, unlikely to remain in the wings if revolution did threaten.[13] What is incontrovertible is that the intransigent Communist militancy of the Third Period was an unmitigated disaster. No advances were made, the second largest Communist Party (CP) in Europe, the KPD, was destroyed, and no other really had counted for much before 1945.

The bitter lessons drawn from the débâcle of the Third Period when Moscow again had misread the prospects for revolution in Europe were gradually applied during 1934. The unexpected and unwelcome victory of Nazism, and the threat to Soviet security that it posed, led to another dramatic about-turn. Now European Communists were to seek not just united fronts with other socialists, but popular fronts with all political forces and parties opposed to Fascism and its potential spread. A fundamental reason for this tactical shift was rooted in Stalin's pursuit of collective security, a system of alliances with Europe's remaining democracies that could act as a deterrent to future Nazi aggression. Continued advocacy of revolution would thwart whatever chances of success this policy had. Another reason was the reaction of many Communists across Europe, especially in France and Czechoslovakia, to the disastrous consequences of the Third Period. In particular, the crushing defeat of the KPD made them sympathetic to the creation of broad coalitions to combat the rise of fascism. Despite opposition from a small ultra-left core of Communists, with varying degrees of commitment the majority of European Communists embraced this new tactic. In fact, some previously hard-line Communists, such as Maurice Thorez, leader of the PCF, even interpreted it as permission for the PCF to enter into the Popular Front government set up by the socialist Leon Blum in 1936, only to be instructed by Georgi Dimitrov, the recently appointed head of the Comintern, that this was not the case.[14]

By the late summer of 1939 it was clear that these new tactics had come to naught too. Collective security remained a mirage, as the British government remained unwilling to enter into any formal alliance with the Soviet Union. In much of Europe, moreover, right-wing authoritarianism was on the rise. Spain was a classic case in point. Here a Popular Front government had come to power in February 1936. The policies of the new Republican government, including a radical redistribution of the land amongst the peasants, provoked resistance from the propertied classes, spearheaded by the army under General Francisco Franco. In the Civil War that erupted in July, Stalin offered military aid to the Republican forces but refused to intervene directly lest this jeopardise the achievement of collective security. Similar reasoning underlay his warnings to the Republican government to moderate its radicalism in case the threat of socialist revolution in Spain so alarm Britain (and France) that they would ally with Nazi Germany to prevent it. To ensure his strictures were complied with his agents in Spain unleashed a campaign of terror against the revolutionary Workers' Party of Marxist Unity, the POUM (that it was influenced by Trotsky no doubt was another reason for the terror), and the anarchists. This internecine strife severely undermined the Republican cause and contributed to its ultimate defeat. But Stalin's murderous assault in Spain had broader consequences. In combination with the Great Terror in the Soviet Union itself, whose victims included many foreign Communists, it alienated those on the Left elsewhere in Europe sympathetic to the concept of the Popular Front, and helped ensure its failure.[15]

These failures precipitated yet another radical change in Soviet policy. As the prospects of a defensive alliance with Britain and France receded in the summer of 1939, and the likelihood of a German invasion of Poland mounted, Stalin plumped for an agreement with Nazi Germany to secure the Soviet Union from the possibility of imminent attack too. The conclusion of the infamous Nazi–Soviet Pact (sometimes referred to as the Molotov–Ribbentrop Pact) on 23 August 1939 had an immediate impact upon the Communist Parties of Europe. To the consternation of many European Communists they were ordered to abandon all attempts to create Popular Fronts and, as the directive issued by the Executive Committee of the Comintern on 9 September instructed, they were told to oppose what now was deemed to be a war between aggressive rival imperialist powers, begun by the Nazi attack on Poland. Dissenting voices were effectively neutered and the majority of Europe's Communists bowed to the line dictated by Moscow. With the Nazi invasion of the Soviet Union in June 1941, Communists in the occupied countries of Europe at last could act to organise resistance movements to often brutal Nazi rule. But the Comintern itself was now dead in the water. According to Dimitrov, Stalin had proposed its dissolution in April 1941. It was finally dissolved on 10 June 1943 at Stalin's behest, in large part to shore up the alliance with Britain and the United States against Nazism.[16] Yet Communism in West Europe was to revive following the Second World War; especially in France and Italy, its credibility was restored largely by its opposition to Nazism after the summer of 1941. Yet before turning to this revival a brief detour to consider Gramsci's explanation for Communist defeat in the West will prove to be illuminating.

Gramsci and Western Marxism

Gramsci has been a continuing source of fascination for both those sympathetic and those unsympathetic to Marxism. His theoretical work, however, is notoriously difficult to fathom, and hence to summarise. Much of it is enshrined in a series of Notebooks that he wrote in prison, under the gaze of the Fascist authorities, which helps explain its lack of clarity. Its central purpose is easier to grasp. Gramsci's concerns were to elucidate why Italy, and the West more generally, had proved to be impregnable to revolution after the Russian model and, consequently, to elaborate a revolutionary strategy better fitted to Western conditions. In response to the former question he summed up his conclusions in a famous quotation:

> In the East, the State was everything, civil society was primordial and gelatinous; in the West there was a proper relationship between State and civil society, and when the State trembled a sturdy structure of civil society was at once revealed. The State was only an outer ditch, behind which there was a powerful system of fortresses and earthworks: more or less numerous from one State to the next, it goes without saying – but this precisely necessitated an accurate reconnaissance of each individual country.[17]

What underlay this oft-quoted statement was the concept of hegemony. It is also a concept that is difficult to pin down, as Gramsci failed to define precisely what he meant by civil society and the state. In places, he argued that 'the State (in its integral meaning: dictatorship + hegemony)' must be 'understood [as] not only the apparatus of government but also the "private" apparatus of "hegemony" of civil society'. Elsewhere he drew a fundamental distinction between them, insisting that civil society was 'the ensemble of organisms commonly called "private" ', where hegemony alone properly operated, in contrast to ' "political society" or "the State" ', which functioned through ' "direct domination" or command'.[18] Contradictions and a level of inconsistency notwithstanding, in employing the concept of hegemony Gramsci reckoned that he had uncovered the fundamental reason why much of the working class in the West had rejected revolution and, essentially, become reconciled to continuing rule by the bourgeoisie. He laid great weight on the dominant culture, or ideology, of the bourgeoisie. Its influence had deflected the majority of the workers from pursuing what he thought their true revolutionary interests were and led them to consent to operating within the existing system. Hegemony, however, did not fall as manna from heaven but rather was constructed and perpetuated by what he termed the 'traditional intellectuals'. They encompassed, it seems, the professional classes, clerics, lawyers, teachers, journalists and other writers, and those employed in technical or white collar positions within the growing economic and political bureaucracies spawned by industrial capitalism. They were wedded to the system which had brought them advancement, status and material benefit.[19] By their collective efforts they had created an image of bourgeois society as the only conceivable one, and thus shored up its legitimacy in the eyes of the majority of workers. As long as the 'great masses' remained in thrall to this image, then the ruling class had no need for the use of repression, or State 'domination', to maintain itself in power. Provided the hegemonic, or ideological, 'fortresses and earthworks' were not breached, Gramsci added, even in times of economic crisis the bourgeoisie had no need to resort to its ultimate weapon, coercion, or rallying behind Fascism or Nazism, to survive.[20]

Gramsci's understanding of hegemony was at the heart of his prognosis of the preconditions necessary for a successful socialist revolution in the West. Let the reader be in no doubt that for Gramsci there was no parliamentary path to socialism. In essence, he averred that an ideological, or cultural, revolution, the creation of a proletarian counter-hegemony sufficiently persuasive to win mass support, had to precede the assault on the political and economic structures of capitalist society. The problem, however, was to determine precisely the agents, or agencies, capable of developing this counter-hegemonic culture. At an early point in his political career, from 1919 until the spring of 1920, Gramsci came close to the views of his contemporary Karl Korsch, a German Maxist. He suggested that the factory councils which had sprung up in the cities of northern Italy, especially those in Turin, would provide the practical political experience whereby many workers would acquire the consciousness required to build such a culture. Thereafter, he increasingly emphasised the Party as central in establishing a new stratum of 'organic intellectuals', whose task was to inculcate in the workers, and their potential allies, the ideological awareness necessary for revolution. Despite his awareness of the dangers of the Party becoming a vanguard of self-appointed intellectuals isolated from 'the mass of members', and so degenerating into a 'hidebound and conservative' bureaucracy (there are echoes of Rosa Luxemburg here), for Gramsci it had a leading role to play. As he rather obliquely stated, in the modern epoch the protagonist of the future, the force alone capable of fashioning an effective revolutionary movement, no longer could be the individual, 'the new Prince', but only 'the political party'.[21]

Gramsci's reflections on hegemony also compelled him to caution that the revolutionary strategy victorious in Russia in 1917 was inappropriate for the West. There, all insurrectionary movements between 1918 and 1923 had ended in failure. Open assault, he concluded, or the 'war of manoeuvre', which had swept away the autocracy and then the Provisonal

Government in 1917, would founder upon the deeply rooted 'trench systems' of developed civil society in the West. Instead, he advocated a 'war of position', a strategy that has some affinities with Kautsky's advocacy of a 'war of attrition'. The immediate task of the Party was to weld together a broad counter-hegemonic movement, embracing the workers and other subaltern strata in bourgeois society (in Italy, he singled out the peasantry as critical), and so create an historic bloc with the commitment and power to overthrow the capitalist order. In effect, he had come to advocate the formation of a broad united front, which he had opposed bitterly in the early 1920s.[22] While this was plausible in theory, doubts remained whether the capitalists would sit idly by and permit such a movement to develop to the point where it was in a position to seize power. Mass consent was one prop of the modern bourgeois state. But when threatened it possessed another, one Gramsci, if not his compratiot Bordiga, tended to minimise: a superior apparatus of repression.

Gramsci's legacy remains contested. Without wishing to minimise his contribution to Marxist theory it was not quite as novel, nor as convincing, as it often has been represented. Other Marxists in the early twentieth century had become aware, if in a more rudimentary manner, that capitalism was not dependent upon coercion alone for its survival. To take but one example, in 1916, Bukharin had grappled with the problem of what he called the modern Leviathan state, one resistant to revolution. He had pointed in more general terms to the ideological mechanisms, 'the church, the press, the school, etc.', that buttressed it. Some two years later Lev Kritsman broached the question of the mechanics of revolution in greater detail and emphasised that its first prerequisite was the creation of a revolutionary ideology capable of mobilisng the majority against the existing order.[23] Moreover, later commentators, including those favourably disposed to Gramsci, focused on the perceived flaws in his conceptualisation of hegemony. Anderson, in particular, emphasised that it was a mistake to conceive of it merely as an ideological construct emanating from civil society. On the contrary, the state remained at its core, especially in the West. The legal and political rights afforded to the workers by liberal states were not illusory, but real. Their very existence lent credence to those who insisted that bourgeois society in fact was fair and just, and underpinned the consent of many workers to operating within its framework. Their consent was reinforced by the fate of the Russian Revolution. There the hopes for democratic socialism, present in 1917, soon were dashed by the emergence of a one-party dictatorship, where all dissenting voices were suppressed with increasing ruthlessness.

The imposition of Stalinist dictatorships in East Europe after 1945 simply confirmed to many workers in the West that liberal democracy offered more freedom, and better material prospects, than Communist revolution did.[24]

Gramsci has also been depicted as a democratic Leninist, and credited with restoring to Communism a tolerance distinctly lacking from Communism in its Stalinist variant. The first judgement, as the patient reader will have gathered, is highly contentious, given the authoritarian premises at the core of Lenin's own interpretation of Marxism. Secondly, despite Gramsci's emphasis on the need to create a counter-hegemony of 'the masses', his own actions and writings betray a lurking intolerance. In the first half of the 1920s he had no truck with alliances with other parties or forces in society, and did not spring to the defence of party democracy. He was as opposed to factionalism as Lenin and had little sympathy for voices later critical of Stalin, such as Trotsky and other oppositionists within the Communist Party of the Soviet Union (CPSU) in the 1920s. Moreover, as Walicki has persuasively argued, his vision of a socialist hegemony was far removed from pluralist democracy. In power, the Party was to seek to rule by 'organised persuasion' as far as possible. Yet rule it would, setting limits on what could and could not be discussed, what would and would not be tolerated. What would happen to those who refused to abide by these prescriptions was not spelled out in any detail, but the implication was ominous.[25] Such a judgement also casts grave doubts on Gramsci as the ideological inspiration of Eurocommunism, which purported to offer its own democratic path to socialism. It is to this theme that we must turn.

The rise and fall of Eurocommunism

Eurocommunism, a term reputedly coined by the Yugoslavian journalist Frane Barbieri in 1975, was a heterogeneous phenomenon whose precise theoretical origins remain disputed. Yet its central purpose was clear. To borrow Trotsky's aphorism about the significance of Lenin's *April Theses*, it can be described as the attempt launched chiefly by the French, Italian and Spanish Communists in the 1970s to re-arm themselves ideologically, in order to build the broader coalitions seen as necessary if they were to acquire some purchase on political power. To understand why this was the case demands a brief survey of the history of Western Communism in practice since the end of the Second World War, and its failure to advance beyond the ghetto of opposition politics.

The Second World War, as Sassoon remarked, provided 'Western Communists their finest hour'. Their remarkable fortitude in opposing Nazism, certainly after the invasion of the Soviet Union in June 1941, restored their credibility, which had been massively damaged by the contortions they had performed in defence of the Nazi–Soviet pact of August 1939. They emerged from the war as major political forces, especially in France and Italy where they won one-quarter and one-fifth of the votes respectively in the first post-war elections. In these countries, and others (Austria, Belgium, Luxemburg and Norway), they had taken part in newly formed coalition governments. Despite their moderation, most evident in their refusal to countenance a revolutionary seizure of power, within two years they again found themselves consigned to the political wilderness, Italy apart. The onset of the Cold War was the primary reason for their expulsion from government, as parties still subordinate to Moscow no longer could be tolerated as partners. The Stalinisation of East Europe, which markedly intensified in 1947, provided added justification for the exclusion of the Communists.[26]

There was a measure of irony to Communist practice in the early post-war years. In effect, the Western CPs had abandoned Leninism, and insurrection, as inappropriate in advanced capitalist democracies. Instead they had opted for an essentially reformist strategy as the German Social Democrats had before the Great War. Yet in theory the old rhetoric survived. David Joravsky wryly pointed out that while practising class conciliation they continued to preach class war.[27] This contradiction provides us with a grasp of what the eventual embrace of Eurocommunism signified. It was a belated attempt to match theory with practice, one which recognised that revolution in the West was not feasible. Participation in electoral politics became the paramount strategy. Equally, its adoption marked an acceptance of the fact that Western Communists on their own had no possibility of achieving majorities in the advanced capitalist societies and that any political breakthrough could only be realised in alliance with other socialist, and democratic, parties. To achieve this objective, many Western Communists felt they had to distance themselves from the dictatorial practices associated with the Soviet Union, especially after its suppression of the Prague Spring in 1968 (Chapter 9). Eurocommunism was a means to these ends.[28]

The principal inspiration behind Eurocommunism arguably was Palmiro Togliatti, leader of the PCI from the late 1920s until his death in

1964, not Gramsci. Gramsci's ideas of the creation of a socialist hegemony, the formation of a historical bloc, and the utilisation of democratic procedures, certainly were used, or abused, to legitimate the project. Boggs, astutely, has pointed out how his ideas were emasculated, particularly by the PCI. While professing its allegiance to the Gramscean tradition, and proclaiming that Eurocommunism was an adaptation of his notion of a 'war of position' to contemporary circumstances, the PCI quietly discarded his conviction that such a war was but a vital preliminary to a 'war of manoeuvre', a mass insurrection to overthrow the bourgeois capitalist order. Its abandonment of revolution led others, including Massimo Salvadori and John Kautsky, to conclude that the roots of Eurocommunism are better found in Karl Kautsky's eventual subscription to electoral politics as a viable road to power.[29]

While the PCI had emerged as the leading left-wing force in Italian politics after 1945, Togliatti recognised that on its own it could not hope to achieve power through the ballot box. Even in alliance with the PSI an electoral majority was not within its reach. In the late 1940s he conceded that an accommodation with political Catholicism – Christian Democracy – which remained the most powerful force in Italy, was required if the PCI ever was to participate in the government of the country. His successor, Enrico Berlinguer, embraced his thinking and developed it to its logical conclusion. Despite the bitter protests of a small left-wing faction, Berlinguer distanced the PCI from the (Maoist-inspired) student and worker militants of the late 1960s, who seemed bent on the violent overthrow of the existing political system. Support for them, he calculated, would jeopardise any prospects of securing the triple alliance, with the PSI and the Christian Democrats (CDs), that he cherished. Once this wave of extremism had ebbed, he emerged as the driving force behind what became known as the 'historic compromise', the formation of a bloc with the PSI and the CDs, arrived at in 1973. Its purpose was twofold. In a series of articles in *Rinascita* Berlinguer argued that an accommodation with the CDs was vital to prevent them drifting towards the resurgent neo-fascist right, whose share of the vote had doubled to almost 11 per cent in 1970 in the wake of student and worker militancy. In Berlinguer's opinion, its rise signalled a clear and immediate threat to democracy, let alone socialism, in Italy. The experience of Chile, where the elected socialist regime of Salvatore Allende was overthrown in 1973 by right-wing reactionaries fronted by General Pinochet and abetted by the United States, reinforced him in this conviction. The fact too that leading CDs, such as Aldo Moro, and many younger priests, were now prepared to accept the Communists as allies in the struggle against neo-fascism and the corruption that plagued Italy provided him with further encouragement. In the longer term, he continued, in a rather inchoate manner, the compromise would permit the introduction of measures of social and economic reform that would advance the country, piecemeal, towards socialism. Eurocommunism as espoused by Berlinguer, it might be suggested, was a new, if half-baked, form of Revisionism. Half-baked or not, Berlinguer's avowedly parliamentary democratic tactics paid off, at least in the short term. In the June 1976 elections the PCI won its highest ever share of the popular vote, 34.6 per cent. While still excluded from the new government, at the time Giaccomo Sani concluded that it stood 'on the threshold of power'.[30]

Sani's optimistic prediction proved to be unfounded. The 'historic compromise' soon floundered. It was renounced by Berlinguer in November 1980, in favour of a vain attempt to resurrect an alliance with the PSI. Historians continue to debate precisely what underlay its failure. Sassoon contended that the PCI committed 'a major tactical blunder' in not insisting on its incorporation into the government after its electoral success in 1976. This blunder left the notoriously corrupt state machine, whose military and policing wings were fiercely anti-communist (Tobias Abse implies even neo-fascist), unreformed, and a tool of patronage in the hands of the CDs. The PCI's control of numerous local and regional governments proved to be no substitute for a share in national power. Equally short-sightedly, it did not insist that the CDs enact a series of economic, political and social reforms to the advantage of the workers as the price of its continued parliamentary support. On the contrary, it rallied to the defence of Italian capitalism, supporting the austerity measures introduced by the CDs to deal with the surge in inflation, chiefly fuelled by the fourfold rise in the price of oil after the 1973 war in the Middle East. It also remained committed to protecting the state from the threats to democracy posed not just by the neo-fascists but also by the Red Brigades on the extreme Left in the late 1970s. As it unsuccessfully sought to distance itself from the violent actions of the latter, which culminated in the assassination of Moro in 1978, it was driven further into the clutches of the CDs.[31] By 1980, the historic compromise had brought the PCI no tangible gains. The prospect of any progress towards power let alone socialist transformation was as distant as it ever had been. Its support declined throughout the 1980s. The collapse of Communism in East Europe impelled it to change its name to the Party of Democratic Unity (PDS) in 1990, which led to the breakaway of a substantial minority faction. Communism in Italy, where hopes once had been so high, again found itself at a dead end.

The flirtation of the French Communist Party (PCF) with Eurocommunism, partial as it was, also ended in failure. The crushing defeats that the historically Stalinist PCF had suffered in the 1968 and 1969 elections drove it to reappraise its strategy. Popular revulsion at the student riots and workers' strikes in 1968, 'the year of the barricades', which the PCF had condemned and even tried to contain, and the Soviet invasion of Czechoslovakia, contributed to the collapse in support for both Communists and Socialists. Union with the Socialists was vital if power was ever to be snatched back from the Gaullists. In the summer of 1972 the PCF, the Socialists and the left-wing Radicals adopted the *Programme commun*. Its core demands included higher wages; the extension of social welfare and public housing; equal rights for women and greater legal protection for workers; nationalisation of the banks and other key industries; increased taxation; and political reform, primarily to limit the powers of the President and increase those of Parliament. Equally significant was what was not included. There was no mention of revolution, or of destroying the existing state. In effect, the PCF tacitly had plumped for a parliamentary path to socialism. Later, in 1976, it confirmed this when it explicitly rejected the concept of the dictatorship of the proletariat, while somewhat paradoxically still clinging to its role as the vanguard of the working class. It went further and conceded that François Mitterand, the socialist leader, had the best chance of winning the Presidency for the Left.[32]

The beneficiaries of the newly forged *Union de la Gauche* (Union of the Left) proved to be the Socialists, who had overtaken the Communists in the 1978 elections. This unanticipated and unwelcome development prompted the PCF leadership to abandon its half-hearted embrace of Eurocommunism. It reverted to its traditional habits and sought to re-impose its own centralised control and discipline over a now declining industrial working class, at the expense of reaching out to new, middle-class radical movements, such as the ecologists and feminists. At its Twenty-Third Congress, in 1979, it rejected the Union of the Left; reaffirmed that it was a revolutionary party (if still one deeply implicated in electoral politics); and committed itself to the destruction of capitalism.[33] Surviving Eurocommunists, it appears, were purged. Its zigzags cost it dearly. In the 1981 elections the Socialists triumphed, while the PCF won its smallest share of the vote since 1945. The crumbs offered by the victorious Mitterand (four Communists were appointed ministers in the new administration) were little comfort. Its decline accelerated during the 1980s and by the end of the decade French Communism was in an even more parlous state than its Italian counterpart.

The rise of Eurocommunism in Spain, to return again to one of the guiding themes set out in the Introduction, can only be understood by reference to the context in which the Spanish Communist Party (PCE) found itself after the Civil War of the late 1930s. Under the Franco dictatorship it was an illegal organisation, which could not operate openly. In fact, most of its members had fled the country. It also suffered from the stigma of its fealty to Stalin's *Realpolitik* during the War, which had fractured the forces of the Left, and led, so many critics of Franco thought, to the defeat of the Republic. Stigma notwithstanding, the PCE was the most potent opposition – its backbone, one might argue – to Franco, especially influential within the illegal trade unions, the *Comisiones Obreras* (Workers' Commissions), that first sprang up in 1958. In the 1950s, long before the French and Italian Parties, it had openly advocated the restoration of unity on the Left, which previously it had done so much to destroy. Such an alliance was seen as vital if the Franco regime eventually was to be overthrown, and to thwart its replacement by another dictatorial regime of the Right. It also was designed to help the PCE to restore its integrity, severely tarnished as a result of its earlier compliance with Stalinism. This was the essence of the PCE's call for National Reconciliation, so Eusebio Mujal-León concluded – one made as early as 1956, as it strove to rebuild its popular support.[34] In the 1960s the PCE distanced itself further from the Soviet Union in its search for national credibility. Its leader, Santiago Carillo, openly criticised the repression of the dissidents after Khrushchev had been ousted; he questioned the legitimacy of the one-party state; and he, as well as many other leading Spanish Communists, welcomed the Prague Spring. The PCE had effectively forsaken Leninism. Carillo's strategy was formally adopted at the Eighth Congress of the PCE, in November 1972. It jettisoned the dictatorship of the proletariat from its programme, and denied that the Soviet system could be regarded as the only model for the construction of socialism.[35]

The death of Franco in November 1975 ushered in a real, if at times halting, transition to liberal democracy, overseen by the newly restored King, Juan Carlos, and Adolfo Suarez, who had been appointed prime minister in July 1976. This transition raised great expectations amongst many Spanish Communists. Yet it did not result in the breakthrough that the PCE had anticipated as the reward for its role in opposing Franco's dictatorship and its abandonment of the sectarian tactics of the Civil War years. In one sense, the PCE had expected too much. The Democratic Front (*Junta Democrática*) that it had succeeded in forming in July 1974 was a ragbag of minority liberal and socialist parties, and some monarchists too. The Socialist Workers' Party (PSOE), by then the strongest left-wing organisation in Spain, and one increasingly confident of its own prospects, spurned Communist advances to persuade it to join this Front. Its refusal doomed the *Junta* to impotence. The majority of Spanish citizens too, scarred by memories of the Civil War when upwards of half a million perished, was content to accept a gradualist path to democracy. It rejected the radical break (*ruptura*) with the old order espoused by the PCE lest it ignite a new conflagration. Fear of alienating this majority explains why it shrank from supporting the strikes and worker demonstrations in favour of a *ruptura* in late 1975 and 1976, and instead retreated into what Patrick Camiller has described as an extremely cautious and moderate parliamentarianism. Moderation brought some reward when the Suarez government legalised the Party in April 1977. In fairness, one must add that Carillo and many other Communists were aware that the consolidation of democratic institutions was a delicate process (the abortive military coup later in February 1981 was clear evidence of this point), which further determined their caution.[36]

In the first free elections since 1936, held in June 1977, the PCE received just over 9 per cent of the vote, while the Socialists garnered 29 per cent. The adoption of Eurocommunism, Spanish-style, had left the PCE far distant from the threshold of power. Still mindful of the fragility of democracy in Spain, the PCE persevered with its own 'historic compromise', which included recognition of the monarchy. Its membership grew, from 15,000 in 1975 to over 200,000 in 1978, small compared with the French and Italian CPs, but its popularity did not increase commensurately. It polled just under 11 per cent in the March 1979 elections, compared with 31 per cent for the Socialists. Repeated failure provoked factional and regional divisions within the Party. The more traditional Communists had opposed Carillo's proposal of 1977 formally to jettison Leninism in a bid to increase the Party's popular support. Ironically, Carillo resorted to Leninist disciplinary strictures to ensure his policy initiative was endorsed by the Ninth Party Congress, in April 1978, when he sought to suppress those factions resistant to his initiative. In response, the more liberal-minded Eurocommunists insisted that the PCE had to transform itself into a more open and democratic party if it was to emerge as a viable contender for power. In the early 1980s Grillo's faction had seized control of the PCE in Catalonia and Madrid, while the liberal Communists gained a stronghold in the Basque region. Growing faction-alism thereafter made sure that the PCE was consigned to the margins of Spanish politics (it polled less than 4 per cent in the October 1982 elections), with the Socialists by far the dominant left-wing force.

In sum, the hopes engendered by the turn to Eurocommunism came to nothing. In the final analysis it was little more than a return to the reformism practised by the German Social Democrats before and after the Great War, so Boggs contended, and failed to provide any vision of a socialist and democratic future. With their support already dwindling during the 1980s, the dramatic collapse of Communism in East Europe and the Soviet Union between 1989 and 1991 sounded the death knell of the Communists in the West.[37]

Chapter 9: Communism in East Europe

Communism in East Europe defies any simple analysis, a problem rooted in the very diversity of the region. The resurgence of stark national differences among the successor states after the Communist order collapsed in 1989 confirmed that the major reason for treating East Europe as an entity was the fact that it had been incorporated into the Soviet bloc after 1945, when, in the main, Stalinism had been imposed upon it. Yet even before the collapse of Communism differences had become evident. In the countries of Central Europe – Czechoslovakia, Hungary, Poland and the German Democratic Republic (GDR) – Communism had survived in power in large part as a result of the reality, or threat, of Soviet military intervention. In the Balkans, Albania, Bulgaria, Romania and Yugoslavia, the Communist regimes had acquired varying levels of indigenous support. Moreover, the Central European states had achieved considerably higher levels of industrialisation and urbanisation than those in the Balkans.[1] Such contrasts notwithstanding, Communism shaped the history of East Europe for four and a half decades after the Second World War, during which time major challenges and revisions to Stalinist orthodoxy sprang up. Despite Romania's spirited and successful defiance of Moscow's attempts to control its economic policy after the late 1950s, and its adoption of an independent foreign policy since the 1960s, it offered nothing new to Communist theory and practice. Neither did Albania nor Bulgaria, nor the GDR despite some half-hearted efforts to introduce a limited degree of economic decentralisation, the 'New Economic System', in the 1960s. The most important challenges emerged in Yugoslavia, Hungary, Czechoslovakia and Poland. Accordingly, it is to the chequered history of Communism in these countries that the bulk of this chapter will be devoted.

171

The establishment of Communist power

In the early years of the Cold War, Communism in East Europe was seen as primarily the creation of the Soviet Union, which had asserted its power over the region as part of its grand design to export revolution. Czechoslovakia apart, the indigenous Communist Parties had found little fertile soil in the inter-war period. Repression at the hands of increasingly dictatorial, right-wing regimes had emasculated them further, while Stalin's purges also took a heavy toll, especially amongst the Polish Communists. However, without denying the historical weaknesses of the Communist Parties in much of East Europe it has long been considered to be too simplistic to attribute the establishment of Communist regimes there simply to the machinations of Moscow, and its forces on the ground, the Red Army and the Soviet secret police. Widespread popular aspirations for radical change, and the building of a new and more just order, existed at the end of the war. As Czesław Milosz, the Nobel prize-winning Polish poet who had worked for the Communist regime before defecting to the West in 1951, pointed out in his famous book *The Captive Mind*, many East Europeans supported far-reaching economic and social reforms, and democratic–socialist governments that would reflect these desires. The Czech reform Communist Zdeněk Mlynář added that many young people either were ignorant of, or closed their eyes to the iniquities of Stalinism, and were convinced that Communism alone could usher in a new dawn of freedom and social justice.[2]

Why this was the case requires an understanding of the inter-war history of East Europe, and of the failings of the new states that had risen from the ashes of the old European empires at the end of the First World War. With the exception of Czechoslovakia (and to a degree the future GDR), they remained backward agrarian societies. The majority of the peasants remained poor and downtrodden. The solution to this problem, fundamentally one of over-population in the countryside, was rapid industrial development. Such development was stymied by a dearth of indigenous and foreign capital, and put beyond reach by the Depression of the 1930s when external markets and investment dried up. Politically, democracy had proved to be a weak plant and in most instances had been replaced by right-wing dictatorships. The return to authoritarianism should have been no surprise, given the absence in East Europe of the liberal traditions that had evolved over many centuries in the West. Authoritarianism also acquired a vicious nationalist complexion. In a region that has been pithily described as an 'ethnic mosaic', the newly independent states were inevitably multinational in composition. The dominant nation in each subjected the minorities within it to ever greater repression. Yugoslavia was the classic case in point, where the Serbs rode roughshod over the claims of the Croats, and others, for equality. But oppression of minorities was endemic, even in democratic Czechoslovakia, where the Slovaks as well as the Germans of the Sudetenland were treated as second-class citizens.[3]

The Second World War also left its mark. In Poland especially, Nazi occupation destroyed the old authoritarian elites. The bloody suppression of the Warsaw uprising of August 1944 by the Nazis led to the elimination of the surviving resistance leaders loyal to the Polish government-in-exile in London. Elsewhere, in Bulgaria, Hungary, Romania and Slovakia, the reputation of the old elites was tarnished beyond repair by collaboration with Nazism. The war also left the Soviet Union paramount in the region, with the power to shape its future, as its Western allies, Britain and the United States, grudgingly conceded. At the time, the Soviet Union was held in some regard by many East Europeans. It had succeeded in industrialising itself, if at a human cost not yet fully comprehended, which had enabled it to bear the brunt of defeating Nazism. The Red Army too had liberated much of East Europe from Nazism. The native Communists also had been prominent in the resistance to Nazism (at least after the sundering of the Nazi–Soviet Pact in June 1941) and their self-proclaimed patriotism secured for them a credibility that they hitherto had lacked. Furthermore, many East European intellectuals, and influential leaders, most notably Eduard Benes, President of Czechoslovakia, had become much more sympathetic towards the Communists. They were prepared to work with them, and to establish friendly relations with the Soviet Union. The major reason for this shift in attitude lay in the Munich agreement of September 1938, and the suspicions of the West that it had nurtured. The policy of appeasement pursued by Britain and (a reluctant) France had resulted in the sacrifice of Czechoslovakia, and encouraged Hitler a year later to unleash a war that led to almost six years of barbaric Nazi rule across East Europe. For Benes in particular, the security of Czechoslovakia against future German revanchism could only be guaranteed by cooperation with the Soviet Union. Most Poles were far less sanguine, having suffered ruthless Soviet occupation too as a consequence of the Molotov–Ribbentrop Pact of August 1939, which had partitioned Poland between Germany and the Soviet Union.[4]

Within three years of the end of the war the rather inchoate notions of democratic socialist transformation, and peaceful co-existence with the Soviet Union, that many East Europeans held were dashed as the iron heel of Stalinism descended upon them. That the Soviet Union wished the states of East Europe to remain within its sphere of influence is not in dispute. Yet there is little evidence, as greater access to the former Soviet archives since 1991 has revealed, that Stalinisation was a predetermined policy. On the contrary, Andrei Zhdanov, whose influence was second only to Stalin's in the early post-war years, apparently persuaded Stalin to support the creation of People's Democracies, radical reformist regimes of the Left, and the idea of separate national paths to socialism.[5] Yugoslavia and Albania, admittedly, were exceptions. There, the Communists, led by Tito (Josip Broz) and Enver Hoxha respectively, defied Stalin's directives to set up People's Democracies and created one-party Communist regimes at the end of the war. Their ability to do this was largely the result of their bitter struggle against Nazi occupation forces, which had given them considerable legitimacy in the eyes of their peoples and left them in control of their territories when the advancing Red Army forced the Nazis to retreat. Tito's commitment to end the oppressive Serbian domination of the inter-war period and replace it with a federative republic, in which equal status would be granted to the minority nations, reinforced the appeal of Communism in Yugoslavia. In Bulgaria too, the Communists had been in the vanguard of the resistance, not against the Nazi occupying forces but rather against the reactionary government, which had become little more than a Nazi puppet. The revolutionary coalition, the Fatherland Front, that had overthrown it with the assistance of the Red Army in the late summer of 1944 had been replaced by a Communist-dominated government by the end of 1945. Even in the historically anti-Russian states, Hungary, Poland and Romania, coalition governments of a sort survived, if increasingly under stringent Soviet control until 1948. Then what effectively were Stalinist regimes were constituted: in March in Romania; in June in Hungary, when the Communist Party 'merged' with the Social Democratic Party to form the Hungarian Workers' Party (HWP); and in December in Poland when the the now 'Stalinised' Communists absorbed the Socialists, to form the Polish United Workers' Party (PUWP). In February, the Czechoslovakian Communists, who had won almost 40 per cent of the vote in the relatively free election of May 1946, had ousted their coalition partners.

The diverse pattern of Communist take-over in East Europe has been detailed in innumerable studies.[6] What is central to the purposes of this book is an explanation of why the Stalinist system was imposed upon East Europe, and its impact upon the subsequent evolution of Communism in the region. The heightening of the Cold War was one major reason. In March 1947 President Truman declared that the United States would step into the breach left by a bankrupt Britain and help the Greek government to resist Communist insurgency. The Communist threat was chiefly indigenous, as Stalin honoured the commitment given to Winston Churchill in October 1944 not to support the Greek Communists. Shortly after, in April and May, the French and Italian Communists were ejected from the coalition governments set up at the end of the Second World War. In June George Marshall, Truman's Secretary of State, offered financial aid to assist the economic recovery of the devastated states of Europe. The readiness of the Czech and Polish governments to accept Marshall Aid alarmed Stalin, who feared that economic dependence on the United States would slowly but surely lead to their political subordination to the United States. Pressure from Moscow compelled these governments to refuse this aid. To ensure that similar waverings did not occur in the future, Stalin abandoned any truck with coalition politics and People's Democracies, in favour of one-party Communist regimes. Stalinism, Soviet-style, was thrust upon them. All remaining opposition, real or potential, was crushed by the secret police, and cultural and intellectual freedom was eliminated. Rapid industrialisation, at the expense of consumerism, the collectivisation of agriculture, and central planning (or command) of the entire economy, was also decreed by Moscow. To reinforce Soviet control over the Communist Parties of East Europe, and those of France and Italy, the Communist Information Bureau (Cominform) was set up in September 1947.[7]

The tightening of Stalinist control also resulted in many Communists themselves suffering imprisonment, some even execution. The reason for this lay in the Titoist heresy. The term 'heresy' is curious since the Yugoslavian Communists hitherto had acted in a quintessentially Stalinist manner. They had set up a highly repressive one-party state; they had nationalised the major industries (and many small enterprises too) and embarked on a policy of crash industrialisation; while they had divided the land to appease the peasant majority that had rallied to them during the war they remained committed to collectivisation; the churches were subjugated; and a brutally efficient secret police, headed by Aleksandar Ranković, set about removing all opposition. The real source of the conflict was not, as Stalin and the Cominform alleged, the deviation of the Yugoslavian Communists towards petty-bourgeois nationalism, manifest in the failure to eliminate the kulaks [*sic*] in the countryside. Rather it hinged on Tito's refusal to bow to Moscow's instructions, especially on foreign policy. Contrary to Stalin's wishes he continued to aid the Greek Communists. Moreover, his potential role as leader of a Balkan Federation, to include Bulgaria and Romania, threatened to create a bloc of Communist states not submissive to Moscow's will. That Yugoslavia was able successfully to defy the Soviet Union was a product of its peripheral geographical position, which made direct intervention by the Red Army difficult; the popular support still enjoyed by the Party; and the purge of those sympathetic to Moscow by Ranković's secret police. But the lesson that Stalin drew was that even Communist governments could not necessarily be trusted to follow his instructions. So-called 'national Communists' elsewhere, those suspected of harbouring any reluctance to do Moscow's bidding, had to be removed if Soviet control was to be assured. Polycentrism was dead, at least until after Stalin's death.[8]

The Yugoslavian road

Expelled in June 1948 from the Cominform, whose headquarters ironically had been in Belgrade, for the best part of a year the Yugoslavian Communists continued along the Stalinist path. When their 'orthodoxy' failed to win them re-admission, the Party leadership rapidly re-thought its strategy and embarked on a distinctively Yugoslavian path to socialism. Its central feature was socialist self-management, described by Misha Glenny as 'a brilliant and seductive theory but a disaster in practice'. In March 1950 Milovan Djilas, the Vice-President, outlined in rudimentary fashion the critique of the bureaucratic degeneration of Communism that he later developed in his *The New Class* (see Chapter 7). To avoid what Tito had condemned as the infectious disease of bureaucratisation developing in Yugoslavia, the Party introduced measures of decentralisation, or self-management. Its logic was to devolve a degree of economic decision-making power into the hands of the federal Republics, the organs of local government (Communes), and elected workers' councils at the enterprise level. State ownership of the means of production, the perceived basis of bureaucratism, was replaced by social ownership, an amorphous, but certainly not syndicalist, concept, as neither workers nor managers were allowed to own shares in their enterprises. Decentralisation, however, was far from complete, with the federal state retaining substantial economic powers. It fixed prices and, until 1956, incomes; it maintained strict control over the banking system; and it determined the overall pattern of investment. Investment was financed by high taxation of enterprise income in the more advanced republics in the north (Croatia and Slovenia), which it redistributed to accelerate the development of the backward regions of the country, the predominantly peasant and poorer south (Kosovo, Macedonia and Montenegro). Collectivisation of agriculture, intensified in 1949, was abandoned and the peasants were confirmed in their ownership of the land. The problem, lack of investment apart, was that the maximum size of peasant holdings, set at ten hectares (24 acres) and increased to 30 hectares only in November 1988, meant that a small-scale, backward and unproductive system of agriculture dominated the countryside.[9]

Rates of industrial growth were high in the 1950s, yet just how much was due to the economic reforms is a moot point, as industry also developed rapidly in the other, still essentially Stalinist economies in East Europe. Continuing deficiencies in Yugoslavian industry, for example low productivity and poor quality goods, combined with a rapidly growing balance of payments deficit, led to further reform in 1965. Then measures first proposed in 1961, but aborted in face of rising prices and unemployment, were revived. Their main thrust was in the direction of even greater decentralisation. Remaining price controls were abolished, while centrally imposed quotas and taxes on enterprises were reduced considerably. In turn, enterprises were now expected to fund much of their future investment from the increased profits at their disposal, assisted where necessary by loans from a newly denationalised and decentralised network of commercial banks. The dinar was devalued, to boost exports and hard currency earnings. Protective tariffs also were lowered, in the hope that exposure to foreign competition would stimulate domestic industry to raise its efficiency. Elements of state intervention survived. The federal government continued both to influence the overall rate of investment, and to transfer resources from the north to assist the development of the south, to the growing resentment of the former.[10]

The attempt by the Yugoslavian Communists to construct a form of market socialism, one which attracted much attention from economists across East Europe, soon revealed its flaws. After 1965 the workers' councils voted themselves highly inflationary wage increases, even in enterprises, making losses. Lacking any personal shares in their enterprises, that would appreciate in value as a result of deferring immediate pay rises in favour of long-term investment, they had no incentive to do otherwise. Neither had the managers, who offered no resistance to the workers' demands. The decentralisation of the banking system exacerbated this problem. Banks at the Republican and Commune level made funds readily available to enterprises under their purview, at unrealistically low rates of interest, so effectively bailing out those making losses. Most frequently these loans were used not for investment purposes but simply to pay for further wage rises well in excess of any growth in productivity. As enterprises became more indebted the banks again stepped in to prevent them going bankrupt. A significant proportion of the capital raised from abroad was squandered in a similar manner, while much of the rest was misinvested in grandiose schemes that never came to fruition; the same mistakes also occurred in Poland in the 1970s. Decentralisation led to regional autarky. The waning power of the central planning agencies allowed the constituent republics to undertake the wasteful duplication of major investment projects, for example, in the generation of their own energy supplies, which could have been provided more cheaply and efficiently by the federal government. At the same time, despite the efforts of the federal authorities, insufficient capital was diverted to the poorer regions to overcome their poverty.[11]

These flaws survived the feeble attempts of the federal government to remedy them in the mid-1970s, and led the economy into crisis. An estimated 40 per cent of enterprises fell increasingly into debt. As personal income outstripped production, exports were sucked in and the country as a whole ran a growing balance of payments deficit. By the early 1980s Yugoslavia owed 20 billion dollars in foreign loans; suffered inflation of 40 per cent; and had between 10 and 16 per cent of its workforce unemployed, as the recession in the West in the 1970s limited greatly the (temporary) emigration of workers surplus to requirements. Belated efforts to resolve these problems by cutting real wages, which culminated in the 1984 law prohibiting loss-making enterprises paying above a decreed minimum wage, were inadequate, and merely provoked strikes. By the end of 1988 foreign debt had risen to 23 billion dollars and unemployment to 20 per cent. Yugoslavia's failure to construct a successful model of market socialism has cast doubts on the viability of such a project. However, as Nove pointed out, the operation of the market had been constrained by the imposition of often arbitrary state controls and intervention. No economic system, he continued, is perfect. For all its deficiencies, he concluded, the Yugoslavian experiment provided many lessons, positive as well as negative, that could prove to be of great potential value in the construction of a socialist economy.[12]

Moreover, just as market capitalism has not necessarily been synonymous with democracy, neither was the bowdlerised form of market socialism in Yugoslavia. Rather than promoting political democratisation, the system of self-management, and the kernel of economic democracy contained within it, were seen by many Communists as a substitute for it. In its 1958 programme the Party, renamed the League of Communists of Yugoslavia (LCY) in 1952, reaffirmed its leading role in the government of the country, and clung to its monopoly of power until the bitter end. It only renounced it at its last Congress, in January 1990. Those, such as Djilas, who came to oppose one-party rule and advocate the establishment of a genuinely pluralist democracy, found themselves imprisoned. Until the mid-1970s power remained heavily concentrated in the capital, Belgrade, in the hands of a still centralised Party, supported by a centralised army and secret police. Short shrift was given to those Communists seeking greater autonomy and decentralisation. This became manifest in the early 1970s when Franjo Tudjman and other nationally-minded intellectuals were imprisoned for leading a nationalist movement (Maspok) seeking greater autonomy for Croatia. However, once dissident national voices had been purged from the LCY, Tito did bend, in order to prevent national resentments threatening the integrity of the state in the future. A new constitution was ratified in 1974, which transformed the country into a confederation of six republics and two autonomous regions. In turn, the Party itself was being transformed into eight effectively separate regional or ethnic organisations, held together only by Tito's ability and power to broker agreements among them. After his death in 1980 enmity among the ethnic parties grew markedly, fuelled by the growing economic crisis. It was brought to boiling point in late 1987 when Slobodan Milošević cynically played the nationalist card. He cast himself as the champion of the interests of the allegedly persecuted Serbian minority in the largely Albanian populated autonomous region of Kosovo, in order to secure the leadership of the Serbian League of Communists. The genie of ethnic nationalism that Tito had striven to contain was released from the bottle and led eventually to the horrors of 'ethnic cleansing' in the 1990s.[13]

Hungary and 'goulash Communism'

Stalin's death brought no immediate change in Hungary, with Mátyás Rákosi and his fellow Stalinist die-hards still firmly in control of the HWP.

However, alarmed that strikes in Hungary would escalate into the mass demonstrations that had erupted in the GDR after Stalin's death and only been quelled by Soviet military force, Malenkov summoned them to Moscow in mid-June. There they were instructed to introduce reforms along the lines of the New Course in the Soviet Union itself. To symbolise this intent, Imre Nagy, minister of the interior in the coalition government formed after the November 1945 elections, but demoted for his continued defence of coalition politics, was recalled. On Moscow's insistence he was appointed Prime Minister, although Rákosi continued to hold the post of First Secretary of the Party. At the meeting of the Hungarian CC on 27–8 June, Nagy launched a swingeing attack on Stalinism, and on Rákosi personally. With Malenkov's support, he reduced the pace of heavy industrialisation and concentrated more resources on the consumer industries. To help overcome food shortages, which had been one cause of the spring strikes, more investment was pumped into agriculture, while the existing collective farms could be dissolved by a majority vote of the peasants within them. Nagy also introduced a 'thaw' in cultural life and curbed the powers of the secret police.[14]

However, Malenkov's fall from grace (Chapter 7) deprived Nagy of his patron in the Kremlin. He was deposed as Premier in March 1955 by the resurgent Stalinists, supported by the hard-liners in the Kremlin. Nagy's reforms were reversed, to the frustration of almost all Hungarians. The halting nature of de-Stalinisation, especially irksome after Khrushchev's rapprochement with Yugoslavia in 1955, seemingly signified the recognition of separate national paths to socialism; and, increasingly intolerable after the revelations contained in his Secret Speech, was the underlying cause of the Hungarian rising in the autumn of 1956. Although victims of the purges of the late 1940s and 1950s were gradually rehabilitated, the Rákosi regime did little else to dismantle the Stalinist system. Even his resignation in July as Secretary of the Party, under pressure from Moscow (Khrushchev's plenipotentiary, A. I. Mikoian, was present at the meeting of the CC where Ernst Gerö was elected to replace him), changed little as the old *apparatchiki* remained strong enough to resist any key changes. Opposition grew rapidly: most vociferously, as the CC itself admitted, amongst the intellectuals grouped around the Petöfi circle, and the students, who toured the country in the summer to agitate for fundamental reforms. Recurring shortages, of food and fuel, stirred the workers to action, as their rancour at the material privileges enjoyed by the Party-state bureaucracy grew. The spark that ignited the Hungarian

Revolution came on 23 October when a demonstration, called by the students in support of the growing popular protests against Stalinism in Poland, mushroomed into a mass movement for independence and democracy. Gerö's appeal to the Soviet Union for assistance in controlling the demonstrations simply fanned the flames of opposition. It removed whatever vestiges of credibility the HWP had. Even the reappointment of Nagy, again recently accused of counter-revolutionary opposition, as Prime Minister on 24 October, still left it powerless to channel popular demands within bounds acceptable to Moscow. His immediate proclamation of a democratic and national path to socialism, and a radical improvement in the workers' standard of living, did nothing to conciliate the opposition and it soon became clear that the HWP had lost all control of the situation.[15]

Nagy now found himself a prisoner of events. Bar sanctioning violent repression he had little choice but to accept the demands of the newly formed revolutionary and workers' councils. They called for a new provisional government, cleansed of all old Stalinists; the speedy restoration of multi-party democracy as well as freedom of speech, press and assembly, and of religion; the abolition of the secret police and an end to arbitrary imprisonment; the removal of Soviet troops; and the immediate withdrawal of Hungary from the Warsaw Pact, to become a neutral country on the model of Austria. Enterprise management was to be transferred into the hands of elected workers' councils, while the wages of the poorest were to be raised. The vast majority of the insurgents were not counter-revolutionary, as the Party later claimed. They had no desire to reverse the transformation of the countryside which had given land to the peasants, nor to privatise industry. In January 1989, Imre Poszgay, the black sheep of the Party who had become the driving force behind democratic reform, conceded that the Hungarian Revolution of 1956 had been a popular uprising. Its immediate objective had been to release the country from its thrall to the Soviet Union. It was not, however, simply a nationalist revolution, as independence was simply the first step along a truly Hungarian (and democratic) path to socialism.[16]

The rising was crushed, by the mass intervention of Soviet troops. On 4 November they were requested to smash 'the sinister forces of reaction' by János Kádár, head of the new Revolutionary Worker-Peasant [sic] Government and self-appointed leader of the renamed Hungarian Socialist Workers' Party. It had formed on 1 November to replace the old and totally discredited HWP, which had disintegrated in the face of the Revolution. Moscow and its Warsaw Pact allies justified military intervention on the grounds of providing 'mutual fraternal aid' to one of its members threatened by subversion, as they did 12 years later in Czechoslovakia. From a Communist point of view the threat of subversion seemed to be real. Kádár, himself a victim of Rákosi's terror, and no died-in-the-wool Stalinist, was prepared to support a considerable measure of de-Stalinisation. Yet he would not accept an end to the Party's monopoly of power, nor neutrality for the country. Communist leaders elsewhere (even Tito assented) backed the suppression of the rising, presumably fearful that if it was not put down they too would be faced with similar challenges. While no democrat, Khrushchev too had little room for manoeuvre. Had he not sanctioned intervention, those critical of his attacks on Stalin in all probability would have been able to mobilise sufficient force, including that of the army, to overthrow him.[17]

Kádár and his coterie had no compunction in crushing the insurgents, once the Red Army had restored a semblance of order. The leaders of the Revolution were either executed (an estimated 2000) or imprisoned (upwards of 20,000). The workers' councils were dismantled and moves toward a multi-party system reversed. Nagy himself took shelter in the Yugoslavian embassy for almost two years. After giving himself up in 1958, he was hanged on 16 June, despite guarantees of his personal safety. Yet once the Party was firmly secured in power again, Kádár gradually shifted course, from the exercise of naked terror to some form of compromise with Hungarian society. As he stated in his famous speech of 9 December 1961, 'Whoever is not against us is with us'. Rákosi and his fellow hardliners, who proclaimed the opposite, were expelled from the Party. The arbitrary power of the secret police was curbed. Intellectual life became increasingly freer; and excluding a brief spell of repression beginning in 1973, when the poet Miklos Hárászti became the first dissident to be put on trial since 1958 for his radical critique of the soullessness of factory life, few were arrested or persecuted for their opinions. What has been described (some would say wrongly) as a system of 'socialist legality' had been introduced. A measure of religious toleration followed the *Concordat* negotiated with the Catholic Church in 1964. Travel to the West was eased substantially. Educational opportunities were extended and in the spirit of Kádár's declaration many non-Communist specialists were promoted to important, and materially privileged, positions within the economic and state administration. These concessions were accompanied by a growing emphasis on improving the standard of living of the majority of ordinary people, and from the late 1950s more resources were devoted to consumer industries, and agriculture. The system that emerged became known as 'goulash Communism', which has affinities with the 'organised consensus' of Brezhnev's Soviet Union. Passivity was purchased by the promise of a rising standard of living, which became a substitute for real political liberalisation. More critical voices dismissed Kádár's strategy as nothing but institutionalised 'bribery', whereby the majority of the population sold its political soul in return for material gain and a limited and uncertain cultural freedom.[18]

To improve economic performance and thus ensure that 'goulash Communism' was sustainable in the long run, economic reform, the New Economic Mechanism (NEM), was introduced in 1968. Similar to the system in Yugoslavia, if without the principle of workers' self-management, the NEM purportedly introduced a considerable element of marketisation, although the plan continued to determine the overall direction and pace of growth and the balance between consumption (individual and social) and investment. The prices of many goods were freed, although basic essentials remained heavily subsidised; enterprises no longer had to fulfil quotas imposed by the centre, with success now measured by profits made on the sale of their products; at least 50 per cent of future investment was to be paid for by investment bank loans, for which each enterprise was charged interest; and material supplies and equipment were no longer provided by the state, but procured through the market. Small-scale private and cooperative enterprises were also legalised. In many instances they were run by state employees with second jobs, which, as Janos Kenedi wryly remarked, absorbed so much of their energies that little was left for their primary occupations! Yet the transition to market socialism remained incomplete. In 1973 more than 50 large enterprises, producing over half of the country's industrial output, again became subject to direct central state control.[19]

Collectivisation of agriculture had been pursued with renewed vigour after 1956, but from the early 1960s Kádár granted the collectives a large measure of independence to manage their own activities – or, as Nigel Swain has pointed out, it was granted to their Party-appointed managers, not the peasants themselves. Delivery quotas and production targets were abandoned, with the state raising prices for agricultural produce sufficiently to ensure that enough food was available. The peasants were also allowed to engage in secondary occupations outside the collective, to supplement their income. Few obstacles were placed in the way of them working their private plots. By 1979, 35 per cent of agrarian production (by value) came from these plots, and from voluntary cooperatives set up by the peasants. Inefficiencies notwithstanding, Hungarian agriculture did work. Its peasantry was considerably better off than its counterparts in East Europe, while its urban population did not experience shortages but had a larger and much more varied range of foodstuffs available to it. Moreover, agriculture (and viniculture) proved to be a major source of export earnings, some testimony to the success of reforms in the countryside.[20]

For most of the 1970s the partially reformed economic system worked reasonably well. Though the overall rate of growth did not rise markedly, there was a period of relative prosperity. The population was better fed and clothed than the others in East Europe, enjoyed a much greater availability of consumer durables, and one family in four owned a car by the end of the decade. Problems unquestionably remained, with decent housing in the cities well beyond the means of the average working family. Critical voices within the country, primarily the unofficial Foundation to Assist the Poor (SZETA) group, estimated that 10 per cent of the population still lived below the official poverty line. Inefficient enterprises continued in business as the state intervened to prevent them closing and causing unemployment. In the opinion of many managers this support merely bred laziness amongst the workers. Inequality also grew. Enterprise managers and their white collar staff were granted considerably higher profit-related bonuses than ordinary workers. Those with second jobs in the legalised private or co-operative sectors also became better off.[21]

The era of prosperity, however, was transient. By the end of the decade storm clouds were looming on the economic horizon. Hungary's substantial trade surplus in food was far from sufficient to stem a growing balance of payments crisis. There were two major sources of this crisis. The most important was the fourfold rise in oil prices after the Arab–Israeli war of 1973; lacking its own energy resources and industrial raw materials, it was forced to import them at rapidly growing cost. The second was that its industry had remained uncompetitive, especially in terms of quality, in a world market that had shrunk under the impact of the oil price rises. To overcome this lack of competitiveness, however, required importing Western equipment and technology to replace outdated plant, which added to the trade deficit. Attempts to tackle these problems, in particular the reduction in subsidies on many goods, and price rises to curb consumption, foundered. Many Hungarians complained that they paid capitalist prices but only received socialist wages. Attempts to revitalise the economy in the early 1980s, by refusing to bail out enterprises that were plainly inefficient and subjecting them to the discipline of market forces, came too late. By 1985 the economic situation was deteriorating markedly: inflation was rising; fears of unemployment as a result of further marketisation grew; indebtedness to the West was the greatest, *per capita*, in East Europe; and agricultural production slumped. The standard of living, already declining for several years, plummeted, and the welfare system lurched into crisis as money began to dry up. Kádár's popularity, always greater than that of the Party, fell sharply as the era of relative prosperity ended, and mounting criticisms of the system were suppressed.[22]

Kádárism was at a dead end. What Kádár had introduced was socialism with something of a human face, but one that was far from democratic. He never challenged the central tenet of Communism in its Leninist variant, the leading role of the Party, nor is there any evidence that he aspired to do so. Neither would Moscow, certainly before the Gorbachev era, have tolerated any such attempt. Looked at historically, his strategy had some affinity with that of the NEP in the Soviet Union in the 1920s (see Chapter 6). He had initiated a measure of economic freedom, but balked at political pluralism. The Party, however softened or civilised, clung to its monopoly of political power. Its objective was to establish some *modus vivendi* with the society it controlled, to create a peaceful co-existence internally that would consolidate its power. In this respect, Kádárism has been depicted as the only surviving manifestation of Khrushchevism, and perhaps the most deftly governed dictatorship of the proletariat ever witnessed. The problem was that the survival of the Party had become increasingly dependent on its ability to keep the 'good times rolling'. A society that had been quiescent in the years of prosperity, 'self policed' in Hárászti's opinion, became more receptive to hitherto ignored dissident voices when the materialism underpinning institutionalised 'bribery' dried up during the 1980s. More ominously, radical elements within the Party then added their voices to the clamour for fundamental reform.[23]

Czechoslovakia and the failure of 'socialism with a human face'

The establishment of a one-party regime in Czechoslovakia had been the work essentially of the Czechoslovak Communists themselves. Before 1948, however, Klement Gottwald, the leader of the Party since 1929, had embraced a (semi-)parliamentary road to socialism, which was endorsed as formal policy in January 1947. In retrospect, Mlynář likened this strategy to Eurocommunism (Chapter 8). It was not at all unrealistic, given the support won by the Communists and their Social Democrat allies in the May 1946 elections to the National Assembly. Their victory was magnified by the ban on the Agrarian Party for alleged collaboration with the Nazis. The promulgation of the Truman Doctrine and the Marshall Plan, combined with the waning of the influence of Zhdanov, led to increasing pressure on Gottwald during 1947 to consolidate Communist power in the country. As Rudolf Slánský, who served as General-Secretary of the Party between 1945 and 1951, concluded, the Cominform resolution of September condemning the 'parliamentary cretinism' of the French and Italians was a warning that the Party had to take heed of. The heightened repression of all non-Communist organisations in the autumn betokened the end to coalition politics. The culmination came with the coup of February 1948, executed by the Party itself, with the aid of a communised police and the willing participation of many workers mobilised into their own militia.[24]

Thereafter, typically Stalinist policies, including a particularly vicious and extensive purge of all real or suspected 'national Communists', was introduced, to which Slánský fell victim. The beneficiaries of the imposition of Stalinism, as had been the case in the Soviet Union itself during the Great Transformation, were the workers. Hundreds of thousands of them gained promotion within the economic and state administration, with many finding themselves in positions for which they had no aptitude or training. Despite Malenkov's New Course, Czech Stalinism persisted long after 1953, testimony to its strong indigenous roots. The purge continued until April 1954 when Gustáv Husák, Party leader after 1968, was imprisoned for his alleged support of Slovak nationalism. Collectivisation was accelerated in 1955. The Party also erected what was claimed to be the largest statue of Stalin in the world in 1955. Even Khrushchev's Secret Speech had little immediate impact. The Party, led by Antonin Novotný after Gottwald's death in 1953, ruthlessly silenced all critics, and enthusiastically backed intervention in Hungary.[25]

Despite what Mlynář has described as Novotný's tardy and tentative introduction of Khrushchevite measures of 'liberalisation', including, in June 1960, short-lived measures of economic decentralisation reminiscent of the *Sovnarkhoz* reform (Chapter 7), problems became evident in the early 1960s. Over-investment in heavy industry, a rigid and re-centralised economic bureaucracy, and the collapse of the market for Czechoslovak exports in other Communist states as they developed their own industries, led to the abandonment of the Third Five-Year Plan in 1963. National income, industrial production and productivity fell. Economic stagnation, and the re-imposition of stringent controls over cultural life after 1964, reawakened criticisms of the existing order in the ranks of the intelligentsia and even of the Party. Economic reforms were introduced in January 1965. Largely the work of the economist Oto Šik, they echoed the Yugoslavian model: central control over the economy was reduced; a substantial role was allowed to market forces in determining the pattern, costs and prices of production; and material incentives were offered to those working in efficient enterprises. The results were mixed, as increased competition did help to raise production but the liberalisation of prices opened the door to a noticeable inflation. Moreover, they roused opposition from conservative bureaucrats, and from many workers, especially the unskilled, fearful that the reforms would threaten either their privileges, or their job security and earnings. A sharp rise in prices in 1967 led to their abrupt abandonment in September.[26]

Increasingly vociferous opposition from the cultural intelligentsia, the fulcrum of pressure for reform according to Vladimir Kusin, which had culminated in open criticism of Novotny's leadership and policies at the Fourth Congress of the Writers' Union in June, was quashed. Dissident writers were expelled from the Union and censorship was tightened. In October student protests in Prague against their sordid living conditions were savagely quelled. Yet the growing unpopularity of Novotný provided the swelling numbers of reform-minded Communists, influenced by the intellectuals' arguments for change, with the opportunity to replace him as First Secretary of the Party. At a meeting of the Central Committee in January 1968, Alexander Dubček, the moderate leader of the Slovak Party, became the new Party Secretary. At the end of March, Novotný also lost his position as state President when the National Assembly elected General Ludvik Svoboda to the post. In April, the old Stalinist Josef Lenart had to surrender the premiership to Oldřich Černík, who promptly formed a clearly reformist government. The Czechoslovakian Communists, arguably, had begun to engineer a successful revolution from above. They revived much of Šik's economic programme, offered some measure of intellectual freedom, and aspired to create what Dubček memorably was to define as 'socialism with a human face'. Kádárism, Czechoslovakian-style, seemed to be imminent and, as soon became evident, much more was to follow. In April, Dubček and the reformist centre of the Party, encouraged by a bolder liberal radical faction, issued the Action Programme, which went far beyond what Kádár himself had ever contemplated. Reaffirming the leading role of the Party, it also called for the restoration of a system of socialist democracy, which implied that non-Communist political organisations would be legalised. Censorship too was to be relaxed, and civil liberties, including freedom of speech, assembly and association, were to be restored. The secret police was to be curbed, with its power to suppress internal dissent or opposition reduced to virtually nil. The economy was to be democratised, with enterprises freed from central directives; workers' councils, to which management would be accountable, were to be elected from below; a market system was to be restored across most of the economy; and the emphasis on heavy industry was to be replaced gradually by greater attention to agriculture and the consumer and service sectors. Planning would remain, but its role was confined to that of mapping out the general contours of the future development of the economy. Mindful of the fate of the Hungarian Revolution, the reform Communists stressed that the country would stay part of the Warsaw Pact. Dubček and his centrist allies hoped that this assurance, and his repeated insistence that the Party remained sufficiently strong to control the degree and pace of the reform process, would reassure the Soviet leadership and so pre-empt intervention to crush what has become known as the Prague Spring.[27]

There is little reason to doubt that Dubcek's commitment to maintain the leading role of the Party was genuine, if with the benefit of hindsight naive and idealistic. In Mlynář's opinion, the objective of the Prague Spring was not the destruction of Communist power, root and branch, but to ensure that the Party became more responsible for its actions. Such accountability, he continued, explained the measures of autonomy granted to the trade unions and the judiciary. However, Soviet fears that the very logic of the reforms dictated the dismantling of the single-party state and the restoration of political democracy were well founded. Šik, himself in the liberal-radical camp, later conceded that this indeed was the case, and a rapidly growing popular movement in favour of change pressed for genuine democratisation. As early as 23 March, Brezhnev and the Communist leaders in Bulgaria, the GDR, Hungary and Poland had warned Dubček to this effect at a meeting held in Dresden. The abolition of censorship in June added to their fears. It permitted the publication of the '2000 Words Manifesto'. Issued on 27 June by the liberal radicals to counter conservative criticisms, it called on both Communists and ordinary workers to organise popular demonstrations, and strikes if necessary, in support of the reform process, and to prepare to resist any intervention designed to thwart it. The Manifesto precipitated a series of frantic negotiations between the Czechoslovakian Party and its Warsaw Pact counterparts in July and August, when Dubček fruitlessly sought to convince the latter that the reforms were not escalating beyond his control. Goaded on by Gomułka and Ulbricht in particular, alarmed that the successful creation of 'socialism with a human face' in Czechoslovakia would incite mass movements for change in Poland and the GDR, a majority in the Soviet Politburo finally voted for military intervention to crush the Prague Spring. On 21 August the Red Army and other Warsaw Pact forces (not the Romanians) rolled into Czechoslovakia, where they met a phalanx of largely passive resistance.

The invasion was justified by what is known as the Brezhnev Doctrine. Published in *Pravda* on 26 September under the title of 'Sovereignty and the International Duties of Socialist Countries', it proclaimed that it was the duty of the Soviet Union and its allies to intervene to protect socialism, wherever it was threatened. Of course, the Soviet Union arrogated to itself the right to decide when such a threat was present! What underlay this doctrine was the concern that the Czechoslovakian Party was on the verge of surrendering what had become the shibboleth of Communism since Lenin's day, its monopoly of political power. Moreover, if it did so and became but one party competing in a pluralist political system, its pledge to remain in the Warsaw Pact would be rendered worthless. National paths to socialism in East Europe were not ruled out entirely, but only those acceptable to Moscow would be tolerated.[28]

Černík, Dubček and others were arrested and taken to Moscow, where at a series of meetings in the Kremlin between 23 and 26 August the Moscow Protocols were imposed upon them. They were forced to accept the reintroduction of censorship, and to ban all non-Communist organisations. The Prague Spring had turned to winter, and the prospects for a more democratic and national path to socialism were stymied. Within a year, the Party had been thoroughly purged of all reformers, though on this occasion there were no executions. The same fate befell the state bureaucracy, the army, the unions, the media and the various associations of the intelligentsia. All suspected of harbouring sympathy for the reform process were dismissed. Once the reformers had been removed, the time seemed to be ripe for the 'Kadarisation' of Czechoslovakia, with Gustáv Husák, who had supplanted Dubček as Party leader in April 1969, in the role of Kádár. The Soviet leadership itself seemed to favour such a 'solution'. However, the outcome was quite different, with the Husák regime conducting a policy of consistent repression, not conciliation. The Morlocks, the surviving Stalinists, had their day after all. Opposition did revive, centred around the human rights group Charter 77. Composed of a few hundred dissident intellectuals, it had little noticeable influence over a demoralised and disenchanted populace. In a statement issued to mark the seventeenth anniversary of the 1968 invasion it painted a depressing picture of the consequences of the rigid and bureaucratic Communism presided over by Husák. An era of economic and techno-logical stagnation similar to that in the Soviet Union had overtaken the country. Corruption was pervasive at all levels of society. A cowed and sullen population had sunk into a political torpor and retreated into its own private consumer world, unwilling to risk discussing any political matters lest this invite denunciation. It worked as little as possible, in order to save its energies to improve its own material position by any means available to it. The only glimmer of hope came from the Soviet Union itself, where the dyed-in-the-wool conservative leadership that had extinguished the Prague Spring at last had given way to a new, potentially more progressive regime under Mikhail Gorbachev. It ended on a note of bitter irony, however, with complaints that Gorbachev's own views were subject to censorship in Czechoslovakia. Nothing was to change until the autumn of 1989.

The Polish vortex

The possibility of a Polish road to socialism in the years following 1945, most often associated with Władysław Gomułka, Secretary of the Polish Workers' Party (PPR), swiftly fell by the wayside when he too was tarred with the brush of Titoism. A Polish road, however, would not necessarily have been a liberal one. Gomułka was opposed to the blanket imposition of the Soviet model on Poland, but was no democrat. He was ever ready to use slander, intimidation and naked violence against all non-Communist opposition, first the popular Peasants' Party, and then the Socialist Party, even before the iron heel of Stalinism descended upon Poland. At the same time, he had begun to criticise the existing cooper-ative and private sectors of the Polish economy from April 1947, and urge the expansion of the state sector, with little prompting from Moscow. Nevertheless, the path that Gomułka had chosen to follow was not tant-amount to Stalinism. He was cautious not to attack the Catholic Church, nor to promote the forced collectivisation of the countryside, as the Cominform demanded, nor to advocate crash industrialisation. More pos-itively, by 1948 the Polish economy had experienced an astonishing recov-ery from the ravages of the war: many devastated towns had been rebuilt; real wages and the standard of living were rising; and industrialisation was beginning to ease poverty in the countryside by absorbing the surplus rural population. These marked economic successes have led a number of commentators, such as Neal Ascherson, to suggest that despite the unpopularity of Gomułka's repressive policies real prospects had existed of creating an independent Communist regime with roots in Polish society. The dismissal of Gomułka in September 1948, followed in December by the elevation of the hard-line Bolesław Bierut to head the newly formed PUWP, meant that this possibility was never fully tested.[29]

A half-hearted variant of Stalinism, according to, the dissident Polish economist W. Brus, was now imposed on the country. All non-Communists, especially the old Socialists and the so-called national Communists, were removed from positions of power in the Party, state and economic apparatus, as well as the trade unions, and replaced by largely unqualified and incompetent Party hacks. Yet Stalinism in Poland proved to be mercifully less murderous than elsewhere in East Europe. Few were executed, with even Gomułka himself surviving in prison. Economically, heavy industry was developed, to the neglect of consumer industries and the standard of living of the people; some attempts were made to collectivise agriculture, but almost 80 per cent of the land was left in private hands; and Poland's resources were exploited for the benefit of the Soviet Union. Unsurprisingly, traditional Polish animosity towards domination by Russia re-emerged and was exacerbated by the regime's attempts to suppress national traditions and institutions, especially the Church, in a misconceived attempt to nurture a new loyalty to the Soviet Union. The appointment of Konstantin Rokossowski, a Soviet Marshal of Polish descent, as defence minister and head of the Polish army, merely raised nationalist antipathy to new heights. The Poles' resentment at the Bierut circle was fostered by its failure to adhere to the spirit of the Malenkov's New Course. Few concessions, economic or cultural, were forthcoming, bar moderately higher prices paid to the peasants for their produce. The result was that discontent simmered just below the surface in the three years after Stalin's death. It was sparked into life, as in Hungary, by Khrushchev's assault on Stalin at the Twentieth Party Congress. Numerous Polish Communists, especially after Bierut's death on 12 March, began to demand the dismantling of Stalinism.

What these demands would have amounted to proved to be academic as in June the Polish working class dramatically intervened – not for the last time. Strikes, nigh on riots, erupted in Poznan, at first in the Ciegelski engineering works, in protest against suddenly imposed price rises, increased work norms and, as Eduard Ochab, the new Party leader conceded, falling wages. More overt political grievances, articulated by dissident intellectuals, soon followed: against the Communist monopoly of power; against censorship and the absence of civic and religious freedoms; and against Polish subservience to the Soviet Union. While the Polish police and army were mobilised to put down strikes in Poznań, with an estimated 53 dead and over 300 wounded, and so remove any pretext for Soviet intervention, the unrest encouraged the growing reformist current in the Party to insist that major changes were necessary to prevent their recurrence. The Seventh Plenary Session of the CC of the PUWP, held between 18 and 28 July, resolved that investment in vast and frequently incompleted industrial projects was to be reduced; wages were to be increased, by 30 per cent on average; additional resources were to be channelled to the countryside to raise agricultural production; and more power was to be devolved to the level of the factories and plants, where workers' councils were to have the right to participate in management decisions. It also called for the promotion of Gomułka, rehabilitated in April, to the leading ranks of the Party.[30]

The Polish Stalinists, the Natolin faction, bitterly opposed these reforms and throughout the late summer and early autumn lobbied for Soviet support to reverse them. The dénouement came at the Eighth Plenary Session of the CC, which convened on 19 October. Having put Soviet forces on alert, Khrushchev himself flew uninvited to Warsaw, to warn the CC against electing Gomułka to the leadership of the PUWP. Faced with the intransigence of the majority of the Party, the readiness of the workers, substantial sections of the army and even the security forces to resist any military intervention by the Red Army, and the rapidly esca-lating threat to Communist power in Hungary, Khrushchev backed down and accepted Gomułka and the Polish reform programme. He was reas-sured by Gomułka's promise to keep Poland in the Warsaw Pact, and, as crucial in light of the subsequent fate of the Prague Spring, by his com-mitment to preserve the Party's monopoly of power, which would enable it to control the process of change.[31] To the bitter disappointment of many Poles, Gomułka's victory did not usher in a new era of democratic socialism, or even a Polish road to socialism markedly independent of that in the Soviet Union. The promises that he had made at the Eighth Plenum came to naught in the next fourteen years. Moves towards eco-nomic decentralisation and the creation of workers' councils foundered in face of the vested interests of the bureaucrats in the central economic ministries, and in the factories. In addition, many Communists also feared decentralisation. It would entail the introduction of a substantial measure of market discipline, which would necessitate a relaxation of price controls and the closure of inefficient and unprofitable factories, and so precipitate mass unrest similar to that in Poznań from an already poor working class. The prospects of a cultural or political 'thaw' also came to nothing. Strict censorship was restored, with *Po Prostu* (Speaking Frankly), the leading mouthpiece of critical intellectuals, closed down as early as October 1957. Repression mounted during the 1960s. For example, in 1966 Jacek Kuroń and Karol Modzelewski were imprisoned for three years for circulating their 'Open Letter', which had attacked bureaucratic abuses. The Catholic Church fared no better, with religious education banned in state schools in January 1961; Church schools subject to close control or even shut down; and permits to build new churches refused. The Party itself degenerated markedly. Its desire to attract members regardless of their qualities led to an influx of out and out careerists whose naked and corrupt misuse of their power led to the split between the Party and society that had been temporarily healed by the 'Polish October' growing ever wider again.[32]

Repression escalated in 1968, in response to student demonstrations against the closure of Adam Mickiewicz's famous play *Dziady* (Grandfathers), lest its anti-Russian sentiments cause offence to the Soviet Union. Demonstrations continued from January until April, which were met with force. On 11 March the police, with the support of some Warsaw workers, savagely attacked students protesting on the streets of the capital. Intellectual opposition was broken, and lay largely dormant for the best part of a decade. The regime also faced challenges from hard-line conservatives, the Partisans led by the minister of the interior, Mieczysław Moczar. A nationalist (blatantly anti-Semitic), authoritarian, and rather puritanical faction, it attacked the materialist self-seeking prevalent within the Party in an attempt to wrest power from Gomułka. Despite its failure, its critique of the corruption endemic in the Party struck a widespread chord and, in combination with Gomułka's reliance on Soviet support for his survival, destroyed the little that was left of his reputation as the champion of Polish interests. With Moczar's removal in November the Technocratic faction, headed by Eduard Gierek, emerged as the leading current in the Party. It put forward an ambitious programme of economic renewal, in an attempt to deflect criticisms of the regime and so stabilise Party rule. Investment in new growth industries was to be increased substantially, with much of the necessary capital and technology to be imported from the West. Enterprises that succeeded in raising productivity were to be rewarded, with higher wages and bonuses for management and workers alike. The problem was that those employed in inefficient factories would not benefit, with their pay and standard of living frozen at best and their job security jeopardised at worst. Agriculture, especially the predominant private sector, was largely ignored, which threatened to compound complaints about the shortage of food, especially of meat.[33]

The lopsided nature of the Technocrats' programme made itself felt in December 1970 when Gomułka imposed substantial increases in food prices. In themselves, such increases were quite logical, as they would help to balance the demand for and supply of food; narrow the gap between the costs of production and prices actually paid; and so reduce the large and growing state subsidies. Logic notwithstanding, the events in Poznan 14 years earlier suggested that opposition by the workers could be anticipated, opposition made even more likely by Gomułka's scant regard for their sensitivities by declaring the increases 13 days before Christmas. Riots erupted in Gdańsk and the other Baltic ports, as well as in Lódz, which the police put down with much bloodshed. In Gdańsk itself 48 were killed and 1165 wounded. As the threat of a national strike that would paralyse the country mounted, the ailing Gomułka, who had suffered a stroke on 18 December, was held responsible for the carnage. He was replaced as First Secretary of the Party by Gierek on 20 December. The Polish workers had won a notable victory, especially when Gierek was forced to rescind the price increases early in 1971.[34]

As the Gierek era began, so it continued. Rather than implementing any measure of political liberalisation, attacking the pervasive corruption in the ranks of the bureaucracy and Party, and reforming the economic system, by promoting decentralisation and the participation of the workers in the management of their enterprises, his strategy remained quintessentially Technocratic. He sought to buy off the working class with a Polish form of 'goulash Communism', based on a dash for rapid economic growth. He hoped that the resulting prosperity, in particular the production of more consumer goods, and wage increases, would breathe new life into Party rule. The means chosen were to borrow ever vaster sums from abroad, to finance the imports of up-to-date Western technology required to modernise Polish industry. In the early years, between 1971 and 1974, the results were encouraging, with Poland becoming one of the three fastest growing economies in the world in 1973. Industrial production increased by 72 per cent; agriculture by 22 per cent, despite the continuing inefficiency of the small collective sector, which received

80 per cent of the investment in the countryside; but wages soared out of control. These achievements notwithstanding, housing and consumer goods were still in short supply. Then, in the second half of the 1970s, boom turned to bust. In June 1976, after a series of poor harvests, the government increased food prices by 60 per cent, to reduce demand. Strikes spread from Radom to other cities and forced the government to retreat hastily lest it face riots on the scale of 1970, and to use its dwindling foreign currency reserves to import food. By the end of the decade the whole economy was in decline as industrial output fell too. A combination of economic mismanagement, including misplaced investment in gigantic, unproductive or abortive projects, and the global economic consequences of the 1973 Arab–Israeli war (a fourfold rise in oil prices, a growth in interest rates from 6 to 20 per cent, and the consequent recession in the West) caused Gierek's strategy to become massively unstuck. Poland no longer could export enough to cover the costs of servicing its foreign debt – 27 billion dollars by 1980. Equally, it could not afford to import the spare parts and materials required to keep its new industries running at full capacity.[35]

The bulk of the population was more unprepared than ever to accept Party-dictated measures of austerity to resolve the crisis. Profoundly alienated from a shamelessly corrupt regime, more and more workers criticised its economic incompetence. Their opposition now transcended simple economics. They also bitterly attacked the 'Red bourgeoisie', as it was pejoratively dubbed, enterprise management, the official trade unions and the Party itself, which clung to its privileges. Their politicisation was reinforced by their renewed links with the dissident intellectuals, who on Kuroń's initiative had set up the Workers' Defence Committee (KOR) to defend workers' imprisoned for their participation in strike action in 1976. More ominously, opposition had extended to embrace students, peasants, and the Church, which ever more openly criticised the regime after the election of Karol Wojtyła, bishop of Kraków, as Pope in October 1978. Many rank and-file Communists, especially those employed in the factories and plants, sided with their fellow workers and urged a renewal (*odnowa*) within the Party itself, to make its officials subject to open and democratic election, before it lost any vestigial influence it had over the working class. Their exhortations were in vain, as the Eighth Party Congress, in February 1980, ignored their pleas.[36]

The discontent pervading Polish society erupted in the summer of 1980. The doubling of meat prices on 1 July provoked strikes across the country. On 14 August the Lenin Shipyard in Gdańsk joined in to secure the reinstatement of Anna Walentynowicz, recently sacked for her efforts to organise opposition to the management. Other factories in Gdańsk and Szczeczin followed suit, although the workers remained in their factories to avoid being shot on the streets as had happened in 1970. An inter-factory strike committee, the embryo of the independent trade union Solidarity (*Solidarność*), was formed under the leadership of Lech Wałęsa, a union activist who had been imprisoned in the 1970s. Faced with what had become a general strike, Gierek appointed Mieczysław Jagielski as deputy premier. He was despatched to negotiate with Wałęsa over the 21-Point Programme promulgated by the inter-factory committee on 23 August, after consultation with the intellectuals in KOR. The Programme contained a number of economic and welfare demands, such as basic wage increases, the indexation of pay to inflation, no work on Saturdays, and improved pensions. It also insisted that the privileges enjoyed by the Party-state bureaucracy be curtailed, and all those sacked for defending workers' rights be re-employed. Its political points were far more problematic as far as the regime was concerned: the release of all political prisoners; freedom of speech and publication and access to the media for all, including the Catholic Church; and, most contentious of all, the right to strike and the creation of free trade unions, which the workers saw as vital to ensure the Party did not renege on its other promises once the immediate crisis was over. A compromise was reached on 31 August when the Gdańsk Agreement was signed, in which many of the 21 Points were conceded by the government. The committee itself, mindful of the sad fate of the Prague Spring, agreed to recognise the leading role of the Party, a position reaffirmed in Solidarity's programme of February 1981. Yet official recognition of Solidarity as an independent union was delayed until 10 November. The reason for the delay lay in the fact that the Polish Communists first needed to gain approval for it from Moscow. The Brezhnev regime had to be persuaded that the recognition of independent unions would not fundamentally threaten the Party's monopoly of power.[37]

A *modus vivendi* appeared to have been established. It was symbolised by the elevation of General Wojciech Jaruzelski to the Premiership on 9 February 1981. Mieczysław Rakowski, who veered between being a liberal and a hard-line Communist, was given responsibility for maintaining harmonious relations with Solidarity, now over nine million strong. The new dawn proved ephemeral. The beating of activists attending a meeting in Bydgoszcz on 19 March, whose purpose was to organise the peasants into their own independent union, convinced the radical wing of Solidarity that no lasting gains could be achieved in compromise with the regime. Deepening economic decline added weight to its argument that much more fundamental economic and political liberalisation alone could resolve the malaise afflicting the country. Quite how it thought to realise these objectives without massive job losses, and without inviting Soviet intervention, was never adequately addressed. By the autumn, the radicals were in the ascendancy. At the First Congress of Solidarity, in September and October, the call for the immediate introduction of workers' control, democratic local elections and the honouring of free access to the media was endorsed. In effect, Solidarity was now contesting the leading role of the Party, and seeking a real share in power itself. After negotiations between Jaruzelski, who also became Party leader on 18 October, and Wałęsa failed, martial law was declared on 13 December. Solidarity was outlawed. Until Party rule could be restored a military Council of National Salvation took charge of the country. *Realpolitik* underlay Jaruzelski's action. The only alternative to martial law seemed to be Soviet intervention, which would have caused bloodshed likely to have been well beyond that seen in Hungary in 1956. In that sense, martial law might be deemed to be a success. Solidarity was forced underground; thousands of worker activists and intellectuals were arrested, though most were released in the next few years; but few Poles lost their lives. In comparison with Hungary after 1956 and Czechoslovakia after 1968 the process of 'normalisation' in Poland was mild indeed.[38]

In another sense, martial law failed dismally. Despite price increases in 1982, a largely rhetorical attempt to introduce economic decentralisation, and a temporary spurt in growth, no lasting cure to Poland's economic plight was found. While Jaruzelski's own purposes are still hard to fathom, it is conceivable that he intended to introduce some form of Kádárism, perhaps even Gorbachevism, as Norman Davies suggested. In his speech imposing martial law he obliquely intimated that once order and discipline had been restored, and the 'extremists' in Solidarity threatening the safety of the country had been curbed, reforms to remove the ills of the old corrupt order would recommence. This was not to be the case. In part, the deep-rooted economic crisis, with foreign debt spiralling out of control as a result of Western sanctions in protest against military rule, precluded it. So too did the refusal of most of the population to cooperate with the regime, which, as Kuroń astutely observed, underlay the need for martial law itself. The Party itself was in a process of rapid disintegration; the Church, ironically, lost much of its credibility by counselling against any radical confrontation with the new regime; and Solidarity survived repeated waves of persecution, albeit with much less committed support than before. And so Poland stumbled on through the 1980s, far from democratic but equally far from totally subdued, with Jaruzelski's government unwilling to implement the more Draconian measures of repression sought by the neo-Stalinist wing of the Party. The deadlock was finally broken by a series of 'roundtable talks' between Solidarity, the Church and the government in early 1989. Within months the Communist order that had survived some 40 years fell, swiftly to be followed by its counterparts elsewhere in East Europe.[39]

* * * *

It became commonplace after 1989 to dismiss the Communist experiment in East Europe as a total disaster. Such a conclusion ignores its achievements. It had overseen a quite remarkable recovery from the ravages of the Second World War. The countries of the region had also undergone varying levels of industrialisation and urbanisation, which had done much to resolve the problems of rural over-population that had plagued them before the Second World War. As Robert Daniels even-handedly concluded, 'the "command-administrative system", mistakenly identified with Marxism', was the foundation for 'the extraordinary period of growth that the Soviet and East European economies experienced from the end of the Second World War until the mid-1970s, even if that growth was conducted wastefully and was skewed toward the industrial base of military power'. Illiteracy, too, had been eliminated, which had opened the door to upward social mobility for many ordinary citizens, often, admittedly, into the burgeoning bureaucracies. Unemployment (as opposed to under-employment) did not exist; welfare provisions were universal; and housing, utilities and transport were provided at nominal cost. In total, these achievements provided the material roots of what numerous East European dissidents, such as the Czech playwright Václav Havel, and Kuroń, have isolated as a characteristic critical to the longevity of most Communist regimes in the region. Provided standards of living continued to rise, albeit gradually, the majority, it seems, was prepared to accept Communist power.[40] The problem was that the failure of the regimes to dismantle root and branch the command system erected in the late 1940s led them into an economic cul-de-sac in the 1980s. They lagged well behind their capitalist rivals; were heavily indebted to the West in most cases; and no longer were able to provide the quantity, or quality, of goods desired by their peoples. As living standards fell, so dissatisfaction mounted, which threatened the social compact whereby ordinary people, however grudgingly, had accepted the Communist monopoly of power. The solution might well have been the introduction of an effective variant of market socialism, not the halfway houses erected in Hungary and Yugoslavia. Vested bureaucratic interests certainly obstructed its implementation. In addition, even more reform-minded Communists had their reservations, fearful that economic pluralism would lead sooner or later to political pluralism, as Šik and Brus had implied, and so destroy the leading role of the Party.[41] Yet despite growing economic problems, and political and social tensions, there was little sign for most of the 1980s that Communism in East Europe would fall like a house of cards. At the time, most observers feared that a return to more direct forms of authoritarianism was most likely. Why this was not to be the case is the matter of the final, substantive chapter of this book.

PART V
Disintegration

Chapter 10: The Collapse of Communism in the Soviet Union and East Europe

The reforms introduced by Mikhail Gorbachev after he became General Secretary of the CPSU have been likened to the periodic attempts in Russian history at 'revolution from above', to modernise the country in order to enable it to catch up with and compete with the West. Peter I in the early eighteenth century, Sergei Witte, minister of finance at the end of the nineteenth century, and finally Joseph Stalin, as we saw in Chapter 6, had launched drives to provide the country with the industrial and resulting military power to defend itself. The reforms of the 'Tsar Liberator', Alexander II, after Russia's defeat in the Crimea in 1856, were more broad ranging. Serfdom was abolished, and elements of legal and political modernisation were introduced, with the aim of enabling a modified autocratic regime to survive. Gorbachev sought to refashion the Communist system in similar ways. Yet his own reforms were to spark off a wave of remarkably peaceful revolutions that swept away, first, almost all the Communist regimes of East Europe in 1989 and, two years later, Soviet Communism itself. At the beginning of the Gorbachev era virtually no one anticipated that Communism would fall in the foreseeable future. Even the surviving dissident minority in the Soviet Union was pessimistic about the possibilities of fundamental change. Nor was the collapse inevitable. In the mid-1980s, outside of Poland, there were no real signs of an imminent political crisis. Without Gorbachev, as Georgii Shakhnarazov, one of his academic advisers, pointed out, the prospects for radical reform would have been stillborn. If Chernenko had been succeeded by a 'hard-liner', such as Viktor Grishin or Grigorii Romanov, the leaders of the Moscow and Leningrad party organisations, it was perfectly conceivable that Communism would have survived for at least another generation. Boris Yeltsin, who emerged to become Gorbachev's most powerful political foe, agreed.

Initially, Gorbachev envisaged neither political liberalisation nor the restructuring (*perestroika*) of the economic system. His objective was to overcome the economic stagnation of the late Brezhnev era. How he planned to achieve this end was far less clear. Roy Medvedev observed that when he came to power he did not possess a master plan for change. Gorbachev himself conceded that his strategy had been 'essentially piecemeal'.[1] Even thereafter his policies were improvised, which is not surprising when one considers that there was no established precedent, or model, for the successful dismantling of a command economy, and the polity built upon it. His early initiatives closely resembled those of the late Iurii Andropov, whose patronage had secured his promotion to the Central Committee in November 1978. Campaigns to eliminate corruption and waste and to enforce discipline in the workplace, combined with substantial investment in the technological modernisation of existing industries still equipped with obsolete plant and equipment, were reckoned adequate to lead to an acceleration (*uskorenie*) in growth. Quite where the resources for the latter would come from was left unanswered. In fact, the anti-alcohol crusade launched by Gorbachev, intended to reduce the losses in productivity caused by drunkenness, cost the government billions of rubles in lost revenue as official sales of alcohol declined by 40 per cent. The sharp fall in earnings from oil exports as prices plunged in the 1980s added markedly to the state budget deficit, which tripled in 1986. Moreover, far from reforming the already over-centralised structures of the command economy, Gorbachev acted as though further centralisation would boost economic performance. In November 1985 he merged the five ministries most directly involved in agriculture into a new committee, the State Agro-Industrial Committee (*Gosagprom*), a 'super' ministry which was set the task of making both the production and processing of food more efficient. In practice, it proved to be yet another unwieldy and inefficient bureaucratic Leviathan. He also set up a completely new body, the State Quality Board (*Gospriemka*), with the responsibility of rejecting substandard goods produced in enterprises across the country. Its only lasting achievement was to alienate many ordinary workers, who suffered reductions in pay for turning out poor quality products.[2]

The evolution of glasnost' *and* perestroika

Surprisingly rapidly, Gorbachev came to the conclusion that such top–down measures were insufficient to revitalise the ailing Soviet economy. He also grasped that the Party-state bureaucracy itself could not be relied upon to carry out thorough-going reform. As he repeatedly complained in his *Memoirs*, the obstruction, or sheer passivity, of local officials, in both the Party and the economic apparatus, meant that the directives for reform issued from Moscow were often simply ignored.[3] During 1986 and the first months of 1987, he re-thought his whole strategy and proposed increasingly radical reforms. They first became evident in culture and politics. As early as February 1986 Gorbachev had called for more openness (*glasnost'*), to reveal the real problems facing the country. The catalyst for its implementation was the explosion at the Chernobyl nuclear power plant on 26 April 1986. The failure to admit at once the catastrophic extent of this disaster, and the ensuing international criticisms levelled against the Soviet government, prompted him to move swiftly to introduce it in practice.

Glasnost', and the still modest relaxation of censorship sanctioned at the Eighth Congress of the Writers' Union in June, encouraged many editors and journalists, most notably Vitalii Korotich of *Ogonëk* (Little Fire) and Egor Iakovlev of *Moscow News*, to bring into the public domain hitherto taboo subjects. Reports on the extent of crime, drug abuse and prostitution cast fresh light on the grimmer aspects of Soviet life. After Gorbachev's own intervention Sakharov was released from internal exile in Gor'kii in December 1986, followed by the freeing of other dissidents in February 1987. The short-lived 'thaw' in the arts licensed some 30 years earlier under Khrushchev took on a new dynamism. With Gorbachev's support, works proscribed under his predecessors finally saw the light of day. Significant landmarks included the publication of Anatolii Rybakov's *The Children of the Arbat* and the release of Tenghiz Abuladze's surrealist film *Repentance*. Both depicted Stalin as a paranoid and vindictive dictator who wrought vengeance on all his real, potential or imagined opponents. They provoked greater demands for the 'blank pages' in Soviet history, as Gorbachev had described them in February 1987, to be filled in. Against the resistance of the bulk of a historical profession impervious to Gorbachev's 'new thinking', he began, haltingly, to do so. He authorised the rehabilitation of prominent victims of the Great Terror, most notably Bukharin in February 1988. His rehabilitation served another purpose, as Roy Medvedev again perceived. Gorbachev now could justify the economic reforms that he was launching as a return to the rightful path of socialist construction, the NEP, whose greatest champion after Lenin's death had been Bukharin (Chapter 6). Gorbachev also declared, in terms reminiscent of Bukharin fifty years earlier, that Stalin's policies had created a form of military feudalism.

Despite continued opposition from ingrained forces of conservatism, *glasnost'* slowly became ever wider and deeper. Sections of Solzhenitsyn's *The Gulag Archipelago*, which depicted Lenin, not Stalin, as the architect of the camp system, were published in 1989 and so raised questions about Gorbachev's professed objective of returning the country to a democratic [*sic*] Leninist path. In July 'anti-Soviet agitation and propaganda' was removed as a criminal offence, while almost a year later, on 12 June 1990, the Supreme Soviet abolished censorship. Private ownership in the media too was legalised, which caused many journalists finally to break from the Party and set up their own papers. A fundamental civil liberty, freedom of expression, suppressed since Lenin's time, had been restored, though its extent initially was limited by the Party's continued control of most printing plants.[4]

In promoting *glasnost'* Gorbachev sought to stimulate criticism of the conservatism and corruption endemic within the system that he had inherited and so to muster support for his reforms, from the intellectuals, the media and, ultimately, ordinary citizens. Many of them, according to the reform Communist Aleksandr Tsipko, found the new freedoms unsettling. The purpose of democratisation (*demokratizatsiia*) within the Party and state bureaucracy, which he first mooted in a speech delivered in Krasnodar on 18 September 1986, was similar: to oust those forces resistant to change that had become entrenched under Brezhnev and promote his own reform-minded supporters. At the CC plenum on 27 January 1987, he underlined that *perestroika* was impossible without openness and democracy, and persuaded the CC to endorse admittedly still limited multi-candidate elections to posts within the Party and the soviets. In the elections to the local soviets held on 12 June, two or more candidates (all approved by the Party) stood in a very small number of constituencies. However, growing pressure for change from below, most notably from an intelligentsia that had rediscovered its voice after two decades of docility, combined with persistent bureaucratic obstruction of *perestroika*, drove Gorbachev further along the path of democratisation in the summer of 1988. The Nineteenth Conference of the CPSU (28 June to 1 July) was a significant turning point. Its most dramatic episode was Boris Yeltsin's assault on the second most powerful figure in the Party,

Egor Ligachev, which Soviet television broadcast to a largely stunned audience. Yeltsin castigated Ligachev, whose fingerprints were all over Nina Andreeva's infamous neo-Stalinist letter in defence of the old order published three months earlier in *Sovetskaia Rossiia* (Soviet Russia), for sabotaging the introduction of effective reform. Gorbachev himself advocated a radical restructuring of the existing system of government, to provide himself with a new lever of change. A Congress of People's Deputies was to be created, with two-thirds of its 2250 members elected democratically. As a sop to the old guard, the remaining third was to be nominated by organisations such as the Party and the trade unions under their control, which, as the future mayor of Leningrad, Anatoly Sobchak, bemoaned, simply led to the appointment of many talentless *apparatchiki* (apparatus men). The Congress itself would elect a new Supreme Soviet from its ranks, to act as the country's legislative body.[5]

On 26 March 1989, elections to the Congress took place. The sceptics were confounded as a number of them were genuinely competitive. Leading Communist officials suffered shattering defeats in a number of major cities, including Moscow (where the recently demoted Yeltsin was victorious), Leningrad and Kiev. A small step towards political pluralism had been made, despite the fact that almost nine-tenths of those elected to the Congress were Communists. Many, however, were not pawns of the old guard, but well-educated professionals who had joined the Party simply to ensure their advancement was not blocked. While not reactionary, most did not embrace the proposals for rapid change urged by the more radical intelligentsia. Gorbachev, who had replaced the aged Andrei Gromyko as President of the Soviet Union on 1 October 1988, was re-elected to this position by the Congress on 25 May 1989. His failure to submit himself to election by a popular vote, which rudimentary Soviet opinion polls indicated that he would have won, proved to be a grave miscalculation and in the future was to undermine his legitimacy. Shortcomings apart, Gorbachev's objective was to create a new and separate power base for himself within a reformed state apparatus, so as to combat the opposition to *perestroika* from the *nomenklatura* that persisted from the Politburo and CC down to provincial level even after his expulsion of many old Brezhnevites. Belatedly, he had paid heed to the gloomy prognosis of Aleksandr Yakovlev, his chief ideological ally, who had warned that the leading circles in the Party would prove resistant to restructuring. In thrall to the economic and military bureaucracies, they would remain a tool of reaction rather than reform.[6]

In 1987 Gorbachev also publicly recognised that 'acceleration' was little more than a stopgap, and quite inadequate to overcome economic stagnation. *Perestroika*, broadly the introduction of elements of the market system, including prices that reflected production costs, profit, etc., would be required. Following the law of 1 May which had legalised, within narrow confines, individual family businesses, he persuaded the CC plenum on 25–6 June to embrace a more fundamental programme of economic reform. Central to it was a new Law on State Enterprises, to come into effect on 1 January 1988. Its purpose was to begin the dismantling of the Stalinist command economy and, cautiously, introduce an increasing degree of marketisation. Building on ideas previously proposed by economists such as Liberman (Chapter 7), this Law decreed that by January 1989 state enterprises were to become self-managing. They were to be freed from centrally imposed targets and take their own decisions on what and how much to produce. They also were to become self-financing, bearing responsibility for their own labour, material and capital costs. Errors of judgement, or sheer inefficiency, were to lead to bankruptcy and closure, while enterprise management was given the right to dispose of any profits earned. Plausible as these proposals seemed, practice proved to be rather different. To ensure the targets for the Twelfth Five-Year Plan were met, the various economic ministries continued to issue orders to the enterprises under their control, which absorbed up to 90 per cent of their productive potential and thus left little scope for autonomous decision-making. Loss-making enterprises continued to be subsidised, to prevent unemployment rising sharply, and over-manning remained endemic. Prices too were not increased to reflect the actual costs of production, as the anticipated rises – of 200 to 300 per cent in many cases – inevitably would be highly unpopular. The difference was made up by the state, which devoted an estimated 12 per cent of its budget to price support in 1987. Little changed, as most commentators have pointed out. The command system just operated in an altered guise, while the over-staffed ministerial bureaucracy, which was to have been cut by one-third, survived essentially intact.[7]

Other reforms soon followed. On 27 May 1988, the Law on Cooperation in the USSR broadened the scope of private enterprise by allowing the formation of cooperatives to provide a range of goods and services. They grew to encompass 4.5 million in 1991, with another 4.5 million employed in individual family businesses. Yet they did not prove to be as successful as Gorbachev had hoped. Most were concentrated in the construction and service sectors and thus produced far too few of the consumer goods in short supply. Moreover, they were burdened by a plethora of state controls, for example, on the prices that they could charge and the hiring of additional labour, and were subject to punitive levels of taxation. Nor were they popular. Many ordinary citizens, 50 per cent according to an opinion poll in November 1989, perceived them to be at best profiteers, little different from black marketeers. Their operations also were subject to harassment from local Party organisations and the economic apparatus, which feared the potential competition that they posed.[8]

Growing food shortages made reforms in agriculture equally imperative. Demand for heavily subsidised and hence under-priced and still scarce produce far exceeded its supply, which resulted in the state having to use its fast dwindling hard currency reserves to import grain. Again, Gorbachev's initial response to this problem was limited, and did not fundamentally contest the principle of collective agriculture. He urged the provision of better storage, transport and processing facilities, to little effect. The continuing shortage of labour in the countryside meant that a significant portion of the harvest still rotted in the fields. Minor incentives, such as allowing the collectives to sell freely whatever they produced in excess of their quotas, had little impact either. Gosagprom, his own creation, accomplished nothing, bar the continued wasteful employment of 2 million state officials until its abolition in March 1989. He also extended across the country the collective contract system that he had pioneered when he had been First Secretary of the Stavropol region in the 1970s. Small groups of peasants (even families) within the collective farms were allowed to negotiate agreed targets with their farm managers and to retain a percentage of the profits made by achieving them. Little was forthcoming from this reform either, in part the result of bureaucratic inertia and opposition, in part because the decline in consumer goods available removed any incentive for the peasants to work harder to increase their income.

As the problem of food supply worsened, on 12 October 1988 Gorbachev broached the idea of the privatisation of agriculture, a policy recently introduced with some success by the Communist regime of Deng Xiaoping in China; 50-year leases of land were to be introduced, to stimulate the development of peasant family farming. Further incentives were given to independent farmers to increase the supply of food: for instance, produce from enlarged individual plots now could be sold freely, with virtually no restrictions. The logic of this approach pointed in the direction of the root-and-branch decollectivisation of agriculture, and the restoration of private property in the countryside. Yet this was not to be the case. Legislation introduced in February 1990 permitted peasants to hold land during their lifetimes and pass it on to their children, but not to sell it, nor to work it with hired labour. Moreover, little thought was given to providing peasant families with the equipment, finance and marketing infrastructure vital to the successful creation of individual peasant farming. A rearguard action was also mounted by the managers of the collectives, who frequently allocated land distant from all amenities and services to those seeking to farm independently. They found allies among the local Party bosses, and those leaders such as Ligachev, who viewed privatisation in any shape or form as antipathetic to the whole Soviet project. The added irony was that relatively few peasants were themselves eager to exchange the basic security, meagre as it was, provided by the collective or state farms (pensions, health insurance, minimum income guarantees) for the uncertainties of an unfamiliar market system. Even after the collapse of the Soviet Union, when private farming was encouraged wholeheartedly, the bulk of the peasantry displayed a singular reluctance to embrace it. Six decades of collectivisation had extirpated whatever entrepreneurial spirit had once existed in the countryside.[9]

The crisis of perestroika

The halting and partial nature of *perestroika* had disrupted the Stalinist economic system, but far from completely dismantled it and replaced it with effective market mechanisms. Perversely, attempts at economic reform had compounded the problem of stagnation. In 1989, production, so the Soviet economist Girsh Khanin calculated, fell by 4.5 per cent, while Soviet consumers experienced growing shortages. Tea, sausage (barely edible, with cats reputedly turning their noses up at it), sugar and other basic commodities were rationed or simply not available. The precipitous decline in revenues from oil and other raw materials in the late 1980s ruled out their import from abroad, particularly when a serious trade deficit also overtook the country in 1989. Proposals to resolve the ever worsening economic crisis, which became catastrophic during 1990 according to the economist and architect of *perestroika* Abel Aganbegyan, by a swift and thorough transition to the market system ultimately were rejected by Gorbachev. Whether the 'Five Hundred Days Plan' for such a transition drawn up by Stanislav Shatalin in the late summer of 1990 would have killed or cured the patient is unknown (arguably the former), as his advocacy of economic 'shock therapy' foundered in face of Gorbachev's own indecisiveness. At the root of his dithering were his fears: of widespread resistance to rapid change, not just from the Party-state bureaucracy, the KGB and the military, but also from a far from reactionary Congress of People's Deputies; of the prospect of mass unemployment, in the tens of millions according to some prognoses, if rapid marketisation allowed unsuccessful factories to go bankrupt; and of galloping inflation, and mass unrest, if state subsidies on prices ended. He later defended his rejection of Shatalin's plan on the grounds that by devolving economic sovereignty to the various Republics it had threatened the political integrity of the Soviet Union, and would have left the federal government bereft of tax-raising powers. With *perestroika* grinding to a halt, production declining, the Soviet people facing increasingly empty shelves, and the state a growing budget deficit, Gorbachev merely tinkered with the economy. He raised the prices of luxury goods by 40 per cent in November 1990; and 50 and 100 ruble notes were removed from circulation in January 1991, in a feeble attempt to reduce the huge surplus of money in circulation, the so-called 'monetary overhang', which was a potential source of hyper-inflation. At best, a 3 per cent reduction was achieved. During 1991 the economy plumbed new depths. GNP, it was estimated, plummeted by 12 per cent; consumption 17 per cent; investment 20 per cent; and prices rose by 103 per cent.[10]

The failure of *perestroika* provoked opposition from different strata of Soviet society, from Gorbachev's friends as well as his foes. Ironically, the political reforms that he had instituted had far outstripped his own intentions. The magnitude of the change that he had engineered was starkly revealed in a series of popular protests, both in the Russian Republic and, more ominously, in the non-Russian Republics. They heralded the transformation of his revolution from above into one from below. As early as July 1989, miners in Siberia had organised mass strikes in response to their worsening economic situation. They demanded that long-promised material improvements, comprising better working conditions, food in greater quantity and quality and higher pensions, be made good. They also advocated further economic and political reform, including workers' control of the mines and the direct election of the President, and attacked the holiest of Communist holies, the leading role of the Party. A series of concessions and compromises bought the miners off. Other workers, possibly the majority, were less in favour of reform. A national opinion poll carried out by Boris Grushin in 1989 suggested that they supported an Andropov-type solution to the country's economic malaise, that is, the restoration of discipline and order in the workplace and better central planning.

Differences notwithstanding, political mobilisation on a mass scale at the grass roots of Soviet society, arguably for the first time since the 1920s, continued to develop. On 4 and 25 February 1990, major demonstrations in support of further democratisation took place in Moscow and a number of other cities, with some corrupt Party bosses sacked in their wake. The intelligentsia, too, which had organised a multitude of informal associations, was showing increasing signs of restlessness. In general, it had rallied behind Gorbachev in his struggle against the Party-state bureaucracy that it saw, according to an opinion poll in *Literaturnaia Gazeta* (Literary Newpaper) in early 1989, as the major block on political and economic reform. During 1989 more and more intellectuals, frustrated by the resistance of the old bureaucrats and the faltering of *perestroika*, urged Gorbachev to introduce market and further democratic reforms swiftly. Others, strong in the middle and lower echelons of the Party, were more cautious, yet still acknowledged the need for further change, if at a moderate pace. The peasants, as we saw previously, for the most part were immured in the idiocy of collective rural life, to paraphrase Marx, at best indifferent, if not opposed to *perestroika*. Strong conservative forces, the foes of change, also survived. The military–industrial complex, the KGB, which Sakharov complained was sabotaging Gorbachev's efforts to release all dissidents, and the Party apparatus, afraid of the threats to their power and privileges (and to the unity of the Soviet Union) posed by *glasnost'* and *perestroika*, were ranged against him.[11]

Most menacingly of all, Gorbachev's regime was confronted by mounting nationalist challenges, from the Baltic to the Black Sea and beyond. Mass protest, resulting in nine deaths, had occurred in Kazakhstan when the First Secretary, Dinmukhamed Kunaev, a native Kazakh, had been replaced by Gennadii Kolbin, a Russian and a protégé of Gorbachev, in December 1986. Whether this was a spontaneous movement, or one inspired by Kunaev and his corrupt clique in a vain attempt to cling on to power, is still not settled. Yet it revealed the potential centrifugal force of minority nationalism. In August 1987, and a year later in 1988, significant numbers of Estonians, Latvians and Lithuanians took to the streets to protest against the infamous Nazi–Soviet Pact of August 1939, which had resulted in the forcible incorporation of their states into the Soviet Union in June 1940. By August 1989 these protests had evolved into mass movements, with up to one million involved, in favour of complete independence from the Soviet Union. In February 1988 the Christian Armenian majority in Nagorno-Karabakh, an enclave within the predominantly Muslim Azerbaijan Soviet Republic since the 1920s, mounted mass demonstrations in favour of merging with the Armenian Soviet Republic. Gorbachev himself refused their request, instead imposing on the region direct rule from Moscow. This solution satisfied neither the Azeris nor the Armenians, who entered into a bloody war in 1990, which continued long after the Soviet Union itself had disintegrated. On 9 April 1989, a demonstration in Tbilisi demanding Georgian autonomy was crushed brutally by Soviet forces under the command of General Igor Rodionov, with 19 left dead. Culpability in this instance lay not with Gorbachev, as Gorbachev consistently claimed, but with the Georgian Party itself, which had called in the military in the first place. It possibly had been encouraged to do so by Gorbachev's opponents in the Politburo centred around Ligachev, as Sobchak, who headed the Commission of Inquiry into the slaughter set up by the Congress of Deputies, implied.[12]

Gorbachev, and more surprisingly Eduard Shevardnadze, his foreign minister and former head of the Georgian Party, had underestimated greatly the power of nationalism that the genie of *glasnost'* and democratisation had let out of the bottle. The proposals that he began elaborating in 1990 to transform the Soviet Union from a 'pseudo-federal' (the phrase is Ronald Suny's) into a genuinely federal, or even confederal, state, a Union of Sovereign Soviet Republics, which would devolve considerable economic and political power to the Republics, were too little, too late. By then numerous Republics, in the Baltic, Belorussia and the Ukraine, were bent on independence after the victories of nationalist and ostensibly pro-democracy candidates in the elections in March 1990. In retrospect, this development presaged the eventual disintegration of the Soviet Union, especially when the Russian Republic, where Yeltsin was elected President on 29 May, also declared its sovereignty in June. Whether Gorbachev could have followed a different path is less certain. For instance, had he heeded Sakharov's advice and recognised the justice of Armenia's claim to Nagorno-Karabakh, the Azeris would have resisted, which would have left him little option but to use military force to enforce this decision. Had he recognised that the Baltic States were an exceptional case and granted them independence in the spring of 1990, as Jonathan Steele subsequently contended that he should, then arguably his conservative foes would have rallied to attempt to oust him. Whether such a coup would have succeeded is a matter of speculation, which we must leave aside, to return to the roots of the dramatic nationalist renaissance within the Soviet Union.[13]

Nationalism is a complex phenomenon, not least in the former Soviet Union. Hindsight suggests that a plethora of national resentments had festered beneath the surface before the later 1980s. Occasionally they flared up, as in August 1978 when mass demonstrations in defence of the Georgian language took place in Tbilisi. While overwhelmingly subterranean, they remained unresolved and unresolvable as long as control from Moscow remained tight. However, the reasons underlying the upsurge of nationalism varied from region to region. In the Central Asian Republics, for example, Gorbachev's allegation that the ruling elites which had consolidated themselves in the Brezhnev era played the nationalist card, and fomented ethnic conflict to mask their own corruption and protect their privileges, was not without foundation. Yet it would be churlish to deny that other real concerns underpinned nationalism there: the in-migration of Russians, which threatened to swamp the indigenous peoples, especially in Kazakhstan; the ecological costs of cotton production, which had led to the drying up of the Aral Sea; the under-development of the region, which continued to be largely a primary producer for Russian industry; and the failure of *perestroika* itself, and subsequent economic decline. In the Baltic States, nationalism was fuelled by memories of the inter-war period of independence destroyed by Soviet annexation; and by fear too that Russians soon would be the majority in Estonia and Latvia; it was also provoked by the environmental damage caused by reckless industrialisation, and stimulated by the hope that economic prosperity would be better achieved outside the decrepit Soviet system. There the native Communists had little choice but to rally behind popular demands for greater autonomy, and ultimately independence. Otherwise they would have been swept from power. Similar motives inspired the nationalists in Moldavia (now Moldova), who also were afraid that Russification would place their own language in danger of extinction. One might add that Gorbachev's preparedness in 1989 to allow the Communist states of East Europe to free themselves from Moscow's tutelage emboldened the minorities in the Soviet Union itself to put forward ever more radical demands.[14]

From crisis to coup

During 1990 and 1991 Gorbachev's revolution from above, to reform but not demolish Communism in the Soviet Union, appeared to be sinking fast. Widespread popular dissatisfaction with *perestroika*, which had caused a sharp and accelerating decline in living standards, led to the growing unpopularity of the Party, and of Gorbachev himself. He was jeered openly during the May Day parade in Moscow in 1990. The forces of conservatism also rallied to put pressure on Gorbachev to restore discipline and order in the country. Gorbachev wavered, trying to appease first one side, then the other. At first, he sought accommodation with those in favour of further democratisation. On 5 February, during a plenum of the CC, he called for a return to political pluralism, the end to the Party's monopoly of power and the legalisation of rival parties. The Congress of People's Deputies that met between 13 and 15 March repealed Article 6 of the 1977 (Brezhnev) Constitution, which had enshrined the leading role of the Party in law. He cajoled the Twenty-Eighth Congress of the CPSU to accept the Party's diminished status when it convened in the first half of July. As Sobchak concluded, the elimination of the leading role of the Party, at the heart of Soviet Communism since 1918 when opposition parties had been banned, portended the return of real power to the soviets, and the creation of a genuinely law-governed state.[15] Gorbachev, it seemed, was set on returning the party to the path of Social Democracy that Lenin had unequivocally rejected!

Later in the year, he changed course, to conciliate the conservatives who were still strong within the military–industrial complex, the Party and state bureaucracy, and the KGB. Why he did so is not perfectly clear. One possible reason was to prevent these forces, spearheaded by Colonels Viktor Alksnis and Nikolai Petrushenko, the leaders of the now radicalised conservative *Soiuz* (Union) coalition, from mounting a coup designed to preserve the unity of the Soviet Union challenged by the rising tide of nationalism. After rejecting the Shatalin plan favoured by the radicals, in December he promoted well-known enemies of reform to key positions in government: Gennadii Ianaev became Vice-President; Valentin Pavlov replaced the ailing Nikolai Ryzhkov as Prime Minister; and Boris Pugo, a notorious hard-liner, was appointed minister of the interior. Leading supporters of *perestroika*, Leonid Abalkin, Evgenii Primakov, Shevardnadze and Aleksandr Yakovlev, who feared that Gorbachev's personnel changes heralded a renewed political clamp-down, either resigned or were sacked. Their worst fears soon appeared to be confirmed, when on 13 January 1991 a nationalist demonstration in Vilnius was brutally repressed, with fifteen killed. This barbarous response in all probability was organised by the KGB, without either Gorbachev's foreknowledge or consent. Shevardnadze accepted this was the most likely case. Yet this does not exonerate Gorbachev, as his appeasement of the forces hostile to Lithuanian independence is likely to have encouraged them to act in a repressive manner. His failure, too, unequivocally to denounce the Vilnius tragedy further undermined his credibility amongst the democratic opposition, with Yeltsin demanding that he resign.[16]

In the spring of 1991 Gorbachev performed another *volte-face*, ditched the conservatives and tried to revitalise the process of reform. On 2 April he at last agreed to the freeing of prices, which did result in triple-digit inflation. Most significant of all, he made fundamental concessions to nationalist sentiment. On 23 April, at Novo-Ogarevo, his *dacha* (country house) outside Moscow, he committed himself to a new Union Treaty, which would restructure the state on confederal lines and devolve substantial economic and political, but not military, powers to the Republics. His concessions were in vain. While Yeltsin and the leaders of eight other Republics were prepared to accept his proposals, the Baltic Republics, Armenia, Georgia and Moldavia were not. Independence was their objective and they categorically refused to enter a new Union of Sovereign States. Critically, the Novo-Ogarevo agreement was the straw that broke the back of the conservatives. It threatened the dissolution of the Soviet state and, at the same time, the historical basis of their power and privileges, the centralised system of *nomenklatura*, which the newly empowered Republics inevitably would resist. Accordingly, on 19 August they mobilised to remove Gorbachev, the day before the new Union Treaty was to come into force, and proclaimed a state of emergency. Prominent among the leaders of the August coup were the men whom Gorbachev himself had recently promoted: Ianaev, Pavlov and Pugo.[17]

For manifold reasons the coup was botched. Poor organisation, including the failure to seize all means of communications, and to arrest Yeltsin, the obvious figurehead of opposition; loss of nerve; and even the drunkenness of some of its leaders, as Steele insinuated, certainly played their part. The refusal of Gorbachev, effectively under house arrest in the Crimea where he was on holiday, to accede to the conspirators' demands that he declare a state of emergency and hand power over to Ianaev, also contributed to their defeat. Most importantly, the major institutions to which the conspirators looked for support in completing the coup swiftly, the army and secret police, were hopelessly split. As Gorbachev pointed out, had General Evgenii Shaposhnikov, in charge of the air force, not disobeyed Defence Minister Dmitrii Iazov's orders, then the planes necessary to destroy the opposition gathered around the 'White House', the seat of the Russian Parliament elected in March 1990, would have taken off. Other generals, including V. Samsonov in Leningrad,

numerous junior officers, and rank-and-file soldiers, repelled at the
prospect of shooting unarmed civilians, were reported to have refused to
fire upon those (a minority) who demonstrated against the coup. Even
more surprisingly, the KGB in Leningrad denounced the whole business,
while it was rumoured that a KGB tip-off had allowed Yeltsin time to avoid
capture. For all the bravery of those who took to the streets in Moscow,
and of striking workers in Leningrad and the coalmines of Siberia,
popular resistance contributed but little to the defeat of the coup. The
majority, in Moscow and across Russia, ignored Yeltsin's call for a general
strike. Had the army, KGB and police been united and resolute in
support of the coup then the resistance that did muster would have
been suppressed, at the expense of much bloodshed.[18] All that the coup
succeeded in doing was to wreck the already fragile bases for a new
Confederation and accelerate the break-up of the Soviet Union (see
Appendix A).

The puzzling question is why key leaders in the military and KGB, as
well as middling officials in the Party-state bureaucracy, refused to rally
behind the coup. Boris Kagarlitsky, a consistent critic of Gorbachev for
his refusal to countenance a return to the revolutionary tradition of
workers' control, and others suggested that they had come to realise, in
a halting manner, that they could protect their own interests better by an
accommodation with Yeltsin and his allies, rather than with Ianaev and
his cronies. For instance, according to recent testimony emanating from
Russia, Vladimir Putin, formerly a KGB officer, and President since 2000,
brokered a deal between Sobchak and the Leningrad KGB in August
1991 whereby the reward for the latter's passivity would be security and
position in the new order. Moreover, many of the old enterprise managers already had taken advantage of the June 1990 law which permitted
state enterprises to convert into joint stock companies, to become their
de facto owners. State property thus was becoming transformed into private property, and the 'New Class' itself (its ranks reinforced by countless
criminals) into a Western-style capitalist class, although the capitalism
that it presided over was more of a Wild West, or East, variety. Yet they did
succeed in enriching themselves. An ex-KGB colonel observed in a BBC
TV *Panorama* interview, in the mid-1990s, that they were not alone. Their
confederates in the Party and secret police had availed themselves of 'the
old boys' network' to ensure that they too benefited materially.
Subsequent studies have lent much credence to this interpretation. Olga
Kryshtanovskaya and Stephen White concluded that as the Soviet Union
collapsed, the 'younger and less compromised' generation of the

nomenklatura had clung on to political and economic power by transforming itself into a new bourgeoisie. As the historian Edward Thompson once remarked, history is the record of unintended consequences. In Gorbachev's case, his ambitions to rejuvenate and humanise Soviet Communism had led, ironically, to a bourgeois revolution![19] Perhaps old Trotsky got a prediction or two right, back in the 1930s, as the reader of the manuscript deftly pointed out. Either the revolution moves on, or it degenerates back to capitalism. I am unsure whether Trotsky is the beacon for the future of a more democratic and better society, but to use a British football colloquial (and quite illiterate) expression, 'the boy did good' as a critic.

East Europe

Two years earlier East Europe had undergone a similar transformation, when a remarkable wave of predominantly non-violent political revolutions had swept the old Communist order away. The material context in which these revolutions took place was akin to that of the Soviet Union, primarily one of economic stagnation, as we saw in Chapter 9. The consequent decline in living standards no longer could be assuaged by using foreign loans to buy consumer goods from abroad. On the contrary, the need to repay previous loans demanded harsh austerity measures, which bore down heavily on the majority of ordinary citizens. That the corrupt ruling elites continued to live in relative luxury further alienated them, and also led growing numbers of reform-minded Communists to question the viability of the existing system. In these circumstances, the social compact whereby political freedom had been exchanged for a mess of pottage broke down. At last, as Gaspar Tamás, a Hungarian political philosopher and activist for democracy, recalled, dissident voices which outside Poland had long been isolated and unpopular found an increasing resonance at the grass roots of society in the late 1980s. In Poland, Solidarity, which had wilted under martial law, revived; in Czechoslovakia, Charter 77 began to garner popular support, as did a still amorphous movement in favour of democracy in Hungary; and elsewhere, even in the highly repressive GDR, small fragile organisations, seeking protection for the environment, promoting peace, and defending religious freedom, sprang up. What this opposition signified, as many commentators have pointed out, was the awakening of an independent civil society, one no longer prepared to accept one-party rule.[20]

However, growing popular discontent in itself is insufficient to account for the dramatic collapse of East European Communism. The critical, and necessary, factor was Gorbachev. He was the Dubček in Moscow long hoped for by dissidents and reformers, who was prepared to allow the Communist Parties of East Europe the freedom to construct socialism with a human face, although the final outcome far exceeded his desires and expectations. There is little doubt that *glasnost'* and *perestroika* in the Soviet Union had inspired those in East Europe seeking a fundamental restructuring of the old order. Gorbachev's own increasingly explicit hints that the Soviet army would not intervene to prevent change gave the reformers added confidence. In face of opposition from conservatives in the Politburo and the military he had renounced the Brezhnev Doctrine (Chapter 9) by the middle of 1988. That these were not empty words became clear in December 1988 when he announced troop withdrawals from Czechoslovakia, the GDR and Hungary. His own attitude towards East Europe became popularly known as 'the Sinatra doctrine'. The term was coined by Gennadii Gerasimov, Gorbachev's appointee as spokesperson for the Ministry of Foreign Affairs, when he pronounced that the countries of East Europe could now do it 'their way'. The reasons for Gorbachev's abandonment of the motif of Soviet policy since the late 1940s, to ensure control of East Europe, were twofold. Ideologically, he seemed genuinely to believe in polycentrism, the right of the states of the region to choose their own path to what he hoped would be a new, and more acceptable, form of socialism. More pragmatically, he reckoned that any Soviet military intervention would shatter the détente with the West that he had done much to revive and, in turn, preclude the possibility of reducing the heavy drain of resources to the Soviet military.[21]

The course of the tumultuous events in East Europe in 1989 and after are well known and are presented in summary form in Appendix B. What remains important is to ascertain precisely who or what precipitated them. In Poland pressure from below played a major part in the fall of the Communist order. Despite government repression, which had caused a decline in its numbers from 10 million to 2 million, the hardcore of Solidarity continued its attack on the regime throughout the 1980s. In the summer of 1988 it attracted growing support, after the Jaruzelski government imposed swingeing price increases on food and other consumer goods. In response to rapidly escalating protests, Jaruzelski sought the cooperation of Solidarity, or at least those within it prepared to cooperate with him, such as Adam Michnik and Wałęsa, to find a peaceful resolution to this new crisis. The outcome was a series of Round Table negotiations between February and April 1989, which resulted in the recognition of Solidarity, and an agreement to hold elections in which 35 per cent of the seats would be openly contested. However, Jaruzelski's attempt at conciliation had come far too late, and in the June elections the Party was routed. After a period of heated and tense debates in the Party, and in Solidarity itself, on 19 August Jaruzelski finally conceded the formation of a coalition government under Tadeusz Mazowiecki, one of Wałęsa's intellectual advisers. Within months the old order was thoroughly dismantled, including the command economy, when crash marketisation, or economic 'shock therapy' as it was called, was introduced by Leszek Balcerowicz, the finance minister, in January 1990.[22]

In Hungary, the transformation began, as it had in the Soviet Union, as an attempted revolution from above. It was triggered by reform Communists, supported by the cultural and technical intelligentsia, who conceded the bankruptcy of the existing economic and political system. The replacement of Kádár as leader of the Party by Karoly Grósz on 22 May 1988 was a partial victory for the reformists. Within nine months, Grósz, who resolutely had defended the leading role of the Party, in turn was removed, to be replaced by a much more radical leadership led by Imre Pozsgay. The transformation of Hungary into a pluralist democracy followed in the autumn of 1989, with the Party agreeing to free elections in September. In October it split into two, with the reformists founding the Hungarian Socialist Party. The old guard retained the title of the Hungarian Socialist Workers', but not Communist, Party. In the elections held in the spring of 1990, between them they mustered only 12 per cent of the vote. The Hungarian Democratic Forum won 42 per cent and under József Antall formed a coalition government with the Independent Smallholders, the new peasant party, and the Christian Democrats.[23]

One other act of the Pozsgay government was to have an unforeseen, yet dramatic impact. In early May 1989 it opened Hungary's borders with Austria. In the late summer thousands of East German citizens flooded into the country, perceiving it to be the exit route to the West, blocked since the construction of the Berlin Wall in 1961, which had cut off free passage from East to West Berlin. Roused by the sight of this exodus, and by a visit of Gorbachev himself to East Germany on 6 October, to commemorate the fortieth anniversary of the founding of the GDR, hundreds of thousands took to the streets in Leipzig on 9 October at the bequest of the New Forum, a dissident organisation formed from small religious and peace groups that had first sprung up in 1987. Erich

Honecker, the leader of the East German Communist Party, and his fellow conservatives, remained intractably opposed to any reforms, and demanded the shooting of the demonstrators. They were overruled by Egon Krenz, the head of the State Security forces, and a number of leading army officers. Gorbachev himself had cautioned against the use of force, and Soviet military advisers in Berlin had encouraged Krenz in his stand against it. The replacement of Honecker by Krenz was to no avail. Mass demonstrations escalated, with between 500,000 and a million on the streets of East Berlin on 4 November. On 8 November the Party threw in the towel, and a new (and short-lived) government led by one of the few East German reform Communists, Hans Modrow, was established within days. The gate in the Berlin Wall, that most palpable monument to Communist dictatorship, was flung open on 9 November.[24]

On 10 November, the Bulgarian Party read the runes. With the support of the army, and the consent of Moscow, Petŭr Mladenov, the leader of the small Bulgarian reformist faction, replaced the old Stalinist Todor Zhivkov as General Secretary. In December he agreed to end the Party's monopolisation of power and to hold democratic elections. In June 1990 the Bulgarian Socialist Party, the Communists under a different name, ultimately won a small majority (intimidation, it seems, contributed to its victory), while the Union of Democratic Forces, led by Zheliu Zhelev, won over a third of the seats in the new parliament. By the end of the year, popular protests, culminating in a general strike, forced the Socialist government from office and a new coalition government was formed.[25]

Communism in Czechoslovakia, where reaction had reigned since the defeat of the Prague Spring, was unable to weather swiftly growing pressure for radical change. On 17 November a mass demonstration in Prague, largely of students, was broken up with great brutality by the police. This action appears to have been deliberately carried out by the Czech secret police, with the assistance of the KGB, in order to discredit the old order and engineer its replacement with a reform Communist government under Mlynář, a fellow student of Gorbachev's in the law faculty of Moscow State University in the early 1950s. Their plan succeeded to an extent, as mass demonstrations continued, in the course of which Havel and his fellow dissidents formed an organisation known as Civic Forum. Faced with mounting and intransigent opposition, in which the hitherto passive working class played an increasingly prominent role, the Party capitulated on 7 December. A coalition government, with a bare majority of pro-democracy figures, was formed on 10 December.

In June 1990 elections were held in which the Communists were defeated, and Havel became President in July.[26]

So far, the Communist regimes of East Europe had fallen with astonishingly little violence and bloodshed. Romania was to prove one exception. The repression of demonstrations for democracy in Timisoara, when the security forces, the hated *Securitate*, shot dead 71 on the weekend of 16–17 December, sparked off mass protests in the capital, Bucharest. Nicolae Ceauşescu, the arch-reactionary Communist leader, and his wife Elena, refused to budge and ordered the mobilisation of the *Securitate*, and the army, to put them down by whatever means necessary. The army hesitated, as did a section of the *Securitate*. In face of continuing intransigence, and growing popular opposition (he was roundly heckled by the protesters in Bucharest when he appealed to them to go home on 21 December), long hidden opponents within the Party, headed by Ion Iliescu, army officers and even some *Securitate* leaders, mobilised to overthrow him. Arrested as they tried to flee the country, the Ceauşescus were shot on Christmas Day, an execution seen on television by a global audience.[27]

The final dominoes to fall were Yugoslavia and Albania. In the former the later 1980s witnessed the dramatic resurgence of ethnic nationalism, with many of the leaders of the Republican Communist Parties playing the nationalist card as they sought to cling on to power. By 1991 the country had all but disintegrated and, Slovenia apart, was wracked by brutal ethnic conflict in the following years. In Albania, which had remained intransigently Stalinist and isolated from Soviet influence since the early 1960s, the Party desperately resisted change and on numerous occasions during 1990 and early 1991 unleashed the security forces against those demonstrating for democracy, but to no avail. In the first genuinely free elections, held in March 1992, the Communists, who had reconstituted themselves as the Albanian Socialist Party, were overwhelmingly defeated and power passed into the hands of the Democratic Party of Albania.[28]

The latter cases apart, most of East Europe underwent what has been termed 'velvet revolutions', in which the Communist elites relinquished power surprisingly swiftly and peacefully. One plausible explanation for why this was so again is rooted in the concept of *nomenklatura* privatisation. Recognising that they could not retain their power and material privileges in the old manner, they surrendered the political dominance that they had long enjoyed. At the same time, they utilised their influence to ensure that they were the main beneficiaries of the marketisation that the new regimes promised to introduce. They deftly positioned themselves to appropriate the vast bulk of the state property that was privatised when the old command economies were dismantled. The old Party-state bureaucracy, in particular the economic managers, were the real victors and became the new economic masters in the new East Europe. What East Europe experienced after 1989 was bourgeois or capitalist revolutions, to varying degrees. That the consequences of these revolutions confounded the expectations of the vast majority of ordinary citizens for a better life is one of the issues to be addressed in the conclusion.

Conclusion

At first sight, European Communism has been an abject failure. There were no Communist revolutions in the advanced capitalist West. Those that did take place in backward Russia and East Europe did not create kingdoms of freedom, nor economic systems capable in the long run of outstripping capitalism. Khrushchev's assertion that 'we will bury you', that the Soviet Union would out-produce the capitalist West, was indeed hare-brained.[1] Yet the Communist project had other achievements to its name. Rudolf Bahro argued that it had succeeded against all odds, albeit at a horrifying human and ecological cost, in modernising the Soviet Union, which preserved its independence in a threatening imperialist world. Its victory over Nazi Germany in the Second World War is clear testimony to this argument.[2] Thereafter living conditions also improved, especially in the first half of the much maligned Brezhnev era, in Moscow, Leningrad, and the other major cities and federal capitals of the Soviet Union, although the provincial towns and the countryside lagged far behind. Its record in East Europe was not without its successes too. The Communist regimes established there after 1945 oversaw recovery from the ravages of the Second World War and, in some cases, considerable levels of industrialisation and urbanisation in what largely had been a backward region.

Less obviously, Communism unwittingly helped to consolidate liberal democratic capitalism. The threat posed by Nazism was broken primarily on the battlefields of the Soviet Union. Subsequently, the Cold War, and the vast military expenditure it engendered, was one of the sources of sustained capitalist economic recovery in the first two and half decades after 1945 ('the long boom'), and again in the 1980s. Finally, the

Communist challenge prompted the capitalist states of West Europe, if not the United States, to introduce extensive measures of welfare reform. Such reform not only did much, in Donald Sassoon's opinion, to 'civilise' capitalism. By increasing considerably the number of state employees as well as payments to the unemployed and poor, it also helped the capitalist world survive the sharp economic downturn of the late 1980s much better than it had the Great Crash of 1929.[3]

Moreover, the experience of the post-Communist regimes perplexed those who expected that free market capitalism would lead to economic prosperity and democracy. As Hobsbawm sardonically commented, '[t]he theories on which the neo-liberal theology was based, while elegant, had little relation to reality'.[4] The free market experiment in Russia and in the new states spawned by the former Soviet Union has proved to be economically disastrous for the majority of their peoples. New oligarchs emerged, mostly drawn from the old ruling elites and the hitherto concealed criminal underworld, who indulged in a shameless exercise in asset stripping to enrich themselves. Joseph Stiglitz, chief economist at the World Bank until 2000, concluded that in the 1990s the fall in gross domestic production in Russia was more than twice what it had been in the Second World War. Admittedly, a recovery took place in Russia after 1998, largely based on continuing high international prices for oil and gas, with growth of up to 7 per cent per year. Sadly, many Russian citizens have had no tangible benefits from this much acclaimed 'economic miracle', and an estimated 30 million remain in poverty. Elsewhere, in Moldova, the Ukraine, the Caucasus and Central Asia economic decline was even worse, and persists. The countries of East Europe experienced a similar fate, although at the beginning of the twenty-first century in some – Poland, Hungary, Slovakia and Slovenia, which abandoned economic shock therapy in favour of a more measured transition to the market system – production had climbed back to the levels of the 1980s. Again the victims of the often mad gallop to uncontrolled capitalism have been millions upon millions of ordinary people who lost their jobs, savings and the welfare provisions provided by Communism. Many are still unemployed and live as paupers, their hopes of a better post-Communist future dashed.[5]

Dire as these consequences have been, they must not blind us to the fact that European Communism in practice collapsed in ignominy. More curiously, its collapse witnessed a resurgence of interest in Marx, especially his understanding of how capitalism functions, in the most unexpected quarters. One New York financier was reported as stating that '[t]he longer I spend on Wall Street, the more convinced I am that Marx was right'.[6] In particular, Marx's uncannily prescient vision of how capitalism would develop, nationally and internationally, has been subject to renewed appreciation. Early in the third millennium there is no doubt that capitalism, as Marx predicted, has become thoroughly globalised. The prospect of a single world market is no longer a pipe-dream. Monopolisation too acquired a new, global dynamic in the 1990s. In the process, a tiny minority has acquired undreamt of wealth. In the advanced capitalist states, lower taxes for the rich and consequent welfare cuts have led to the growth of an impoverished and alienated underclass, most pronounced in the United States. In the Third World, poverty has remained endemic, as many countries have struggled to service the debts owed to the West. For example, the debt burden of the countries of sub-Saharan Africa rose fivefold between 1975 and 1995. Then the advanced First World, encompassing a quarter of the world's population, were in receipt of three-quarters of global income, however unequally distrib-uted, while the other three-quarters lived in poverty. Little has changed since.

Moreover, since the late 1990s the global triumph of capitalism has seemed less secure than it did at their beginning. In the spring of 1998 the president of the Sony Corporation, Norio Ohga, feared that in Japan, the much-touted exemplar of capitalism's dynamism in the second half of the twentieth century, the economy was 'on the verge of collapse'.[7] Should its economy fall into 'a deflationary spiral', the rest of the world would suffer, especially the 'tiger economies' of South-east Asia. George Soros, global speculator *par excellence*, has expressed similar fears. In the long run, he argued, uncontrolled capitalism is unsustainable. It is par-ticularly vulnerable to the instability of international financial markets, which, if not regulated by new global institutions, will cause it to come 'apart at the seams'.[8] One possible solution, proposed by the economist James Tobin, was a global tax on currency speculation, though quite how it would be enforced remains nebulous. The conservative British philoso-pher Roger Scruton similarly cautioned that 'the failure of socialism [sic] does not let capitalism off the hook'. The free market, functioning without any constraints (Scruton opines in favour of religious and moral constraints), will lead merely to economic and social disintegration.[9]

To date, these prophecies of doom have not come to pass. Global capitalism has survived. Even the sharp decline on the New York stock exchange in April 2000, which reawakened fears that a crash in the United States, the world's largest economy, would lead to a global depression similar to that of the 1930s, now appears to have been but a passing blip. By 2003 the United States again had become the powerhouse of global capitalism when its economic growth reached the dizzy heights of 6 per cent. But doubts persist. Many economists still question the permanence of economic recovery in the United States as its budget and balance of payments deficits, already in the hundreds of billions of dollars, mount daily. The costs of the war against Iraq in 2003, and of its continuing occupation, have added markedly to these deficits. The bills will have to be paid one day, and boom can swiftly turn to bust. Japan appears to have survived the worst of its economic doldrums, but growth has been halting at best. Much of the European Union, another powerhouse of capitalism since the 1960s, remains stagnant in 2005. With few exceptions the historically poor and wretched of the earth continue to wallow in backwardness and impoverishment, unlikely breeding-grounds for democracy. These are some of the reasons why it is premature to hail the triumph of liberal capitalism globally.

Recent academic work has echoed this sombre message. White concluded his study of Marx's thought with this observation:

> But in recent years capitalism has been on the march. It has made deep inroads in the Third World. Its development has been encouraged in the former socialist countries of the former Soviet Union and Eastern Europe. And in the West policies of privatization and deregulation have been carried out and more and more areas of national life have been modelled on market relations. ... Capitalism seems set to become the Universal economic system throughout the world, and to subordinate all spheres of human life to its circulation and reproduction. If it does so then one can expect that it will reach its point of culmination in the way that Marx believed it would.[10]

However, there is little sign that 'the spectre of Communism' that Marx once thought was hovering over Europe will return to haunt the world in the new millennium. After the destruction of the twin towers in New York on 11 September 2001, the most immediate threat to the capitalist West, especially the United States, apparently emanates from a fundamentalist terrorism, justified by a one-sided and extreme reading of Islamic thought. The carnage in London in July 2005 caused by suicide bombers lend weight to this conclusion. Yet protests against the rampant inequalities and environmental damage caused by the onward march of capitalism have resurfaced, even in the prosperous First World. 'Le monde n'est pas a vendre' (The world is not for sale), the slogan adopted by French critics of globalisation, and daubed on many a hillside in southern France, has caught the imagination of many. Whether these protests will intensify and spread is a moot point. What they confirm, as Michael Hardt and Antonio Negri contended in their recent book *Empire*, is that global capitalism in the twenty-first century remains challenged, if not just from the industrial proletariat as Marx had thought when he was writing in the nineteenth century. Precisely what the contribution of Marxism to these new challenges might be still has to be answered. However valuable his insights into the functioning of capitalism and the inequalities and injustices that it produces are, Marx, as we have seen, provided little practical guidance for the construction of a more egalitarian and democratic society. Moreover, as a nineteenth-century figure, he understandably had little direct to say about its ecological costs. It is futile, therefore, simply to seek salvation in his gospels, however much the few surviving keepers of that fundamentalist flame might protest. What the practice of those who claimed Marx as their spiritual fount also makes clear is what must be avoided, in particular Soviet-style Communism.

It is presumptuous to conclude that the collapse of Communism has signified the end of history and the triumph of a stable and secure, liberal capitalist new world order. Two months after '9/11' Fukuyama reiterated his belief that a combination of liberal democracy and free market capitalism was the only way forward for the world. He cautiously conceded that Islamic societies had proved to be one exception to his prognosis.[11] Other exceptions have emerged, most strikingly the growth of violent, even murderous, ethnic nationalisms, especially evident in former Yugoslavia during the 1990s, and in some of the successor states of the old Soviet Union. It is not the task of historians to predict, as history provides no blueprints for the future. Whether history offers any lessons is another, at times contested, question. Manfred Steger wisely concluded in the Epilogue to his recent study of Bernstein that the problem of 'real human suffering' has been far from resolved.[12] Indeed he could have added that suffering and inequality have grown in the last quarter-century. As long as they persist, so will the aspiration to construct the institutions that will help overcome it. Communism as practised is dead. The inspiration underlying it arguably survives.

Appendix A: The Disintegration of the Soviet Union

23 August 1987	Protest marches in Baltic Republics in favour of independence.
20 June 1988	Nationalist People's Front formed in Estonia.
August 1988	Nationalist demonstrations in Baltic Republics.
October 1988	Popular Fronts established in all Baltic Republics.
25 February 1989	Demonstration in Tbilisi protesting against annexation of Georgia in 1921.
9 April 1989	Nationalist demonstration in Tbilisi repressed brutally.
6 December 1989	Lithuanian Supreme Soviet abolishes leading role of Communist Party in republic; and permits opposition parties; similar reform in Latvia on 28 December.
20 December 1989	Lithuanian Communist Party declares its independence of CPSU, supports creation of independent and democratic Lithuania.
January 1990	Armenia–Azerbaijan civil war over Nagorno-Karabakh.
4 March 1990	Popular Fronts victorious in elections in Baltic States.
11 March 1990	Lithuania unilaterally declares its independence.
30 March 1990	Estonia proclaims sovereignty.
4 May 1990	Latvia proclaims sovereignty, and seeks independence.

12 June 1990	Russian Republic proclaims sovereignty.
9 February 1991	Referendum in Lithuania massively for independence.
3 March 1991	Similar results in referenda in Estonia and Latvia.
17 March 1991	In referendum, majority in favour of continuation of Soviet Union, but Armenia, Estonia, Georgia, Latvia, Lithuania and Moldavia refused to participate.
31 March 1991	Referendum in Georgia massively for independence.
9 April 1991	Georgia unilaterally declares its independence.
23 April 1991	Novo-Ogarev agreement between Gorbachev, Yeltsin and 8 Republics to formulate new Union Treaty.
26 May 1991	Zviad Gamsakhurdia becomes popularly elected president of Georgia.
12 June 1991	Boris Yeltsin popularly elected president of Russian Republic.
17 June 1991	Draft Union Treaty approved by participants in Novo-Ogarev agreement, to be ratified finally on 20 August.
20 August 1991	Estonia declares its independence.
21 August 1991	Latvia declares its independence; Lithuania adheres to 1990 declaration of independence.
24 August 1991	Ukrainian parliament votes for independence.
25 August 1991	Belarus parliament votes for independence.
27 August 1991	Moldovan parliament votes for its independence.
30 August 1991	Azerbaijan declares its independence.
31 August 1991	Kyrgyzstan and Uzbekistan declare their independence.
5 September 1991	Crimean parliament declares independence from Ukraine.
9 September 1991	Tajikistan declares its independence.
23 September 1991	Armenia declares its independence.
27 October 1991	Turkmenistan declares its independence.
7 December 1991	Russia, Ukraine and Belarus form Commonwealth of Independent States.
31 December 1991	Formal dissolution of Soviet Union.

Appendix B: The Collapse of Communism in East Europe

November 1988	Hungarian Communist Party introduces multi-party system.
5 June 1989	Massive Solidarity victory in Polish elections.
19 August 1989	Solidarity-led government formed under Tadeusz Mazowiecki as Prime Minister.
September–October 1989	Mass emigration of East German citizens to Austria, via Hungary and West German embassy in Prague.
19 September 1989	Communist regime in Hungary agrees to free elections in 1990.
October 1989	Mass demonstrations against Communist government in GDR in East Berlin, Dresden and Leipzig.
18–19 October 1989	Leading role of Communist Party in Hungary abandoned; opposition parties legalised.
8–17 November 1989	New government formed in East Germany under reform Communist Hans Modrow, including non-Communists.
9 November 1989	Berlin Wall crumbles; 40,000 East Germans visit West Berlin.

10 November 1989	Todor Zhivkov resigns as General Secretary of Bulgarian Communist Party in favour of reform Communists led by Petŭr Mladenov.
17 November to 10 December 1989	Mass demonstrations in Czechoslovakia lead to creation of democratic opposition (Civic Forum), then to formation of non-Communist-dominated coalition government.
11 December 1989	Communist Party monopoly in Bulgaria ended as free elections called.
16–26 December 1989	Brutal repressions of demonstrations in Timisoara precipitate mass movement in Bucharest, supported by army, that ousts Ceauşescu government in Romania; Nicolae and Elena Ceauşescu executed on Christmas Day; Ion Iliescu, opposition Communist, heads new government, which ends Communist Party monopoly on power and promises free elections.
28–9 December 1989	Alexander Dubček elected chairman of Czechoslovak parliament; Václav Havel elected President by parliament.
March–April 1990	Hungarian Democratic Forum wins elections, non-Communist coalition formed.
20 May 1990	Former Communists in National Salvation Front win elections in Romania.
8–9 June 1990	Non-Communists win elections in Czechoslovakia.
10–17 June 1990	Former Communists win elections in Bulgaria.
3 October 1990	German reunification.
7 December 1990	Strikes force resignation of Communist-led government in Bulgaria.
31 March 1991	Albanian (Communist) Workers' Party wins elections.
6 June 1991	Communist government in Albania resigns.

13 October 1991	Union of Democratic Forces wins in Bulgarian election.
15 October 1991	Broad coalition formed in Romania.
9 December 1991	Majority in Romania vote for multi-party government.

Notes

Chapter 1: Introduction

1. F. Fukuyama, *The End of History and the Last Man* (New York: Free Press, 1992), p. xi.
2. E. J. Hobsbawm, *Age of Extremes: The Short Twentieth Century, 1914–1991* (London: Michael Joseph, 1994), p. 498.
3. J. D. White, *Karl Marx and the Intellectual Origins of Dialectical Materialism* (London: Macmillan, 1966), p. 1.
4. E. Bernstein, *The Preconditions of Socialism* (Cambridge: Cambridge University Press, 1993), p. 159; 'The Bolshevist Brand of Socialism', in *Selected Writings of Eduard Bernstein, 1900–1921* (Atlantic Highlands, NJ: Humanities Press, 1996), p. 190.
5. A. Walicki, *Marxism and the Leap to the Kingdom of Freedom: The Rise and Fall of the Communist Utopia* (Stanford, CA: Stanford University Press, 1995), p. 6.

Chapter 2: The 'Founding Fathers'

1. E. J. Hobsbawm, *The Age of Capital* (London: Weidenfeld & Nicolson, 1975), p. 111.
2. Bernstein, *Preconditions*, p. 28.
3. I. Berlin, *Karl Marx* (London: Fontana, 1995), p. 90; D. McLellan, *Karl Marx: His Life and Thought* (St Albans: Paladin, 1976), p. 151.
4. R. Hilton et al., *The Transition from Feudalism to Capitalism* (London: Verso, 1976), p. 9.

5. Cited in R. I. Kowalski, *The Bolshevik Party in Conflict: The Left Communist Opposition of 1918* (London: Macmillan, 1991), p. 41.
6. J. V. Femia, *Marxism and Democracy* (Oxford: Oxford University Press, 1993), p. 165; N. Harding, *Leninism* (London: Macmillan, 1996), p. 6.
7. M. Meisner, *Li Ta-chao and the Origins of Chinese Marxism* (Cambridge, MA: Harvard University Press, 1967), p. 128.
8. H. Marcuse, *Reason and Revolution* (London: Routledge & Kegan Paul, 1973), p. 318.
9. E. J. Hobsbawm (ed.), *Pre-Capitalist Economic Formations* (London: Lawrence & Wishart, 1964), p. 33.
10. White, *Karl Marx*, p. 206; H. Wada, 'Marx and Revolutionary Russia', in T. Shanin (ed.), *Late Marx and the Russian Road* (London: Routledge & Kegan Paul, 1983), p. 49.
11. Walicki, *Communist Utopia*, p. 49; White, *Karl Marx*, p. 247.
12. L. Colletti, *From Rousseau to Lenin* (New York: Monthly Review, 1972), p. 8.
13. J. Schumpeter, *Capitalism, Socialism and Democracy* (London: Routledge, 1996 reprint), p. 39; McLellan, *Karl Marx*, p. 132; C. J. Arthur (ed.), *Engels Today: A Centenary Appreciation* (London: Macmillan, 1996), p. x; Berlin, *Karl Marx*, p. 90.
14. A. J. Polan, *Lenin and the End of Politics* (London: Methuen, 1984), p. 6; C. Boggs, *The Socialist Tradition: From Crisis to Decline* (London: Routledge, 1995), p. 34.
15. R. N. Hunt, *The Political Ideas of Marx and Engels, II: Classical Marxism 1850–1895* (Pittsburgh: University of Pittsburgh Press, 1984), pp. 330–2.
16. Ibid., p. 155; D. Doveton, 'Marx and Engels on Democracy', *History of Political Thought*, xv (1994), pp. 577–80.
17. S. Arnold, *Marx's Radical Critique of Capitalist Society: A Reconstruction and Evaluation* (Oxford: Oxford University Press, 1990), p. 142.
18. Cited in T. Wohlforth, 'The Transition to the Transition', *New Left Review*, 130 (1981), p. 81.
19. A. Nove, *The Economics of Feasible Socialism* (London: George Allen & Unwin, 1983), pp. 44, 50.
20. Schumpeter, *Capitalism*, pp. 180–4.
21. Boggs, *Socialist Tradition*, pp. 36–50.

Chapter 3: German Social Democracy

1. M. Donald, *Marxism and Revolution: Karl Kautsky and the Russian Marxists, 1900–1924* (New Haven, CT: Yale University Press, 1993),

p. 5; K. Kautsky, *Selected Political Writings* (Basingstoke: Macmillan, 1983), p. vii.

2. R. McKibbin, 'Why was there No Marxism in Great Britain', *English Historical Review*, 99 (1984), pp. 297–301.

3. A. S. Lindemann, *A History of European Socialism* (New Haven, CT: Yale University Press, 1983), pp. 139–43.

4. W. A. Petz (ed.), *Wilhelm Liebknecht and German Social Democracy: A Documentary History* (Westport, CT: Greenwood, 1994), pp. 163, 188–9.

5. W. H. Guttsman, *The German Social Democratic Party, 1875–1933* (London: George Allen & Unwin, 1980), p. 80.

6. Petz, *Liebknecht*, p. 163; S. Berger, *Social Democracy and the Working Class in Nineteenth- and Twentieth-Century Germany* (Harlow: Longman, 2000), p. 75.

7. Petz, *Liebknecht*, pp. 230–3, 242; V. I. Lenin, *Collected Works*, vol. 4 (Moscow, 1960), p. 235.

8. Bernstein, *Preconditions*, p. 33; S. Pierson, *Marxist Intellectuals and the Working-Class Mentality in Germany, 1887–1912* (Cambridge, MA: Harvard University Press, 1993), pp. 19–26.

9. M. Salvadori, *Karl Kautsky and the Socialist Revolution, 1880–1938* (London: Verso, 1979), pp. 41–9; D. Geary, *European Labour Protest, 1848–1939* (London: Croom Helm, 1984), pp. 95–7.

10. N. Harding (ed.), *Marxism in Russia: Key Documents, 1879–1906* (Cambridge: Cambridge University Press, 1983), pp. 370–1.

11. Petz, *Liebknecht*, pp. 180–2, 199; the quotation from Kautsky is taken from Donald, *Marxism*, p. 30.

12. J. H. Kautsky, *Karl Kautsky: Marxism, Revolution and Democracy* (New Brunswick: Transaction, 1994), pp. 60ff.; H. Schurer, 'The Russian Revolution of 1905 and the Origins of German Communism', *Slavonic and East European Review*, 39 (1961), p. 461.

13. Berger, *Social Democracy*, p. 83; G. P. Steenson, *Karl Kautsky, 1854–1938: Marxism in the Classical Years* (Pittsburgh: University of Pittsburgh Press, 1991), p. 129.

14. Kautsky, *Selected Political Writings*, pp. 16–31; M. C. Howard and J. E. King, *A History of Marxian Economics*, vol. 1: *1883–1929* (Princeton, NJ: Princeton University Press, 1989), pp. 81–4.

15. Luxemburg's arguments are reproduced in H. Tudor and J. M. Tudor (eds), *Marxism and Social Democracy: The Revisionist Debate, 1896–1898* (Cambridge: Cambridge University Press, 1988), esp. pp. 225, 253–8, 271–2.

16. Ibid., pp. 260–2, 268–9; Salvadori, *Kautsky*, pp. 65–70.

17. C. E. Schorske, *German Social Democracy, 1905–1917: The Development of the Great Schism* (Cambridge, MA: Harvard University Press, 1955), pp. 24–6.

18. Luxemburg's article is best translated in Harding, *Key Documents*, pp. 295–309; Kautsky's letter is cited in Kautsky, *Karl Kautsky*, pp. 23–4.

19. For Maynes's thesis, see D. E. Barclay and E. D. Weitz (eds), *Between Reform and Revolution: German Socialism and Communism from 1840 to 1990* (New York: Berghahn, 1998), pp. 20–1; Kautsky, *Karl Kautsky*, p. 23.

20. Berger, *Social Democracy*, p. 84; Salvadori, *Kautsky*, pp. 109–14.

21. K. Kautsky, *The Road to Power: Political Reflections of Growing into the Revolution* (Atlantic Highlands, NJ: Humanities Press, 1996), pp. xlii–xliv; see too, Kautsky, 'The Mass Strike', *Selected Political Writings*, pp. 53–73.

22. Schorske, *German Social Democracy*, pp. 265–7, 277–9.

23. M. Vajda, *The State and Socialism: Political Essays* (London: Allison & Busby, 1981), p. 91; Bernstein's arguments can be found in Tudor and Tudor, *Revisionist Debate*, pp. 52–3; Berger, *Social Democracy*, pp. 89–90.

24. J. Riddell (ed.), *Lenin's Struggle for a Revolutionary International: Documents, 1907–1916: The Preparatory Years* (New York: Monad Press, 1984), pp. 54–9; Pierson, *Marxist Intellectuals*, pp. 212–18.

25. Riddell, *Lenin's Struggle*, pp. 34–5, 88.

26. A more detailed exposition of Hilferding's analysis can be found in Kowalski, *Bolshevik Party*, pp. 25–30.

27. Kautsky, *Karl Kautsky*, pp. 10–12.

Chapter 4: Russian Marxism

1. R. Blick, *The Seeds of Evil: Lenin and the Origins of Bolshevik Elitism* (London: Steyne, 1995), p. 47; D. Volkogonov, *Lenin: Life and Legacy* (London: HarperCollins, 1994), pp. 20–1; M. Liebman, *Leninism under Lenin* (London: Jonathan Cape, 1975), p. 98; N. Harding, *Lenin's Political Thought*, vol. 1 (London: Macmillan, 1977), pp. 4–5.

2. V. Myakotin, 'Lenin (1870–1924)', *Slavonic Review*, 2 (1923–4), p. 473; J. Frankel (ed.), *Vladimir Akimov and the Dilemmas of Russian Marxism, 1895–1903* (Cambridge: Cambridge University Press, 1969), p. 98.

3. L. H. Haimson, *The Russian Marxists and the Origins of Bolshevism* (Cambridge, MA: Harvard University Press, 1955), p. 110.

4. L. H. Haimson et al. (eds), *The Making of Three Russian Revolutionaries: Voices from the Menshevik Past* (New York: Cambridge University Press, 1987), pp. 121, 313 for the views of Akselrod and Denike.

5. Lidiia Dan's account can be found in ibid., pp. 111–12; Harding, *Lenin's Political Thought*, vol. 1, p. 53, and ch. 5 passim.

6. P. S. McKinsey, 'The Kazan Square Demonstration and the Conflict between Russian Workers and *Intelligenty*', *Slavic Review*, 44 (1985), pp. 101–3; S. I. Kanatchikov, *A Political Worker in Tsarist Russia: The Autobiography of S. I. Kanatchikov* (Stanford, CA: Stanford University Press, 1986), pp. 106, 142, 248.

7. Harding, *Key Documents*, pp. 199–200.

8. Ibid., pp. 176–87; R. Pipes, *Social Democracy and the St Petersburg Labour Movement, 1885–1897* (Cambridge, MA: Harvard University Press, 1963), p. 124.

9. J. L. H. Keep, *The Rise of Social Democracy in Russia* (Oxford: Oxford University Press, 1963), p. 58; Frankel, *Akimov*, p. 176; *On Agitation* and other critical sources later cited on the Economist controversy are well translated in the important collection in Harding, *Key Documents*.

10. P. B. Struve, 'My Contacts and Conflicts with Lenin, II', *Slavonic Review*, XIII (1934), p. 76; Harding, *Key Documents*, pp. 26–7.

11. R. Service, *Lenin: A Political Life*, vol. 1: *The Strengths of Contradiction* (Basingstoke: Macmillan, 1985), p. 79.

12. N. Valentinov, *The Early Years of Lenin* (Ann Arbor: University of Michigan Press, 1970), p. 149; for Dan's recollection, see Haimson, *Menshevik Past*, p. 171.

13. Denike's account is in ibid., p. 323; Service, *Lenin*, vol. 1, p. 145.

14. P. B. Struve, 'My Contacts and Conflicts with Lenin, I', *Slavonic Review*, XII (1933–4), p. 593.

15. Nicolaevsky's account is in Haimson, *Menshevik Past*, pp. 244, 292.

16. G. Swain (ed.), 'Editor's Introduction', *Protokoly Soveshchaniya Rasshirennoi Redaktsii 'Proletariya' Iun' 1909* (Millwood, NY: Kraus, 1982), p. vii.

17. L. H. Haimson, 'The Problem of Social Stability in Urban Russia, 1905–1917', *Slavic Review*, 23–4 (1964–5), passim; for counter to Haimson, see V. Bonnell, *Workers' Politics and Organisations in St Petersburg and Moscow, 1900–1914* (Berkeley: University of California Press, 1983), pp. 441–55.

Chapter 5: War and Revolution

1. Riddell, *Lenin's Struggle*, pp. 111–12, 120–4.
2. Ibid., pp. 175–7, 413–14, 451–2.
3. R. Service, *Lenin: A Political Life*, vol. 2: *Worlds in Collision* (London: Macmillan, 1995), pp. 80–1.
4. Kowalski, *Bolshevik Party*, pp. 44–52, for a more detailed exposition of Lenin's thinking on imperialism.
5. Riddell, *Lenin's Struggle*, pp. 318–21, 513–16; L. Haimson and C. Tilly (eds), *Strikes, Wars and Revolutions in an International Perspective: Strike Waves in the Late Nineteenth and Early Twentieth Centuries* (Cambridge: Cambridge University Press, 1989), p. 531.
6. R. I. Kowalski, *The Russian Revolution, 1917–1921* (London: Routledge, 1997), pp. 54, 83–5.
7. A. Rabinowitch, *Prelude to Revolution: The Petrograd Bolsheviks and the July 1917 Uprising* (Bloomington: Indiana University Press, 1968), p. 41.
8. R. Pipes, *The Russian Revolution, 1899–1919* (London: Fontana, 1990), pp. 485–6; A. Rabinowitch, *The Bolsheviks Come to Power* (London: New Left Books, 1979), pp. xvii–xxi, emphasises the disunity and lack of discipline within the Bolshevik Party.
9. Kowalski, *Russian Revolution*, pp. 55–9, 135–6, 150–2.
10. I. Getzler, 'Iulii Martov: the Leader who Lost his Party in 1917', *Slavonic and East European Review*, 72 (1994), pp. 432–4; O. H. Radkey, *The Agrarian Foes of Bolshevism* (New York: Columbia University Press, 1958), pp. 369–74.
11. Haimson and Tilly, *Strikes*, pp. 434–5, 495–6; J. Riddell (ed.), *The German Revolution and the Debate on Soviet Power: Documents, 1918–1919. Preparing the Founding Congress* (New York: Pathfinder, 1986), pp. 16–17.
12. Schorske, *German Social Democracy*, pp. 308–20.
13. C. B. Burdick and R. H. Lutz (eds), *The Political Institutions of the German Revolution, 1918–1919* (Stanford, CA: Stanford University Press, 1966), pp. 6–7, 17–18.
14. Riddell, *German Revolution*, pp. 36–40.
15. Ibid., pp. 94–105, 143–4, for Kautsky and Daumig; Burdick and Lutz, *Political Institutions*, pp. 156–8, for Dittman.
16. Ibid., pp. 119–49, for the Cabinet debate of 28 December on the sailors' rising.
17. Riddell, *German Revolution*, pp. 56–8, 262–4; E. D. Weitz, *Creating German Communism, 1890–1990: From Popular Protests to Socialist State* (Princeton, NJ: Princeton University Press, 1997), pp. 101–9, 131.

18. Geary, *European Labour Protest*, pp. 157–63; J. E. Cronin, 'The Crisis of State and Society in Britain, 1917–1922', in Haimson and Tilly, *Strikes*, p. 472.
19. Hobsbawm, *Age of Extremes*, pp. 68–9; W. E. Mosse, 'The February Revolution: Prerequisites of Success', *Soviet Studies*, XIX (1967–8), pp. 100–8; B. Moore, Jr, *Injustice: The Social Bases of Obedience and Revolt* (London: Macmillan, 1978), pp. 302–10.

Chapter 6: The Rise of Stalinism

1. P. Baldwin (ed.), *Reworking the Past: Hitler, the Holocaust and the Historians' Debate* (Boston, MA: Beacon Press, 1990), p. 43; M. Malia, *The Soviet Tragedy: A History of Socialism in Russia, 1917–1991* (New York: Free Press, 1994), pp. 8, 499–500; Walicki, *Communist Utopia*, pp. 2, 5.
2. D. W. Lovell, *From Marx to Lenin: An Evaluation of Marx's Responsibility for Soviet Totalitarianism* (Cambridge: Cambridge University Press, 1984), pp. 188–97; R. Service, *Lenin: A Political Life*, vol. 3: *The Iron Ring* (Basingstoke: Macmillan, 1995), p. xix.
3. S. F. Cohen, 'Bolshevism and Stalinism', in R. C. Tucker (ed.), *Stalinism: Essays in Historical Interpretation* (New York: W. W. Norton, 1977), p. 12; R. Medvedev, *Lenin and Western Marxism* (London: Verso, 1981), p. 20.
4. R. Pipes, *Russia under the Bolshevik Regime, 1919–1924* (London: Fontana, 1994), pp. 501–6; R. C. Tucker, *Stalin in Power: The Revolution from Above, 1928–1941* (New York: W. W. Norton, 1990), pp. xiv, 9, 21; T. H. von Laue, 'Stalin in Focus', *Slavic Review*, 42 (1983), pp. 383–6.
5. V. Serge, *Memoirs of a Revolutionary* (Oxford: Oxford University Press, 1967), pp. 133–4; J. R. Millar and A. Nove, 'A Debate on Collectivisation: Was Stalin Really Necessary?', in C. Ward (ed.), *The Stalinist Dictatorship* (London: Arnold, 1998), p. 148; S. Kotkin, '1991 and the Russian Revolution: Sources, Conceptual Categories, Analytical Frameworks', *Journal of Modern History*, 70 (1998), p. 400.
6. R. C. Elwood (ed.), *Resolutions and Decisions of the Communist Party of the Soviet Union*, vol. 1 (Toronto: University of Toronto Press, 1974), pp. 254–7.
7. Cited in Kowalski, *Bolshevik Party*, pp. 72–3.
8. L. Kritsman, *Geroicheskii period russkoi revoliutsii* (Moscow: Gosudarstvennoe izdatel'stvo, n.d.), p. 68; S. Malle, *The Economic*

Organisation of War Communism (Cambridge: Cambridge University Press, 1985), p. 324.

9. R. Kowalski, ' "Fellow Travellers" or Revolutionary Dreamers? The Left Social Revolutionaries after 1917', *Revolutionary Russia*, 11 (1998), pp. 6–8, 11.

10. Serge, *Memoirs*, p. 115; Kritsman, *Geroicheskii period*, p. 204; Osinski, cited in Kowalski, *Bolshevik Party*, p. 118.

11. S. Louw, 'In the Shadow of the Pharaohs: the Militarisation of Labour Debate and Classical Marxist Theory', *Economy and Society*, 29 (2000), pp. 239–62; Serge, *Memoirs*, p. 115; Service, *The Iron Ring*, pp. 207–14, for opposition to Lenin.

12. L. Lih, 'The Mystery of the ABC', *Slavic Review*, 56 (1997), pp. 50–1; M. N. Pokroskii, *Sem' let proletarskoi diktatury* (Moscow: Istpart, 1923), p. 8.

13. J. C. McClelland, 'The Utopian and the Heroic: Divergent Paths to the Communist Educational Ideal', in A. Gleason et al. (eds), *Bolshevik Culture: Experiment and Order in the Russian Revolution* (Bloomington: Indiana University Press, 1985), p. 114; T. F. Remington, *Building Socialism in Bolshevik Russia: Ideology and Industrial Organisation* (Pittsburgh: University of Pittsburgh Press, 1984), pp. 115–16.

14. D. P. Koenker, 'Urbanisation and Deurbanisation in the Russian Revolution and Civil War', in D. P. Koenker et al., *Party, State and Society in the Russian Civil War* (Bloomington: Indiana University Press, 1989), p. 81.

15. N. I. Bukharin, *The Politics and Economics of the Transition Period* (New York: Bergman, 1979), pp. 128, 150–6.

16. R. C. Tucker, *Stalin as Revolutionary, 1879–1929* (London: Chatto & Windus, 1974), pp. 296–304.

17. Kowalski, *Bolshevik Party*, pp. 134–7, for a fuller account.

18. For 'circular flow', see R. Sakwa, *The Rise and Fall of the Soviet Union, 1917–1991* (London: Routledge, 1999), p. 145; M. von Hagen, *Soldiers in the Proletarian Dictatorship: The Red Army and the Soviet Socialist State, 1917–1930* (Ithaca, NY: Cornell University Press, 1990), pp. 5–8.

19. L. Lih (ed.), *Stalin's Letters to Molotov* (New Haven, CT: Yale University Press, 1995), p. 86.

20. Translations of Bukharin's key writings in defence of the NEP are in R. B. Day (ed.), *N. I. Bukharin: Selected Writings on the State and the Transition to Socialism* (Nottingham: Spokesman, 1982); Preobrazhenskii's critical essays are in D. A. Filtzer (ed.), *The Crisis of*

Soviet Industrialisation: Selected Essays (White Plains: Greenwood, 1980).

21. R. Gregor (ed.), *Resolutions and Decisions of the Communist Party of the Soviet Union*, vol. 2 (Toronto: University of Toronto Press, 1974), pp. 315, 322; Stalin's speech can be found in R. Sakwa, *Rise and Fall*, p. 188.

22. J. Hughes, *Stalin, Siberia and the Crisis of the New Economic Policy* (Cambridge: Cambridge University Press, 1991), pp. 209–10.

23. J. Hughes, 'Capturing the Russian Peasantry: Stalinist Grain Procurement and the "Ural–Siberian Method" ', *Slavic Review*, 53 (1994), pp. 77–8; C. Read, *The Making and Breaking of the Soviet System* (Basingstoke: Macmillan, 2001), pp. 66–72, 92.

24. N. S. Timasheff, *The Great Retreat: The Growth and Decline of Communism in Russia* (New York: Dutton, 1946), p. 388.

25. S. Fitzpatrick, *Cultural Revolution in Russia, 1928–1931* (Bloomington: Indiana University Press, 1978), pp. 11, 38–40.

26. Sakwa, *Rise and Fall*, pp. 199–200, for Riutin's speech; J. Haslam, 'Political Opposition to Stalin and the Origins of the Terror', *Historical Journal*, 29 (1986), pp. 399–400.

27. Haslam, ibid., pp. 412–15; J. A. Getty and O. V. Naumov, *The Road to Terror: Stalin and the Self-Destruction of the Bolsheviks, 1932–1939* (New Haven, CT: Yale University Press, 1999), pp. 444–8.

28. O. Khlevnyuk, 'The Objectives of the Great Terror, 1937–1938', in J. Cooper et al. (eds), *Soviet History, 1917–1953: Essays in Honour of R. W. Davies* (Basingstoke: Macmillan, 1995), pp. 168–9.

29. Getty and Naumov, *Road to Terror*, pp. 493–8.

30. Ibid., p. 588; V. N. Zemskov, 'Zakliuchennye v 1930-e gody; sotsial'-no-demograficheskie problemy', *Otechestvennaia istoriia*, 4 (1997).

31. R. Bahro, *The Alternative in East Europe* (London: New Left Books, 1976), especially part I; S. Kotkin, *Magnetic Mountain: Stalinism as a Civilisation* (Berkeley: University of California Press, 1995), pp. 355–66.

Chapter 7: Late Stalinism to Gorbachev

1. C. Ward, *Stalin's Russia* (London: Arnold, 1999), pp. 214, 225; L. K. Adler and T. G. Paterson, 'Red Fascism: the Merger of Nazi Germany and Soviet Russia in the American Image of Totalitarianism, 1930s–1950s', *American Historical Review*, LXXV (1970), pp. 1046–8.

2. W. O. McCagg, Jr, *Stalin Embattled, 1943–1948* (Detroit: Wayne State University Press, 1978); T. Dunmore, *The Stalinist Command Economy: The Soviet State Apparatus and Economic Policy, 1945–1953* (London: Macmillan, 1980); W. G. Hahn, *Post-war Soviet Politics: The Fall of Zhdanov and the Defeat of Moderation, 1946–1953* (New York: Cornell University Press, 1982); Y. Gorlizki, 'Stalin's Cabinet: the Politburo and Decision Making in the Post-War Years', *Europe–Asia Studies*, 53 (2001), pp. 291–312.

3. A. Nove, *Stalinism and After* (London: Allen & Unwin, 1981), pp. 97–8.

4. Sakwa, *Rise and Fall*, pp. 297–302.

5. V. Shamberg, 'Stalin's Last Inner Circle', *The Harriman Review*, 10 (1997), pp. 36–7; D. Brandenberger, 'Stalin, the Leningrad Affair and the Limits of Postwar Soviet Russification', *Russian Review*, 63 (2004), pp. 253–4.

6. N. I. Khrushchev, *Khrushchev Remembers* (London: Sphere, 1971), pp. 220–5; A. Knight, *Beria: Stalin's First Lieutenant* (Princeton, NJ: Princeton University Press, 1993), pp. 151–63.

7. Khrushchev, *Khrushchev Remembers*, pp. 309, 319.

8. W. J. Tompson, *Khrushchev: A Political Life* (Basingstoke: Macmillan, 1997), pp. 134–42.

9. S. F. Cohen, 'The Stalin Question since Stalin', in *Rethinking the Soviet Experience* (Oxford: Oxford University Press, 1985), pp. 98–9.

10. P. J. D. Wiles, *The Political Economy of Communism* (Oxford: Oxford University Press, 1964), pp. 43–6.

11. G. W. Breslauer, *Khrushchev and Brezhnev as Leaders: Building Authority in Soviet Politics* (London: George Allen & Unwin, 1982), pp. 55–60.

12. K. Simis, *USSR: Secrets of a Corrupt Society* (London: Dent, 1982), pp. 30–3; Tompson, *Khrushchev*, pp. 264–74.

13. Read, *Making and Breaking*, p. 159; A. Yakovlev, *The Fate of Marxism in Russia* (New Haven, CT: Yale University Press, 1993), p. 80.

14. S. F. Cohen, 'Promises Kept', *New Statesman*, 5 August 1983; R. Medvedev, 'Russia after Brezhnev', *Marxism Today*, September 1982, pp. 23–4.

15. Jonathan Steele's contemporary report, *Guardian*, 5 August 1980.

16. Sakwa, *Rise and Fall*, p. 426; Steele's report, *Guardian*, 4 August 1980.

17. A. Nove, 'Economic Reforms in the USSR and Hungary: a Study in Contrasts', in A. Nove and D. M. Nuti (eds), *Socialist Economics* (Harmondsworth: Penguin, 1972), pp. 354–60; R. Sakwa, *Soviet Politics in Perspective* (London: Routledge, 1998), pp. 226–7.

18. Sakwa, *Soviet Politics*, p. 213.

19. A. Amalrik, *Will the Soviet Union Survive until 1984?* (London: Allen Lane, 1970), pp. 15, 31–3; T. Deutscher, 'Intellectual Opposition in the USSR', *New Left Review*, 96 (1976), p. 111.

20. V. Zaslavsky, *The Neo-Stalinist State: Class, Ethnicity and Consensus in Soviet Society* (Brighton: Harvester, 1982), especially pp. 134–41.

21. Ibid., especially pp. 106–11; G. E. Smith, 'Ethnic Nationalism in the Soviet Union: Territory, Cleavage, and Control', *Government and Policy*, 3 (1985), pp. 55–9.

22. Sakwa, *Soviet Politics*, pp. 213–14.

23. M. Ellman and V. Kontorovich, 'The Collapse of the Soviet System and the Memoir Literature', *Europe–Asia Studies*, 49 (1997), pp. 260, 275; Sakwa, *Rise and Fall*, pp. 418–20, for Andropov's speech on the economy.

24. T. Zaslavskaia, 'The Novosibirsk Report', *Survey*, 28 (1984), pp. 88–108.

Chapter 8: Communism in West Europe since the First World War

1. E. Hobsbawm, *Revolutionaries* (London: Weidenfeld & Nicolson, 1973), p. 16.

2. P. Anderson, *Considerations on Western Marxism* (London: New Left Books, 1976), p. 29.

3. R. S. Gottlieb, *Marxism, 1844–1990: Origins, Betrayal, Rebirth* (London: Routledge, 1992), pp. 124–5.

4. D. Sassoon, *One Hundred Years of Socialism: The West European Left in the Twentieth Century* (London: Fontana, 1997), p. 77.

5. A. Gramsci, *Further Selections from the Prison Notebooks* (London: Lawrence & Wishart, 1995), p. xvi; Anderson, *Considerations*, p. 31.

6. F. Claudin, *The Communist Movement: From Comintern to Cominform* (Harmondsworth: Penguin, 1975), pp. 56–62.

7. J. Degras (ed.), *The Communist International, 1919–1945: Documents*, vol. 1 (London: Cass, 1956), pp. 166–73; K. McDermott and J. Agnew, *The Comintern: A History of International Communism from Lenin to Stalin* (London: Macmillan, 1996), pp. 17–23.

8. E. D. Weitz, *Creating German Communism*, pp. 129–31, 158–9; E. Hobsbawm, *Interesting Times: A Twentieth-century Life* (London: Abacus, 2002), p. 69.

9. McDermott and Agnew, *Comintern*, pp. 15, 58–68; K. Middlemass, *Power and the Party: Changing Faces of Communism in Western Europe* (London: André Deutsch, 1980), pp. 30–3.

10. Claudin, *Communist Movement*, pp. 132–4.

11. Hobsbawm, *Revolutionaries*, pp. 48–9; McDermott and Agnew, *Comintern*, pp. 34–8.

12. McDermott and Agnew, *Comintern*, pp. 68–78.

13. Hobsbawm, *Interesting Times*, pp. 67–9; Weitz, *Creating German Communism*, p. 187.

14. A. Dallin and F. I. Firsov, *Dimitrov and Stalin, 1934–1943: Letters from the Soviet Archives* (New Haven, CT: Yale University Press, 2000), p. 34.

15. McDermott and Agnew, *Comintern*, ch. 4 passim.

16. I. Banac (ed.), *The Diary of Georgi Dimitrov, 1933–1939* (New Haven, CT: Yale University Press, 2003), p. xxxv; McDermott and Agnew, *Comintern*, pp. 206–7.

17. A. Gramsci, *Selections from Prison Notebooks* (London: Lawrence & Wishart, 1971), p. 238.

18. Ibid., pp. 12, 239, 261.

19. Ibid., pp. 5–14.

20. Ibid., pp. 235, 275–6.

21. Ibid., pp. 147, 236–8.

22. Ibid., p. 235; P. Anderson, 'The Antinomies of Antonio Gramsci', *New Left Review*, 100 (1976–7), pp. 55–61.

23. Day (ed.), *Bukharin*, p. 27; L. Kritsman, 'The Heroic Period of the Russian Revolution', trans. R. I. Kowalski, *Revolutionary Russia*, 2 (1989), p. 3.

24. Anderson, *Antinomies*, pp. 28–30.

25. Walicki, *Communist Utopia*, pp. 426–31.

26. D. Sassoon, 'The Rise and Fall of West European Communism', *Contemporary European History*, 1 (1992), p. 149.

27. D. Joravsky, 'Communism in Historical Perspective', *American Historical Review*, 99 (1994), p. 842.

28. Boggs, *Socialist Tradition*, p. 107.

29. Boggs, *Socialist Tradition*, pp. 109, 119; Kautsky, *Karl Kautsky*, pp. 167–70.

30. G. Sani, 'The PCI on the Threshold of Power', *Problems of Communism*, XXV (1976), p. 46.

31. Sassoon, *One Hundred Years*, pp. 578, 585–7, 592; T. Abse, 'Judging the PCI', *New Left Review*, 153 (1985), pp. 19, 25–33.

32. Sassoon, *One Hundred Years*, pp. 534–8; A. Levi, 'Eurocommunism: Myth or Reality?', in P. F. della Torre et al., *Eurocommunism: Myth or Reality?* (Harmondsworth: Penguin, 1979), p. 22.

33. Boggs, *Socialist Tradition*, pp. 125–6.

34. E. Mujal-León, 'Decline and Fall of Spanish Communism', *Problems of Communism*, XXXV (1986), pp. 1–2.
35. Levi, '*Eurocommunism*', p. 25.
36. P. Camiller, 'The Eclipse of Spanish Communism', *New Left Review*, 147 (1984), p. 123.
37. Boggs, *Socialist Tradition*, pp. 116–18.

Chapter 9: Communism in East Europe

1. G. Swain and N. Swain, *Eastern Europe since 1945* (London: Macmillan, 1993), pp. 6–7; M. Vajda, *The State and Socialism*, p. 123.
2. C. Milosz, *The Captive Mind* (London: Mercury, 1962), pp. x, 89–90; Z. Mlynář, *Night Frost in Prague: The End of Humane Socialism* (London: Hurst, 1980), pp. 1–6.
3. R. Bideleux and I. Jeffries, *A History of Eastern Europe* (London: Routledge, 1998), pp. 435–40.
4. Ibid., pp. 509–12.
5. G. Roberts, *The Soviet Union in World Politics: Coexistence, Revolution and Cold War, 1945–1991* (London: Routledge, 1999), pp. 18–19.
6. Classic, if now dated, accounts include Z. Brzezinski, *The Soviet Bloc: Unity and Conflict* (Cambridge, MA: Harvard University Press, 1960); and M. McCauley (ed.), *Communist Power in Europe, 1944–1949* (London: Macmillan, 1977).
7. B. Fowkes, *The Rise and Fall of Communism in Eastern Europe* (London: Macmillan, 1995), p. 52; R. C. Tucker, 'The Cold War in Stalin's Time: What the New Sources Reveal', *Diplomatic History*, 21 (1997), p. 275.
8. R. V. Daniels (ed.), *A Documentary History of Communism and the World* (Hanover, NH: University Press of New England, 1994), pp. 114–17; Dallin and Firsov, *Dimitrov and Stalin*, p. 260.
9. Daniels, *Documentary History*, pp. 121–5; M. Glenny, *The Rebirth of History: Eastern Europe in the Age of Democracy* (Harmondsworth: Penguin, 1990), p. 120.
10. W. Brus, *Socialist Ownership and Political Systems* (London: Routledge & Kegan Paul, 1975), pp. 71–5; D. A. Dyker, 'Yugoslavia: Unity out of Diversity', in A. Brown and J. Gray (eds), *Political Culture and Political Change in Communist States* (London: Macmillan, 1979), p. 95.
11. Nove, *Economics of Feasible Socialism*, pp. 134–8.
12. Ibid., pp. 140–1; E. Primorac and M. Babic, 'Systemic Changes and Unemployment Growth in Yugoslavia, 1965–1984', *Slavic Review*, 48 (1989), p. 195.

13. S. K. Pavlowitch, *Tito: Yugoslavia's Great Dictator, a Reassessment* (Columbus, OH: Ohio State University Press, 1992), pp. 78–9; P. Shoup, 'Crisis and Reform in Yugoslavia', *Telos*, 79 (1989), pp. 135–6, 147; Glenny, *Rebirth of History*, pp. 121–5.

14. J. K. Hoensch, *A History of Modern Hungary, 1867–1986* (London: Longman, 1988), pp. 208–10.

15. P. E. Zinner (ed.), *National Communism and Popular Revolt in Eastern Europe: A Selection of Documents on Events in Poland and Hungary, February–November 1956* (New York: Columbia University Press, 1956), pp. 328–9, 338–40, 410.

16. Ibid., pp. 422, 433–4, 456–7; S. Crawshaw, *Independent*, 29 December 1989.

17. Ibid., pp. 474–8; M. Tatu, 'Intervention in Eastern Europe', in S. S. Kaplan, *Diplomacy of Power: Soviet Armed Forces as a Political Instrument* (Washington, DC: Brookings Institution, 1981), pp. 215–23.

18. Kádár's speech, in Daniels, *Documentary History*, pp. 226–8; F. Feher and A. Heller, *Hungary 1956 Revisited* (London: George Allen & Unwin, 1983), p. 148.

19. A. Nove, 'Economic Reforms in the USSR and Hungary', pp. 341–6; J. Kenedi, *Do It Yourself: Hungary's Hidden Economy* (London: Pluto, 1981), p. 58; L. Csaba, 'Some Lessons from Two Decades of Economic Reform in Hungary', *Communist Economies*, 1 (1989), pp. 18, 22.

20. N. Swain, *Collective Farms Which Work?* (Cambridge: Cambridge University Press, 1985), p. 182.

21. Hoensch, *Modern Hungary*, pp. 248–9, 261–2.

22. Fowkes, *Rise and Fall of Communism*, pp. 180–2.

23. M. Hárászti, *The Velvet Prison: Artists under State Socialism* (Harmondsworth: Penguin, 1989), pp. 96, 182; Feher and Heller, *Hungary 1956 Revisited*, pp. 118–20.

24. Z. Mlynář, 'August 1968', in G. R. Urban, *Communist Reformation: Nationalism, Inter-nationalism and Change in the World Communist Movement* (London: Temple Smith, 1979), pp. 120–2; V. Kusin, *The Intellectual Origins of the Prague Spring: The Development of Reformist Ideas in Czechoslovakia* (Cambridge: Cambridge University Press, 1971), pp. 8–12.

25. H. G. Skilling, *Czechoslovakia's Interrupted Revolution* (Princeton, NJ: Princeton University Press, 1976), pp. 25–32.

26. Mlynář, 'August 1968', p. 127.

27. R. V. Daniels, *A Documentary History of World Communism*, vol. 2 (London: I. B. Tauris, 1985), pp. 329–36; Kusin, *Intellectual Origins*, p. 135.

28. Mlynář, 'August 1968', pp. 138–9; O. Sik, 'Egalitarianism in Socialist Society', in Urban, *Communist Reformation*, pp. 151, 170; Tatu, 'Intervention', pp. 223–39. The Doctrine is reprinted in Daniels, *Documentary History*, pp. 240–2.

29. N. Ascherson, *The Polish August: The Self-Limiting Revolution* (Harmondsworth: Penguin, 1981), pp. 47–8; W. Brus, 'Stalinism and the "People's Democracies" ', in Tucker (ed.), *Stalinism*, pp. 243, 247–8.

30. Zinner, *National Communism*, pp. 132, 145–86, for the Resolution of the CC.

31. Ibid., pp, 239, 256–7.

32. Ascherson, *Polish August*, pp. 72–4; G. C. Ference (ed.), *Chronology of 20th-Century Eastern European History* (Detroit and Washington, DC: Gale Research, 1994), pp. 282–5.

33. Ascherson, *Polish August*, pp. 91–2, 96–8.

34. N. Davies, *Heart of Europe: A Short History of Poland* (Oxford: Oxford University Press, 1986), pp. 368–9.

35. D. M. Nuti, 'Poland: Economic Collapse and Socialist Renewal', *New Left Review*, 130 (1981), pp. 24–7; M. Vale (ed.), *Poland: The State of the Republic: Two Reports by the Experience and Future Discussion Group (DiP) Warsaw* (London: Pluto, 1981), pp. 135–7.

36. Ibid., pp. 147–9; O. MacDonald, 'The Polish Vortex: Solidarity and Socialism', *New Left Review*, 139 (1983), pp. 11–13.

37. The 21-Point Programme and Gdańsk Agreement can be found in L. H. Legters (ed.), *Eastern Europe: Transformation and Revolution, 1945–1991* (Lexington: D. C. Heath, 1992), pp. 253–4, 255–62; Solidarity's Programme is in Daniels, *Documentary History*, pp. 297–301.

38. Solidarity's radical October programme is translated in Legters, *Eastern Europe*, pp. 268–89; the declaration of martial law is in Daniels, *Documentary History*, pp. 301–3; Fowkes, *Rise and Fall of Communism*, pp. 166–8.

39. W. Wesolowski, 'Transition from Authoritarianism to Democracy', in Legters, *Eastern Europe*, p. 303.

40. R. V. Daniels, *The End of the Communist Revolution* (London: Routledge, 1993), p. 179; Havel and Kuroń are cited in V. Tismaneanu (ed.), *The Revolutions of 1989* (London: Routledge, 1999), pp. 198, 234.

41. A. Arato, 'The Budapest School and Actually Existing Socialism', *Theory and Society*, 16 (1987), pp. 614–15.

Chapter 10: The Collapse of Communism in the Soviet Union and East Europe

1. R. Medvedev and G. Chiesa, *Time of Change: An Insider's View of Russia's Transformation* (London: I. B. Tauris, 1991), p. 38; S. White, *Gorbachev and After* (Cambridge: Cambridge University Press, 1992), vol. 2, p. 223; M. Gorbachev, *Memoirs* (London: Doubleday, 1997), p. 288.
2. R. Sakwa, *Gorbachev and His Reforms, 1985–1990* (Hemel Hempstead: Philip Allen, 1990), pp. 271–2, 288.
3. Gorbachev, *Memoirs*, pp. 242, 250, 290.
4. Medvedev and Chiesa, *Time of Change*, p. 107; J. Miller, *Mikhail Gorbachev and the End of Soviet Power* (London: Macmillan, 1993), pp. 77–81, 90–100.
5. A. S. Tsipko, *Is Stalinism Really Dead?* (San Francisco: HarperCollins, 1990), p. 10; M. Galeotti, *Gorbachev and His Revolution* (London: Macmillan, 1997), pp. 89–93; A. Sobchak, *For a New Russia* (New York: HarperCollins, 1992), p. 22.
6. A. Yakovlev, *The Fate of Marxism in Russia* (New Haven, CT: Yale University Press, 1993), pp. 109–11; Gorbachev, *Memoirs*, pp. 365–6.
7. Sakwa, *Gorbachev*, pp. 278–82.
8. Miller, *Mikhail Gorbachev*, pp. 103–4.
9. A. Brown, *The Gorbachev Factor* (Oxford: Oxford University Press, 1997), pp. 142–5.
10. Ibid., pp. 152–3; Gorbachev, *Memoirs*, pp. 473, 494–5.
11. Opinion polls and cited in H. Smith, *The New Russians* (London: Hutchinson, 1990), pp. 88–91; Gorbachev, *Memoirs*, pp. 271, 469f.
12. For a chronology of the rise of minority nationalism, see Appendix A; Sobchak, *For a New Russia*, pp. 53–69.
13. E. Shevardnadze, *The Future Belongs to Freedom* (London: Sinclair-Stevenson, 1991), p. 35; J. Steele, *Eternal Russia: Yeltsin, Gorbachev and the Mirage of Democracy* (London: Faber & Faber, 1994), p. 32.
14. Gorbachev, *Memoirs*, p. 435; J. Hiden and P. Salmon, *The Baltic Nations and Europe* (London: Longman, 1991), pp. 130–1; G. E. Smith, 'The Soviet State and Nationalities Policy', in G. E. Smith (ed.), *The Nationalities Question in Post-Soviet States* (London: Longman, 1995), pp. 13–18; M. Ellman and V. Kontorovich, 'The Collapse of the Soviet System and the Memoir Literature', *Europe–Asia Studies*, 49 (1997), p. 268.
15. Sobchak, *For a New Russia*, pp. 86–7.

16. Miller, *Mikhail Gorbachev*, pp. 160–71; Shevardnadze, *The Future*, p. 177.
17. Brown, *Gorbachev Factor*, pp. 285–93.
18. Steele, *Eternal Russia*, pp. 59–79.
19. B. Kagarlitsky, *The Disintegration of the Monolith* (London: Verso, 1992), pp. vii–ix, 100–2; O. Kryshtanovskaya and S. White, 'From Soviet *Nomenklatura* to Russian Elite', *Europe–Asia Studies*, 48 (1996), pp. 724, 729.
20. G. M. Tamás, 'The Legacy of Dissent', in Tismaneanu, *Revolutions*, 181–97.
21. Steele, *Eternal Russia*, pp. 148–9.
22. Fowkes, *Rise and Fall of Communism*, pp. 177–80.
23. M. Frankland, *The Patriots' Revolution: How Eastern Europe Toppled Communism and Won its Freedom* (London: I. R. Dee, 1992), pp. 104–13.
24. Swain and Swain, *Eastern Europe*, pp. 201–4.
25. Ference, *Chronology*, pp. 95–8.
26. Ibid., pp. 152–7.
27. Fowkes, *Rise and Fall of Communism*, pp. 188–9.
28. M. Ignatieff, *Blood and Belonging: Journeys into the New Nationalism* (London: Chatto & Windus, 1993), pp. 16–19; Ference, *Chronology*, pp. 49–56.

Conclusion

1. Sassoon, *One Hundred Years*, p. 737.
2. Bahro, *The Alternative*, pp. 58–61.
3. Sassoon, *One Hundred Years*, pp. 776–8; Hobsbawm, *Age of Extremes*, p. 574.
4. Hobsbawm, *Age of Extremes*, p. 564.
5. J. Stiglitz, *Globalisation and Its Discontents* (Harmondsworth: Penguin, 2002), ch. 5, passim, pp. 187–8.
6. J. Cassidy, in *Independent on Sunday*, 7 December 1997.
7. *Guardian*, 3 April 1998.
8. *Independent on Sunday*, 1 November 1998.
9. Ibid., 16 August 1998.
10. White, *Karl Marx*, p. 367.
11. *Guardian*, 11 November 2001.
12. M. B. Steger, *The Quest for Evolutionary Socialism: Eduard Bernstein and Social Democracy* (Cambridge: Cambridge University Press, 1997), p. 254.

Select Bibliography

1903 Second Ordinary Congress of the RSDLP, trans. B. Pearce (London: New Park Publications, 1978).

Amalrik, A., *Will the Soviet Survive until 1984?* (London: Allen Lane, 1970).

Anderson, P., *Considerations on Western Marxism* (London: New Left Books, 1976).

Arnold, S., *Marx's Radical Critique of Capitalist Society: A Reconstruction and Evaluation* (Oxford: Oxford University Press, 1990).

Arthur, C. J. (ed.), *Engels Today: A Centenary Appreciation* (London: Macmillan, 1996).

Bahro, R., *The Alternative in East Europe* (London: New Left Books, 1976).

Banac, I. (ed.), *The Diary of Georgi Dimitrov, 1933–1939* (New Haven, CT: Yale University Press, 2003).

Barclay, D. A. and Weitz, E. D. (eds), *Between Reform and Revolution: German Socialism and Communism from 1840 to 1990* (New York: Berghahn, 1998).

Berger, S., *Social Democracy and the Working Class in Nineteenth and Twentieth-Century Germany* (Harlow: Longman, 2000).

Berlin, I., *Karl Marx* (London: Fontana, 1995).

Bernstein, E., *The Preconditions of Socialism* (Cambridge: Cambridge University Press, 1993).

——, *Selected Writings of Eduard Bernstein, 1900–1921* (Atlantic Highlands, NJ: Humanities Press, 1996).

Blick, R., *The Seeds of Evil: Lenin and the Origins of Bolshevik Elitism* (London: Steyne, 1995).

Boggs, C., *The Socialist Tradition: From Crisis to Decline* (London: Routledge, 1995).

Bonnell, V., *Workers' Politics and Organisations in St Petersburg and Moscow, 1900–1914* (Berkeley: University of California Press, 1983).

Breslauer, G. W., *Khrushchev and Brezhnev as Leaders: Building Authority in Soviet Politics* (London: George Allen & Unwin, 1982).

Bukharin, N. I., *The Politics and Economics of the Transition Period* (New York: Bergman, 1979).

Burdick, C. B. and Lutz, R. H. (eds), *The Political Institutions of the German Revolution, 1918–1919* (Stanford, CA: Stanford University Press, 1966).

Chase, W. J., *Enemies within the Gates: The Cominterm and the Stalinist Repression, 1934–1939* (New Haven, CT: Yale University Press, 2001).

Claudin, F., *The Communist Movement: From Comintern to Cominform* (Harmondsworth: Penguin, 1975).

Cohen, S. F., *Rethinking the Soviet Experience* (Oxford: Oxford University Press, 1985).

Colletti, L., *From Rousseau to Lenin* (New York: Monthly Review, 1972).

Dallin, A. and Firsov, F. I., *Dimitrov and Stalin, 1934–1943: Letters from the Soviet Archives* (New Haven, CT: Yale University Press, 2000).

Day, R. B. (ed.), *N. I. Bukharin: Selected Writings on the State and the Transition to Socialism* (Nottingham: Spokesman, 1982).

Degras, J. (ed.), *The Communist International, 1919–1945: Documents*, vol. 1 (London: Cass, 1956).

Donald, M., *Marxism and Revolution: Karl Kautsky and the Russian Marxists, 1900–1924* (New Haven, CT: Yale University Press, 1993).

Dunmore, T., *The Stalinist Command Economy: The Soviet State Apparatus and Economic Policy, 1945–1953* (London: Macmillan, 1980).

Femia, J. V., *Marxism and Democracy* (Oxford: Oxford University Press, 1993).

Ference, G. C. (ed.), *Chronology of 20th-Century Eastern European History* (Detroit and Washington, DC: Gale Research, 1994).

Filtzer, D. A. (ed.), *The Crisis of Soviet Industrialisation: Selected Essays* (White Plains: Greenwood, 1980).

Fitzpatrick, S., *Cultural Revolution in Russia, 1928–1931* (Bloomington: Indiana University Press, 1978).

Fowkes, B., *The Rise and Fall of Communism in Eastern Europe* (London: Macmillan, 1995).

Frankel, J. (ed.), *Vladimir Akimov and the Dilemmas of Russian Marxism, 1895–1903* (Cambridge: Cambridge University Press, 1969).

Fukuyama, F., *The End of History and the Last Man* (New York: Free Press, 1992).

Geary, D., *European Labour Protest, 1848–1939* (London: Croom Helm, 1984).

Getty, J. A. and Naumov, O. V. (eds), *The Road to Terror: Stalin and the Self-Destruction of the Bolsheviks, 1932–1939* (New Haven, CT: Yale University Press, 1999).

Gleason, A. et al. (eds), *Bolshevik Culture: Experiment and Order in the Russian Revolution* (Bloomington: Indiana University Press, 1985).

Gorlizki, Y. and Khlevnyuk, O., *Cold Peace: Stalin and the Soviet Ruling Circle, 1945–1953* (Oxford: Oxford University Press, 2004).

Gottlieb, R. S., *Marxism, 1844–1990: Origins, Betrayal, Rebirth* (London: Routledge, 1992).

Gramsci, A., *Selections from Prison Notebooks* (London: Lawrence & Wishart, 1971).

——, *Further Selections from the Prison Notebooks* (London: Lawrence & Wishart, 1995).

Guttsman, W. H., *The German Social Democratic Party, 1875–1933* (London: George Allen & Unwin, 1980).

Hagen, M. von, *Soldiers in the Proletarian Dictatorship: The Red Army and the Soviet Socialist State, 1917–1930* (Ithaca, NY: Cornell University Press, 1990).

Hahn, W. G., *Post-war Soviet Politics: The Fall of Zhdanov and the Defeat of Moderation, 1946–1953* (New York: Cornell University Press, 1982).

Haimson, L. H., *The Russian Marxists and the Origins of Bolshevism* (Cambridge, MA: Harvard University Press, 1955).

Haimson. L. H. et al. (eds), *The Making of Three Russian Revolutionaries: Voices from the Menshevik Past* (New York: Cambridge University Press, 1987).

Haimson, L. and Tilly, C. (eds), *Strikes, Wars and Revolutions in an International Perspective: Strike Waves in the Late Nineteenth and Early Twentieth Centuries* (Cambridge: Cambridge University Press, 1989).

Harding, N., *Lenin's Political Thought*, vol. 1 (London: Macmillan, 1977).

—— (ed.), *Marxism in Russia: Key Documents, 1879–1906* (Cambridge: Cambridge University Press, 1983).

——, *Leninism* (London: Macmillan, 1996).

Hilton, R. et al., *The Transition from Feudalism to Capitalism* (London: Verso, 1976).

Hobsbawm, E. J. (ed.), *Pre-Capitalist Economic Formations* (London: Lawrence & Wishart, 1964).

Hobsbawm, E., *Revolutionaries* (London: Weidenfeld & Nicolson, 1973).

——, *The Age of Capital* (London: Weidenfeld & Nicolson, 1975).

——, *Age of Extremes: The Short Twentieth Century, 1914–1991* (London: Michael Joseph, 1994).

Hobsbawm, E., *Interesting Times: A Twentieth-Century Life* (London: Abacus, 2002).

Howard, M. C. and King, J. E., *A History of Marxian Economics*, vol. 1: *1883–1929* (Princeton, NJ: Princeton University Press, 1989).

Hughes, J., *Stalin, Siberia and the Crisis of the New Economic Policy* (Cambridge: Cambridge University Press, 1991).

Hunt, R. N., *The Political Ideas of Marx and Engels*, vol. II: *Classical Marxism, 1850–1895* (Pittsburgh: University of Pittsburgh Press, 1984).

Kanatchikov, S. I., *A Political Worker in Tsarist Russia: The Autobiography of S. I. Kanatchikov*, trans. R. E. Zelnik (Stanford, CA: Stanford University Press, 1986).

Kautsky, J. H., *Karl Kautsky: Marxism, Revolution and Democracy* (New Brunswick: Transaction, 1994).

Kautsky, K., *Selected Political Writings* (London: Macmillan, 1983).

——, *The Road to Power: Political Reflections of Growing into the Revolution* (Atlantic Highlands, NJ: Humanities Press, 1996).

Keep, J. L. H., *The Rise of Social Democracy in Russia* (Oxford: Oxford University Press, 1963).

Khrushchev, N. I., *Khrushchev Remembers* (London: Sphere, 1971).

Knight, A., *Beria: Stalin's First Lieutenant* (Princeton, NJ: Princeton University Press, 1993).

Koenker, D. P. et al. (eds), *Party, State and Society in the Russian Civil War* (Bloomington: Indiana University Press, 1989).

Kotkin, S., *Magnetic Mountain: Stalinism as a Civilisation* (Berkeley: University of California Press, 1995).

Kowalski, R. I., *The Bolshevik Party in Conflict: The Left Communist Opposition of 1918* (London: Macmillan, 1991).

——, *The Russian Revolution, 1917–1921* (London: Routledge, 1997).

Kritsman, L., *Geroicheskii period russkoi revoliutsii* (Moscow: Gosudarstvennoe izdatel'stvo, n.d.).

Lenin, V. I., *Collected Works* (Moscow: Progress, 1960–70).

Lih, L. (ed.), *Stalin's Letters to Molotov* (New Haven, CT: Yale University Press, 1995).

Lindemann, A. S., *A History of European Socialism* (New Haven, CT: Yale University Press, 1983).

Lovell, D. W., *From Marx to Lenin: An Evaluation of Marx's Responsibility for Soviet Totalitarianism* (Cambridge: Cambridge University Press, 1984).

McCagg, W. O., Jr, *Stalin Embattled, 1943–1948* (Detroit: Wayne State University Press, 1978).

McDermott, K. and Agnew, J., *The Comintern: A History of International Communism from Lenin to Stalin* (Basingstoke: Macmillan, 1996).

McLellan, D., *Karl Marx: His Life and Thought* (St Albans: Paladin, 1976).

Malia, M., *The Soviet Tragedy: A History of Socialism in Russia, 1917–1991* (New York: Free Press, 1994).

Malle, S., *The Economic Organisation of War Communism* (Cambridge: Cambridge University Press, 1985).

Marcuse, H., *Reason and Revolution* (London: Routledge & Kegan Paul, 1973).

Medvedev, R., *Lenin and Western Marxism* (London: Verso, 1981).

Meisner, M., *Li Ta-chao and the Origins of Chinese Marxism* (Cambridge, MA: Harvard University Press, 1967).

Middlemass, K., *Power and the Party: Changing Faces of Communism in Western Europe* (London: André Deutsch, 1980).

Moore, B., Jr, *Injustice: The Social Bases of Obedience and Revolt* (Basingstoke: Macmillan, 1978).

Nove, A., *Stalinism and After* (London: Allen & Unwin, 1981).

——, *The Economics of Feasible Socialism* (London: George Allen & Unwin, 1983).

Petz, W. A. (ed.), *Wilhelm Liebknecht and German Social Democracy: A Documentary History* (Westport, CT: Greenwood, 1994).

Pierson, S., *Marxist Intellectuals and the Working-Class Mentality in Germany, 1887–1912* (Cambridge, MA: Harvard University Press, 1993).

Pipes, R., *Social Democracy and the St Petersburg Labour Movement, 1885–1897* (Cambridge, MA: Harvard University Press, 1963).

——, *The Russian Revolution, 1899–1919* (London: Fontana, 1990).

——, *Russia under the Bolshevik Regime, 1919–1924* (London: Fontana, 1994).

Pokrovskii, M. N., *Sem' let proletarskoi diktatury* (Moscow: Istpart, 1923).

Polan, A. J., *Lenin and the End of Politics* (London: Methuen, 1984).

Rabinowitch, A., *Prelude to Revolution: The Petrograd Bolsheviks and the July 1917 Uprising* (Bloomington: Indiana University Press, 1968).

——, *The Bolsheviks Come to Power* (London: New Left Books, 1979).

Radkey, O. H., *The Agrarian Foes of Bolshevism* (New York: Columbia University Press, 1958).

Radosh, R. et al. (eds), *The Soviet Union and the Spanish Civil War* (New Haven, CT: Yale University Press, 2001).

Read, C., *The Making and Breaking of the Soviet System* (Basingstoke: Macmillan, 2001).

Remington, T. F., *Building Socialism in Bolshevik Russia: Ideology and Industrial Organisation* (Pittsburgh: University of Pittsburgh Press, 1984).

Resolutions and Decisions of the Communist Party of the Soviet Union, vol. 1, ed. R. C. Elwood (Toronto: University of Toronto Press, 1974).

Resolutions and Decisions of the Communist Party of the Soviet Union, vol. 2, ed. R. Gregor (Toronto: University of Toronto Press, 1974).

Riddell, J. (ed.), *Lenin's Struggle for a Revolutionary International: Documents, 1907–1916: The Preparatory Years* (New York: Monad Press, 1984).

—— (ed.), *The German Revolution and the Debate on Soviet Power: Documents, 1918–1919: Preparing the Founding Congress* (New York: Pathfinder, 1986).

Sakwa, R., *Soviet Politics in Perspective* (London: Routledge, 1998).

——, *The Rise and Fall of the Soviet Union, 1917–1991* (London: Routledge, 1999).

Salvadori, M., *Karl Kautsky and the Socialist Revolution, 1880–1938* (London: Verso, 1979).

Sassoon, D., *One Hundred Years of Socialism: The West European Left in the Twentieth Century* (London: Fontana, 1997).

Schorske, C. E., *German Social Democracy, 1905–1917: The Development of the Great Schism* (Cambridge, MA: Harvard University Press, 1955).

Schumpeter, J., *Capitalism, Socialism and Democracy* (London: Routledge, 1996 reprint).

Serge, V., *Memoirs of a Revolutionary* (Oxford: Oxford University Press, 1967).

Service, R., *Lenin: A Political Life*, vol. 1: *The Strengths of Contradiction* (London: Macmillan, 1985).

——, *Lenin: A Political Life*, vol. 2: *Worlds in Collision* (London: Macmillan, 1995).

——, *Lenin: A Political Life*, vol. 3: *The Iron Ring* (London: Macmillan, 1995).

Shanin, T. (ed.), *Late Marx and the Russian Road* (London: Routledge & Kegan Paul, 1983).

Simis, K., *USSR: Secrets of a Corrupt Society* (London: Dent, 1982).

Steenson, G. P., *Karl Kautsky, 1854–1938: Marxism in the Classical Years* (Pittsburgh: University of Pittsburgh Press, 1991).

Swain, G. (ed.), 'Editor's Introduction', *Protokoly Soveshchaniya Rasshirennoi Redaktsii 'Proletariya' Iun' 1909* (Millwood, NY: Kraus, 1982).

Swain, G. and Swain, N., *Eastern Europe since 1945* (London: Macmillan, 1993).

Thatcher, I., *Trotsky* (London: Routledge, 2003).

Timasheff, N. S., *The Great Retreat: The Growth and Decline of Communism in Russia* (New York: Dutton, 1946).

Tismaneaunu, V. (ed.), *The Revolutions of 1989* (London: Routledge, 1999).

Tompson, W. J., *Khrushchev: A Political Life* (London: Macmillan, 1997).

Torre, P. F. della et al., *Eurocommunism: Myth or Reality?* (Harmondsworth: Penguin, 1979).

Tucker, R. C., *Stalin as Revolutionary, 1879–1929* (London: Chatto & Windus, 1974).

—— (ed.), *Stalinism: Essays in Historical Interpretation* (New York: W. W. Norton, 1977).

——, *Stalin in Power: The Revolution from Above, 1928–1941* (New York: W. W. Norton, 1990).

Tudor, H. and Tudor, J. M. (eds), *Marxism and Social Democracy: The Revisionist Debate, 1896–1898* (Cambridge: Cambridge University Press, 1988).

Vajda, M., *The State and Socialism: Political Essays* (London: Allison & Busby, 1981).

Valentinov, N., *The Early Years of Lenin* (Ann Arbor: University of Michigan Press, 1970).

Volkogonov, D., *Lenin: Life and Legacy* (London: HarperCollins, 1994).

Walicki, A., *Marxism and the Leap to the Kingdom of Freedom: The Rise and Fall of the Communist Utopia* (Stanford, CA: Stanford University Press, 1995).

Ward, C. (ed.), *The Stalinist Dictatorship* (London: Arnold, 1998).

——, *Stalin's Russia* (London: Arnold, 1999).

Weitz, E. D., *Creating German Communism, 1890–1990: From Popular Protests to Socialist State* (Princeton, NJ: Princeton University Press, 1997).

White, J. D., *Karl Marx and the Intellectual Origins of Dialectical Materialism* (London: Macmillan, 1966).

——, *Lenin: The Practice and Theory of Revolution* (Basingstoke: Palgrave Macmillan, 2001).

Wiles, P. J. D., *The Political Economy of Communism* (Oxford: Oxford University Press, 1964).

Yakovlev, A., *The Fate of Marxism in Russia* (New Haven, CT: Yale University Press, 1993).

Zaslavsky, V., *The Neo-Stalinist State: Class, Ethnicity and Consensus in Soviet Society* (Brighton: Harvester, 1982).

Index

Abuladze, Tenghiz, 105
Adorno, Theodor, 152
Aganbegyan, Abel, 210
agitation and propaganda, 64–6
Akimov, Vladimir P., 60, 68, 71
Akselrod, Pavel Borisovich, 60–1, 69, 72,
    74–6, 78
Albania, 171
    and collapse of Communism, 222
    and establishment of Communist
        regime, 174
Alksnis, Viktor Colonel, 215
Amalrik, Andrei, 143
Andreeva, Nina, 206
Andropov, Iurii, 146–7, 204
Armenia, 212–13, 216
Austria, 37, 164, 181
    strikes in, 92
Azerbaijan, 212–13

Babeuf, François, 2
Bahro, Rudolf, 125, 224
Bakunin, Mikhail Alexandrovich, 30
Baltic states, 212–16
Bavaria, 81
    Revolution in, 94
    Soviet Republic in, 98, 153
Bebel, August, 39–40
    and Union of German Workers'
        Societies, 39
    and Erfurt programme, 41
Belgium, 37, 82, 164

Belorussia, 213
Benes, Eduard, 173
Beria, Lavrentii, 128, 131–2, 134
Berlinguer, Enrico, 165–6
Bernstein, Eduard, 34, 42, 67, 83, 93,
    125, 228
    and *Anti-Duhring*, 24
    on Bolshevism, 4
    and Erfurt programme, 41
    and mass strike, 52
    and nationalism, 54
    and Revisionism, 45–7
    The Preconditions of Socialism, 4, 12,
        45–7
Bierut, Bolesław, 191
Bismarck, Otto von, 39–40, 82
Blagoev, Dmitrii, 63
Bogdanov, Aleksandr Aleksandrovich,
    73, 75–7
Bolsheviks, 3, 71, 76–8, 83
    and change of name to
        Communist, 106
    and Conciliationism, 79–81
    and construction of socialism, 105
    and dictatorship, 99
    and Lenin's domination,
        79–80
    and splits within, 60
    see also Russian Social Democratic
        Labour Party
Bordiga, Amadeo, 155, 162
Brest–Litovsk, Treaty of, 93, 106

Brezhnev, Leonid, 138
  and agriculture, 140
  Doctrine, 189, 219
  and economic successes, 140
  and era of stagnation, 139, 141, 145
  and failure of economic reform,
    141–2
  and organised consensus, 144
  and political stagnation, 142–3, 145
  and Prague Spring, 188–9
Britain, 2
  and absence of revolution in,
    99–100
  Labour Party, 38, 82
  Socialism in, 2, 37–8
  strikes in, 92
Brusnev, Mikhail Ivanovich, 62
Bukharin, Nikolai Ivanovich, 79, 86,
    113, 134
  and Comintern, 156
  and defence of NEP, 115–16,
    119, 206
  and dictatorship, 112
  execution of, 123
  and rehabilitation, 205
  and state, 88, 109, 162
  and 'War Communism', 108
  *Economics of the Transformation
    Period*, 108
Bukovskii, Vladimir, 143
Bulgaria, 171, 173
  and establishment of Stalinist regime,
    174
  and collapse of Communism, 221
bureaucratisation, 114–15, 121, 206
  Djilas's analysis of, 135, 176

Cabet, Étienne, 2–3
Carillo, Santiago, 168–9
Ceauşescu, Elena and Nicolae, 222
Central planning, 30–1, 136–7,
    141–2
Černík, Oldrich, 187, 189
Chaikovskii, Nikolai, 62
Chernenko, Konstantin, 147, 203
Chernyshevskii, Nikolai Gavrilovich, 60
China, 1, 118, 156, 209
Cold War, 128–9, 175

Communism, 1–2, 7
  and achievements in East Europe, 198,
    224
  and achievements in Soviet Union,
    125–6, 224
  and collapse in East Europe, 218–23
  and collapse in Soviet Union, 217–18
  and consequences of collapse, 225
Communist Information Bureau
    (Cominform), 175–6, 186, 190
Communist International (Comintern),
    6, 153
  Second Congress, 154
  and dissolution of, 159
  and Popular Fronts, 158–9
  and subordination to Soviet Union,
    154, 156, 159
  and Third Period, 156–7
  Twenty-One Conditions, 154
Communist Party (of the Soviet
    Union), 106
  Seventh Congress, 106
  Tenth Conference, 108–9
  Tenth Congress, 112
  Fifteenth Conference, 120
  Fifteenth Congress, 118–19
  Seventeenth Congress, 122
  Nineteenth Conference, 206–7
  Twentieth Congress, 133–4
  Twenty-Second Congress, 137
  Twenty-Eighth Congress, 215
  Anti-Party Group, 136
  and 'circular flow of power', 114, 124,
    136
  and dictatorship, 107, 112, 114
  and Left Opposition, 115–17
  and partiinost', 112–13
  see also Andropov; Brezhnev;
    Chernenko; Gorbachev;
    Khrushchev; Lenin; Stalin
Czechoslovakia, 171–4, 182
  and Charter 77, 189, 218
  and collapse of Communism,
    221–2
  and economic reforms of 1960s,
    187–8
  and establishment of Stalinist regime,
    174, 186

Czechoslovakia – *continued*
  and invasion of 1968, 189–90
  and national minorities, 173, 186
  and Prague Spring, 187–90
Czechoslovakian Communist Party,
    155–7
  and '2000 Words Manifesto', 188
  and Action Programme, 187–8
  and Hungarian Revolution, 186

Dan, Fedor, 70, 72, 76
Dan, Lidiia, 63–4, 70–1
Daniel, Iulii, 143
Daumig, Ernst, 96
David, Eduard, 82
Deich, Lev, 60
democratic centralism, 72, 79, 112
Dimitrov, Georgi, 156, 158
dissidence, 143, 203
  divisions within in Soviet
    Union, 143
  influence on Gorbachev, 145
  weakness in Soviet Union, 144
Dittmann, Wilhelm, 95–6
Djilas, Milovan, 134–5, 176, 179
'Doctors' Plot', 131
Dubček, Alexander, 187–9

Ebert, Friedrich, 95–7
economism, 65–9
Eisner, Kurt, 94
Emancipation of Labour Group (ELG),
    60–1
Engels, Friedrich, 3–4
  and Blanquism, 19
  Darwin's influence on, 23
  and dictatorship of the proletariat,
    26–8
  and economic determinism,
    14–16, 23
  and economics of socialism, 29–31
  and First International, 11–12
  and historical materialism, 12–13
  and League of the Just/Communist
    League, 11
  and nationalism, 32–4
  and parliamentary road to
    socialism, 27

  and Paris Commune, 27–8
  and peasants, 24–6
  and socialist state, 26–9
  and the Russians, 22–3
  and voluntarism, 19–20
  Anti-Duhring, 23–4
  The Communist Manifesto, 11, 13–14, 17,
    20, 32
  The German Ideology, 12, 15–16,
    20, 32
  The Holy Family, 17–18
  *The Peasant Question in France and
    Germany*, 24–5
  The Peasant War in Germany, 25
  *Russia and the Social Revolution
    Reconsidered*, 22
Eurocommunism, 6, 26, 152, 163–4
  in France, 167
  in Italy, 164–7
  in Spain, 167–70
Ezhov, Nikolai, 123

Fabians, 45–6
First International (International
    Working Men's Association),
    11–12, 39
Fischer, Ruth, 155–6
France, 82, 92, 100, 151
  Eurocommunism in, 167–8
  socialism in, 2, 37–8
Franco, Francisco, 123, 158, 168
Frank, Ludwig, 52
Frankfurt School, 152
French Communist Party (PCF),
    155–7, 175
  Twenty-Third Congress, 167
  and decline during 1980s, 168
  and Eurocommunism, 167–8
  and Popular Front, 158
  and revival during Second World War,
    159, 164
French Revolutionary Socialist Party
    (PSDF), 50
French Section of the Workers'
    International (SIFO), 50, 55,
    81, 155
French Socialist Party (PSF), 49, 167
Fukuyama, Francis, 1, 228

Georgia, 135, 213–14, 216
German Communist Party, 97–8, 155–7
German Democratic Republic (GDR), 171–2, 218
and anti-Stalinist demonstrations, 180
and collapse of Communism, 220–1
German Social Democratic Party (SPD), 3, 5, 18, 28, 37, 81
and Anti-Socialist Law, 40–1
and Erfurt programme, 41–2
and First World War, 81–2, 93
and Gotha programme, 3, 40
Halle Congress, 41
and imperialism, 55
and mass strike, 51–3
and nationalism, 54–5
and origins, 40
and reformism, 42–5, 50–1
and Revisionism, 45–50
and revolution, 95–8
split in First World War, 93
see also Bernstein; Independent Social Democratic Party; Kautsky; Luxemburg; Spartacists
Germany, 151
and council movement, 93–7
and failed insurrections in 1920s, 155
Liberals in, 38–9, 41
revolution in, 94–8
and strikes against war, 86, 92–3
Gerö, Ernst, 180–1
Gierek, Eduard, 193–6
Gomułka, Władysław, 189, 190–4
see also Polish United Workers' Party
Gorbachev, Mikhail Sergeevich, 7, 27, 147, 185, 190 203–4
and agriculture, 209–10
and August coup, 216–17
and Congress of People's Deputies, 207, 211, 215
and crisis of perestroika, 210–14
and democratisation, 206, 215
and East Europe, 214, 219–21
and economic stagnation, 204
and glasnost', 205–6
and minority nationalism, 212–16
and perestroika, 206–10
as President, 207
and reflections on Brezhnev era, 142
and Union of Sovereign States, 216
and uskorenie, 204, 207
Gottwald, Klement, 185–6
Gramsci, Antonio, 6, 152
and Eurocommunism, 163, 165
and theoretical contribution, 159–63
Greece, 175–6
Grigorenko, Petr, 143
Grishin, Viktor, 204
Gromyko, Andrei, 207
Grósz, Karoly, 220
Guesde, Jules, 49
Gulag, 120, 122, 124, 134

Haase Hugo, 82, 93
Hárászti, Miklos, 182, 184
Havel, Václav, 198, 221–2
Hilferding, Rudolf, 85, 89
Finance Capital, 56–7
historical materialism, 12–13
Honecker, Erich, 220
Horkheimer, Max, 152
Hoxha, Enver, 174
Hungary, 171, 173, 218
and agrarian reforms, 183–4
and collapse of Communism, 220–1
and economic crisis of 1980s, 184–5
and establishment of Stalinist regime, 174
and Foundation to Assist the Poor (SZETA), 184
and New Economic Mechanism (NEM), 183
and revolution of 1956, 181–2
Soviet Republic in, 99, 153
Hungarian Workers' [Communist] Party (HWP), 174, 179–81
renamed Hungarian Socialist Workers' Party, 181
and rupture of, 220
Husák, Gustáv, 186, 189

Iagoda, Genrikh, 123
Iakovlev, Egor, 205
Ianaev, Gennadii, 215–16

Independent Social Democratic Party
  (USPD), 83–4
  in Bavaria, 94
  and revolution, 94–7
  see also German Social Democratic
    Party
Italian Communist Party (PCI), 155,
  157, 175
  and change of name, 166–7
  and decline in 1980s, 166
  and Eurocommunism, 164–7
  and revival during Second World War,
    164
Italian Socialist Party (PSI), 155, 165
Italy, 38, 92, 100, 151, 155, 164–7

Jagielski, Mieczysław, 196
Jaruzelski, Wojciech, 196–8, 219–20
Jaurès, Jean, 47, 49

Kádár, János, 156–7, 189
  compared with Khrushchev, 185
  and Kádárism, 182–5, 187, 197
Kaganovich, Lazar, 136–7
Kamenev, Lev Borisovich, 88, 90–1,
  122–3, 131, 156
Kanatchikov, Semen, 64
  and impact of economism, 67–8
Kautsky, Karl, 16, 34, 37, 83–4, 93, 125
  and Anti-Duhring, 24
  and class consciousness, 44
  and dictatorship of the
    proletariat, 28
  and Erfurt programme, 41, 47
  and Eurocommunism, 165
  and imperialism, 57, 84–5
  and parliamentary road to socialism,
    49, 96, 165
  and peasantry, 43
  and reformism, 50–1
  and Revisionism, 47–8
  The Agrarian Question, 43
  Bernstein and the Social Democratic
    Programme, 47
  The Class Struggle, 47
  The Driving Forces of the Russian
    Revolution, 43
  The Mass Strike, 52–3

The Materialist Conception of
  History, 12
The Road to Power, 53
Kazakhstan, 212, 214
Kenedi, János, 183
Kerensky, Aleksandr, 87, 92, 100
Khrushchev, Nikita, 104, 128,
  131, 205
  and abatement of terror,
    136, 138
  and comparison with Gorbachev,
    138–9
  and consumerism, 133, 138–9, 144
  and denunciation of Stalin, 133–5,
    137, 191
  and economic reform, 136–7
  and fall from power, 138–9
  and Hungarian revolution, 180–2
  and political reforms, 137–8
  Secret Speech, 133–5, 180
  and 'virgin lands', 133, 137
Kirov, Sergei, 122
Korotich, Vitalii, 205
Korsch, Karl, 30, 161
Kosygin, Alexei, 139
  and economic reform, 141–2
Kremer, Arkadii, 64
Krenz, Egon, 221
Kritsman, Lev, 108, 126, 162
Kulaks, 107, 119–20
Kun, Bela, 99
Kuroń, Jacek, 193, 197–8
  and Workers' Defence Committee,
    195–6
Kuskova, Elena, 68–9
Kuznetsov, Alexei, 130

Lange, Oskar, 30–1
Lassalle, Ferdinand, 12, 25
  and General Union of German
    Workers, 39–40
League of Communists of
  Yugoslavia, 179
League of the Just, 38
Left Communists, 106, 112–13
Left Socialist Revolutionaries, 91,
  107, 111
Lenart, Josef, 187

Lenin, Vladimir Ilich, 34, 55, 105,
    163, 206
  in 1917, 87–91
  and agitation, 65
  and bourgeoisie, 75–7
  and class consciousness, 19, 44, 70
  and Comintern, 153–4
  and commune state, 88, 103
  and dictatorship, 109, 111
  and Economism, 69–70
  and First World War, 84–6
  and Hilferding, 57
  and imperialism, 84–6
  and liquidationism, 75–6
  and nationalism, 33, 78–9
  and New Economic Policy, 109–11
  and party organisation, 70–1, 112
  and peasants, 25–6, 77–8, 91–2, 106
  and revolutionary state, 28, 88
  and uneven development of
    capitalism, 85
  and workers' control, 108, 111
  Better Fewer, but Better, 111
  April Theses, 88–9, 163
  Imperialism, the Highest Stage of
    Capitalism, 84–6
  On Party Unity, 112
  One Step Forward, Two Steps
    Backward, 72
  Our Revolution, 111
  State and Revolution, 28, 88, 109
  Two Tactics of Social Democracy in the
    Democratic Revolution, 73, 77
  What is to be Done?, 67–70, 90
'Leningrad Affair', 130–1
Leninism, 59–60, 103–4, 125
Levi, Paul, 154
Liberman, Evsei, 141, 208
Liebknecht, Karl, 82–3, 86, 98
Liebknecht, Wilhelm, 39–40, 44
  and Erfurt programme, 41–2
  and Union of German Workers'
    Societies, 39
Ligachev, Egor, 207, 213
Liubarskii, Konstantin, 145
Lominadze, Beso, 129
Luxemburg, Rosa, 34, 81
  and affinities with Gramsci, 161
  and class consciousness, 49
  and First World War, 81, 83
  and imperialism, 49, 58, 83
  and mass strike, 51–2
  murder of, 98
  and reformism, 50–1
  and Revisionism, 48–9, 51
  The Accumulation of Capital, 49, 58
  Organisational Questions of Social
    Democracy, 50–1
  Reform and Revolution, 48–9
  Theses on the Tasks of International Social
    Democracy, 83
  see also Bolsheviks; Leninism

Macdonald, Ramsay, 47
Malenkov, Georgii, 128–31, 137, 180,
    186, 191
  and Anti-Party Group, 136
  and fall from power, 133–4
  introduces 'New Course', 132
  and 'peaceful co-existence', 132
Marcuse, Herbert, 19
market socialism, 30–1, 142 , 147, 177–8,
    188, 199, 208
Marshall Plan, 175, 186
Martov, Julius, 55, 69, 75, 91
  and agitation, 64–5
  and dictatorship of the proletariat, 28
  and First World War, 84
  and party organisation, 70–2
  see also Mensheviks
Martynov, A. S., 66, 71
Marx, Karl, 3, 112
  ambiguities and lacunae in, 4–5, 13,
    26–31, 34
  and Blanquism, 19
  and class consciousness, 18
  and Communist League, 11
  and contemporary capitalism, 226–8
  and dictatorship of the proletariat,
    26–8
  early writings, 13
  and economic determinism,
    14–16, 23
  and economics of socialism, 29–31
  and historical materialism, 12–13
  and First International, 11–12

Marx, Karl – *continued*
and League of the Just, 18
and nationalism, 32–4
and Paris Commune, 26
and parliamentary road to
socialism, 27
and peasants, 24–6
and politics of socialism, 26–9,
88, 125
and the Russians, 20–3
and voluntarism, 19–20
Against Carl Herzen, 16
Capital, 14–15, 17, 21
The Civil War in France, 26–8
The Critique of the Gotha Programme, 3–4,
25, 30, 40
The Communist Manifesto, 11, 17,
20, 32
*A Contribution to the Critique of Political
Economy*, 13, 16, 19
*Economic and Philosophic Manuscripts of
1844*, 30
*The Eighteenth Brumaire of Louis
Bonaparte*, 17, 27
The German Ideology, 12, 15–16, 20
The Holy Family, 17–18
The Poverty of Philosophy, 13, 18
Marxism–Leninism, 60, 125, 128
Mazowiecki, Tadeusz, 220
Medvedev, Roy, 104, 143, 204–5
Medvedev, Zhores, 143
Mensheviks, 71–6, 83, 91, 107, 111
Internationalists, 84, 87, 91
Michels, Robert, 50
Michnik, Adam, 219
Millerand, Alexandre, 49
Milošević, Slobodan, 179
Milosz, Czesław, 172
Mitterand, François, 167
Mlynář, Zdeněk, 172, 185–6, 188, 221
Moczar, Mieczysław, 198
Modrow, Hans, 221
Modzelewski, Karol, 193
Moldavia (Moldova), 214, 216
Molotov, Viacheslav Mikhailovich, 115,
120, 123, 133–4, 137
and Anti-Party Group, 136
Moro, Aldo, 165–6
Myakotin, V., 60

Nagy, Imre, 179–81
and 'national Communism', 176
nationalism, 4, 54, 82
ethnic nationalism, 179, 222, 228
Great Russian, 130–1, 145
minority nationalism in Soviet Union,
145–6, 212–14
Nazi–Soviet pact, 159, 173
'New class', 121, 217
Djilas's analysis of, 134–5
New Economic Policy (NEP), 109, 185
and absence of democracy, 111
crisis of, 117–19
debate over, 115–19
roots of, 110
Noske, Gustav, 55, 98
Novosibirsk Report, 146–7
Novotný, Antonin, 186–7

Ochab, Eduard, 192
Osinskii, N., 16, 108, 113
Otechestvennye Zapiski, 21

Pavlov, Valentin, 215–16
permanent revolution, 20, 73–4
see also Trotsky
Petőfi circle, 180
Piatakov, Grigorii Leonidovich, 79, 85,
113–14, 123
Plekhanov, Georgii Valentinovich, 22, 60,
65–6, 70, 75, 78
and class consciousness, 62–3
and conversion to Marxism, 61
and economic determinism, 23
and First World War, 83–4
and party organisation, 63, 71
and revolution in Russia, 61–2
Our Differences, 61
Pliusch, Leonid, 143
Podgornyi, Nikolai, 139
Pokrovskii, Mikhail Nikolaevich, 7, 109
Poland, 33, 155, 171, 173, 178, 204
Catholic Church in, 190–2,
195–6, 198
and collapse of Communism in,
219–20
and Gdańsk riots, 194
and economic crisis of 1970s,
195–6

Poland – *continued*
and establishment of Stalinist regime, 174, 190
and martial law, 196
and 'Polish October', 191–2
and Solidarity, 196–8, 218–20
and Stalinism in, 191
Polish United Workers [Communist] Party (PUWP), 174, 191–2
Eighth Congress, 195
Natolin faction in, 192
and *odnowa*, 195
Partisan faction in, 193
and Prague Spring, 189
Technocratic faction in, 193–4
polycentrism, 219
Poszgay, Imre, 181, 220
Potresov, Aleksandr Nikolaevich, 70, 83
Prague Spring, 142, 164, 168, 187–90
Preobrazhenskii, Evgenii, 116
and critique of NEP, 117
ABC of Communism, 109
Prokopovich, Sergei Nikolaevich, 63, 68
Pugo, Boris, 215–16
Putin, Vladimir, 217

Rabochee Delo, 66, 68, 70
Rabochaia Mysl', 67–9
Radek, Karl Bernadovich, 100, 113, 123
Rákosi Mátyás, 179–80, 182
Rakowski, Mieczysław, 196
Ranković, Aleksandar, 175–6
Riutin, Mikhail, 122
Rokossowski, Konstantin, 191
Romania, 171, 173
and collapse of Communism, 222
and establishment of Stalinist regime, 174
Romanov, Grigorii, 204
Russia
and Civil War, 99, 106–7
February Revolution, 87–8
October Revolution, 91–2
see also Russian Social Democratic Labour Party
Russian revolution, 87–92
and comparison with Germany and the West, 98–100

Russian Populists, 21, 60–1
Russian Social Democratic Labour Party (RSDLP), 59
Second Congress, 70–1, 78
Third Congress, 78
Fourth (Unity) Congress, 74–6
and splits within, 70–80
see also Bolsheviks; Lenin; Mensheviks; Plekhanov; Trotsky
Rybakov, Anatolii, 205

Sakharov, Andrei, 143, 205, 212–13
Scheidemann, Philipp, 95
Schumpeter, Joseph, 24, 31
Schweitzer, J. B. von, 40
Second International, 5, 26, 37, 81
and imperialism, 54–5
strength of reformism in, 51
and Revisionism, 49–50
see also German Social Democratic Party
Serge, Victor, 105, 108
Shatalin, Stanislav, 210–11, 215
Shepilov, Dmitrii, 133
and Anti-Party Group, 136
Shevardnadze, Eduard, 213, 215
Šik, Oto, 187–8, 199
Siniavskii, Andrei, 143
Slánský, Rudolf, 186
Slovakia, 153, 173
Sobchak, Anatoly, 207, 213, 215, 217
socialism, 2–3
'scientific socialism', 3
with a human face, 7, 185, 189
Socialist revolutionaries, 77, 91, 107, 111
see also Left Socialist revolutionaries
Solzhenitsyn, Alexander, 143
The Gulag Archipelago, 206
One Day in the Life of Ivan Denisovich, 135
The State of the Nation, 140
Sorin, Vladimir, 112–13
Soviet Communism, *see* Andropov; Brezhnev; Chernenko; Gorbachev; Khrushchev; Lenin; Stalin
Soviets, 75, 112–13
Spain, 123, 151, 158
and Eurocommunism, 168–70

Spanish Communist Party (PCE), 155
  Eighth Congress, 168
  Ninth Congress, 169
  and Eurocommunism, 168–70
  and growing factionalism within,
    169–70
Spanish Socialist Workers' Party (PSOE),
  169–70
Spartacists, 83, 93
  and foundation of German
    Communist Party, 97
  rising of, 97–8
  see also German Social Democratic
    Party
Spiridonova, Maria, 107
Stalin, Iosif Vissarianovich, 88, 109,
  117–20, 163
  and collectivisation, 119–20, 129
  and Comintern, 157–9
  and Concordat with Orthodox
    Church, 129
  and deportation of national
    minorities, 134
  and 'Doctors' Plot', 131
  and foreign policy, 123
  and industrialisation, 115, 118–21, 129,
    204
  Khrushchev's denunciation of, 133–5,
    137
  and 'Leningrad Affair', 130–1
  and opposition to, 122
  and postwar repression, 128–30
  and rise to power, 114
  and socialism in one country, 116
  and terror, 122–4
  victims of, 120, 124
  see also Communist Party of the Soviet
    Union
Stalinism, 5–7, 103–4, 110, 121,
  127–31
  and imposition of in East Europe, 164,
    171, 174–6
  interpretations of, 124–6
  Neo-Stalinism, 139
Stinnes–Legien pact, 96
Struve, Petr Bernardovich, 63, 66
Suarez, Adolfo, 168–9
Suslov, Mikhail, 145

Svoboda, Ludwik, 187
Syrtsov, Sergei, 122

Takhtarev, Konstantin Mikhailovich, 67
Timasheff, Nicholas, 121–2, 135, 137
Tito (Josip Broz), 174, 179
  and Balkan Federation, 176
  and Hungarian Revolution, 182
  and non-Stalinist path to socialism,
    176–7
  see also Yugoslavia
Togliatti, Palmiro, 134, 164–5
totalitarianism, 103, 127–8
  and Marxist roots, 103
Tsipko, Aleksandr, 206
Trotsky, Leon Davidovich, 37, 60, 80,
  105, 113, 115, 119, 134, 156, 163
  and Brest-Litovsk, 93
  as Commissar of War, 107
  and dictatorship, 109, 112
  and fate of Communism in Soviet
    Union, 218
  and labour militarisation, 108
  and party organisation, 71–2
  and permanent revolution, 20, 73–4
  Our Political Tasks, 71–2
  Results and Prospects, 73–4
  The Revolution Betrayed, 124
Truman Doctrine, 175, 186
Tsereteli, Irakli, 87–8
Tudjman, Franjo, 179

Ukraine, 122, 213
Ulbricht, Walter, 189
Union of Russia Social Democrats
  (Abroad), 66, 68, 71
Union of Struggle for the Liberation of
  the Working Class, 65
Uritskii, Moisei, 107

Valentinov, Nikolai, 60, 113
Vollmar, George von, 25–6, 47
  and reformism, 42–4
Voznesenskii, Nikolai, 130

Wałęsa, Lech, 196–7, 219
'war communism', 108–9
Warsaw Pact, 181, 188–9

Webb, Beatrice and Sidney, 46
Weitling, Wilhelm, 38
Western Marxism, 6, 151–2
  and Gramsci, 163
Winstanley, Gerrard, 2
Woytyła, Karol, 195

Yakovlev, Aleksandr, 207, 215
Yeltsin, Boris, 204, 206–7, 213
  and August coup, 216–17
Yugoslavia, 171
  and collapse of Communism, 222
  and economic crisis of 1980s, 178
  and establishment of Communist
    regime, 174
  and ethnic nationalism, 222

  and independent path to socialism,
    176–7
  and market socialism, 177–8
  and national minorities, 173, 179

Zaslavskaia, Tatiana, 146–7
  see also Novosibirsk Report
Zaslavsky, Victor, 144–5
Zasulich Vera Ivanovna, 21, 60, 70
Zetkin, Clara, 82, 154
Zimmerwald Left, 83, 86–7
Zhdanov Andrei, 128–30, 174
'Zhdanovshchina', 129
Zinoviev, Grigorii Evseevich, 77, 90–1,
    122–3, 131
  and Comintern, 154, 156